Latter-day Dissent

Copyright © 2010, Philip Lindholm
Cover design copyright © 2010 by Greg Kofford Books, Inc.

All rights reserved. No part of this book may be reproduced in any form or by any means without permission in writing from the publisher, Greg Kofford Books. The views expressed herein are the responsibility of the authors and do not necessarily represent the position of Greg Kofford Books, Inc.

2015   14   13   12   11   5   4   3   2   1

www.koffordbooks.com

Library of Congress Cataloging-in-Publication Data

Latter-day dissent : at the crossroads of intellectual inquiry and ecclesiastical authority / edited and with an introduction by Philip Lindholm.
   p. cm.
 Includes bibliographical references and index.
 ISBN 978-1-58958-128-9 (alk. paper)
 1. Mormon intellectuals—United States—Interviews. 2. Church of Jesus Christ of Latter-day Saints—Discipline. 3. Excommunication—Church of Jesus Christ of Latter-day Saints. I. Lindholm, Philip, 1980-
  BX8693.L38 2010
  262.9'893320922--dc22
                                 2010022586

Latter-day Dissent

At the Crossroads of Intellectual Inquiry and Ecclesiastical Authority

Edited and with an Introduction by
Philip Lindholm

GREG KOFFORD BOOKS
SALT LAKE CITY, 2011

Contents

Foreword by Diarmaid MacCulloch vii
Introduction ix
Acknowledgments xxxv

Chapters

1   Lynne Kanavel Whitesides 1

2   Paul James Toscano 21

3   Maxine Hanks 53

4   Lavina Fielding Anderson 85

5   D. Michael Quinn 105

6   Janice Merrill Allred 131

7   Margaret Merrill Toscano 157

8   Thomas W. Murphy 183

9   Donald B. Jessee 209

Index 229

Foreword

The Church of Jesus Christ of Latter-day Saints is a fascinating religious system because of its origins in a recent and well-documented historic setting. Representatives of its older parent—Christianity—are often given to ridiculing the Latter-day Saints, careless of how the beginning of their own faith might look if it were not so remote in time and had not Christian canonical literature emerged out of circumstances of extreme obscurity and complexity. Over the last two hundred years, a huge effort of historical criticism and analysis has gone into investigating Christian origins. It has been one of the most remarkable concentrations of human talent and creativity in intellectual history; yet those involved in that effort have often found themselves subject to much harassment and vilification. Those who have sought to bring similar scrutiny to bear on Islam still face real personal danger. So this book offers fascinating parallels to these other investigations of religious doctrine and practice.

Religious belief is by its nature very close to madness. It has brought human beings to acts of criminal folly as well as to the highest achievements of goodness, creativity, and generosity. The fascination of the historical study of religion is to gauge what is folly and what is high achievement. It is always difficult to stand inside a religion and view it objectively; worse still to judge what is "true" about a package of ideas which has shaped one's own identity. Those who try are liable to be unpopular with their fellow believers and equally open to ridicule from those who have no sympathy with the belief-package and feel that the effort is not worthwhile. So the testimonies contained in this book are acts of courage and witnesses to a painful effort to seek integrity, when strong efforts were being made either to make them change their minds or at least keep their intellectual adventures to themselves. They deserve sympathy and admiration.

Diarmaid MacCulloch
Professor of the History of the Church
Saint Cross College, Oxford
Feast of Saint Faith of Conques 2008

Audiatur et altera pars.
"Let the other side also be heard."

Introduction

"As church membership continues to expand, things like the excommunication in a single month of a group of LDS intellectuals, collectively known as the September Six, will become far more significant—and not just to members of the faith." —Jan Shipps in *Sojourner in the Promised Land*, 115.

This volume collects, for the first time in book form, stories from the "September Six," a group of intellectuals officially excommunicated or disfellowshipped from the LDS Church in September of 1993 on charges of "apostasy" or "conduct unbecoming" Church members.[1] Their experiences are significant and yet are largely unknown outside of scholarly or more liberal Mormon circles, which is surprising given that their story was immediately propelled onto screens and cover pages across the Western world. From the *L.A. Times* to the BBC, the *Wall Street Journal* to Connie Chung, the media was intrigued when the LDS Church almost simultaneously banned six of its own intellectuals from speaking in church, taking the sacrament, entering an LDS temple, and wearing sacred garments.

Beginning in 2003, ten years after "the purge," I interviewed five members of the September Six to collect their ongoing stories, compare their reflections, and assess the implications. I then proceeded to speak with three other intellectuals who had faced disciplinary proceedings since the September Six events. Finally, after interview requests with General Authorities were denied, I was referred to meet with Donald B. Jessee of the LDS Church's Public Affairs Department who addressed many of the controversial claims made by the aforementioned intellectuals. In the end, it became clear that the Church understood the expulsion of the September Six as an appropriate exercise of ecclesiastical authority, while the September Six sought to move intellectual inquiry in the Church beyond the existing desiderata of Latter-day dissent.

Doctrinal Purity

In the immediate aftermath of September 1993, many outsiders accused the LDS Church of being a monolithic institution that punished member critiques with expulsion. Some Church members agreed, including Scott G. Kenney (the founding editor of *Sunstone* magazine and first director of Signature Books) and Steve Benson (the Pulitzer Prize-winning editorial cartoonist and grandson of Prophet/President Ezra Taft Benson). Both rescinded their Church membership in protest of the September Six events, while LDS Church leaders, for their part, claimed that action against the intellectuals was taken out of a "responsibility to preserve the doctrinal purity of the church" and that they were "united in this objective."[2]

The tension between the Church and its intellectual critics highlights the difficulty of accommodating congregational diversity while maintaining doctrinal unity—a difficulty hearkening back to the very heart of ancient Christianity. Many of the earliest Christians, from the Apostle Paul to the heresiologists of the second and third centuries,[3] struggled to be exclusive of heresy while inclusive of people.[4] The LDS Church has similarly sought to find and sustain this delicate balance. However, equilibrium was climactically disrupted in the years leading up to 1993 when a robust and internal intellectual movement gained momentum. This diverse group disagreed with the Church's stance on sensitive subjects such as academic freedom, revisionist history, feminist theology, women and the priesthood, homosexuality, and concepts of priesthood authority. And although led by LDS members, the investigations were not conducted in Church meetings and publications, but in academic settings and independent journals like *Dialogue*, *Sunstone*, and the Mormon Women's Forum. They resulted in the expulsion of the September Six.

A number of important events foreshadowed the discipline of the September Six in 1993. For decades, intellectuals had written dissenting views of Mormon history, scholarship, and gender issues. Tensions arose in the 1940s and 1950s with the work of historians Dale Morgan, Juanita Brooks, and Fawn M. Brodie, who was excommunicated in 1946 for her groundbreaking biography of Joseph Smith. Tensions continued through the 1960s and 1970s with writers for liberal publications like *Dialogue, Sunstone,* and *Exponent II* before erupting in 1979 with Sonia Johnson's excommunication for her pro-ERA activism. Church discipline of scholars reappeared again in 1986 with the censure of Linda King Newell and Valeen Tippets Avery for their prize-winning biography *Mormon Enigma: Emma Hale Smith—Prophet's Wife, "Elect Lady," Polygamy's Foe* (New York: Doubleday, 1984) and went so far as to bar Pulitzer Prize-winning scholar Laurel Thatcher Ulrich from speaking at BYU in 1993.

In May 1993, just months before the September Six events, the Church-owned-and-operated Brigham Young University did not renew the teaching contracts of faculty members Cecilia Konchar Farr and David Clark Knowlton. Farr, among other things, taught postmodern and feminist theories and publicly supported pro-choice rights, while Knowlton publicly discussed the religious factors behind terrorism against LDS missionaries and buildings in Latin America. Following their departure, BYU history professor Martha Sonntag Bradley, then co-editor of *Dialogue*, chose to resign from the BYU history faculty rather than face dismissal, and she was followed by professors John and Martha Beck that same summer. Meanwhile, professor Gail Turley Houston was placed on academic probation in August 1993 and terminated in 1996 for her feminist views and defense of Professor Farr, while Professors Scott Abbott and Eugene England resigned under fire in 1998.

Despite the brewing troubles at BYU, people were shocked by the September Six purge. To focus disciplinary action against six high-profile members in just one month was unprecedented in Mormonism since the 1840s (in the succession crisis that erupted after Joseph Smith's death) and the late 1860s (when the Godbeites challenged Brigham Young's domination of Utah). The LDS intellectuals had clearly struck a key issue—the latitude of public discussion on Latter-day Saint theology and practice —and the Church was forced to respond. In so doing, it did not distinguish between those intellectuals participating in forms of personal dissent and others engaging in academic inquiries; both were treated as apostasy because they were conducted in public. The transgression of the September Six, then, was *public* expression of their views, which gave other LDS intellectuals certain cause to reconsider sharing either personal or scholarly critiques of Mormonism in the public sphere.

In 1994, Professor David Wright of Brandeis University and editor Brent Lee Metcalfe were excommunicated for their work in *New Approaches to the Book of Mormon: Explorations in Critical Methodology* (Salt Lake City: Signature Books, 1993). In 1995, author Janice Allred was excommunicated for her writings about the Mother in Heaven. In 2000, Professor Margaret Toscano was excommunicated for her theological reflections, and in 2002, Professor Thomas Murphy was nearly excommunicated for his anthropological work on Mormonism. In addition, many other unnamed intellectuals were called into disciplinary interviews that did not result in excommunication.

Church disciplinary action was driven by LDS leaders who felt that Church unity was threatened by independent public discourse on LDS thought, and they even made a statement in the 1998 edition of the Church's *General Handbook of Instructions* that warned members against participating in public symposia.[5] In like fashion, Apostles Dallin H. Oaks and Boyd K. Packer encouraged discernment. As early as 1989, Oaks cautioned the faithful to beware of "alternative voices" that may be "pursuing selfish personal interests, such as property, pride, prominence, or power."[6]

Oaks did not explicitly prohibit members from attending or presenting papers at independent forums, but he did tell Church leaders and employees to "avoid official involvement, directly or indirectly." He also emphasized the benefit of the "spiritual quality control" afforded when involved with Church-sponsored dialogues. Packer agreed with Oaks in May of 1993, and went on to outline the threefold threat to the Church posed by the "gay-lesbian movement, the feminist movement ..., and the ever-present challenge from the so-called scholars or intellectuals [who] have made major invasions into the membership of the Church."[7]

The 1998 statement on symposia in the Church's *General Handbook of Instructions*, in conjunction with the remarks of Oaks and Packer, succeeded in clarifying the Church's disapproval of certain independent intellectual forums. It also further estranged many intellectuals in their already strained relationship with the Church. While some intellectuals, including some members of the September Six, had already become distant from the institutional Church, many others considered their work to be a faithful engagement with precisely those issues that were threatening its stability. As a result, they felt unjustifiably alienated by the very institution they sought to upbuild. They felt it was dialogue—not correlation—that would sustain the LDS Church into the twenty-first century.

The Correlation and Dialogical Movements

The roots of intellectual tensions leading up to 1993 had been planted decades earlier in the mid-twentieth century with the rise of New Mormon History and the correlation movement. Revisionist scholars like Dale Morgan, Fawn McKay Brodie, Juanita Brooks, Sterling McMurrin, O. C. Tanner, Everett Cooley, and Brigham D. Madsen employed their academic training and methods to study all aspects of LDS thought and history. The result was an alternative perspective rooted in a spirit of free inquiry, which paid less attention to ensuring the production of faith-promoting research.

As revisionist historians were gaining momentum in the 1960s and 1970s, the Church was embracing the principles of correlation, and reinstituted its Correlation Committee in 1961. Like its predecessors from 1907 onward,[8] the new committee sought to strengthen and unify Church teachings and programs, and it proved efficient under the ambitious leadership of the relatively youthful Apostle Harold B. Lee. In fact, so successful was the Correlation Committee that by 1987, the now-named Correlation Department was responsible for approving *all* Church publications and programs. This action had far-reaching implications for LDS intellectuals, many of whom came to be viewed with utmost suspicion. Even though free inquiry remained largely unrestricted in any formal fashion (and still does), intellectuals, and particularly those based in Utah, were watched more closely than in years past.[9]

A key example of the effects of correlation was the closing of the LDS Church Historian's office in 1981 at the height of new scholarly ventures led by Leonard Arrington. The first official Church historian to be a scholar by training, Arrington had mentored a group of young scholars including D. Michael Quinn, Jill Mulvay Derr, Maureen Ursenbach Beecher, Thomas G. Alexander, James B. Allen, Davis Bitton, and others, and set them to work on numerous Church history projects that mobilized still other scholars to produce a new multi-volume history of the Church. Some LDS leaders, though, were disquieted by the scholarly history in process, and they took action. In 1981, Arrington lost his position, office, and support for further projects when the History Division was transferred en masse to BYU as the newly created Joseph Fielding Smith Institute for Latter-day Saint History. The more tolerant days of the 1950s when President David O. McKay protected University of Utah Professor Sterling McMurrin from threatened excommunication had dissipated in the face of doctrinal and organizational mainstreaming in the 1960s and 1970s.[10] As a result, frustrated scholars and intellectuals gradually, and perhaps unintentionally, evolved into a group with values antithetical to those of correlation, which will be referred to here as *the dialogical movement*.

Where the correlation movement sought conformity in order to foster doctrinal integrity in the community, the dialogical movement aspired to procure independent forums for intellectual dialogue and debate that would more readily engage with the diverse views actually held by the LDS membership. The dialogical movement found inspiration in the types of free exchange pioneered at the meetings of the "Swearing Elders" (Sterling McMurrin, O. C. Tanner, Everett Cooley, Brigham Madsen, William Mulder, Lowell Bennion, T. Edgar Lyon, and others, founded in 1949). It also drew strength from later organizations, like the scholarly Mormon History Association

(f. 1965), *Dialogue* (f. 1966), and *Sunstone* (f. 1974), which came to serve as bastions of independent intellectual thought. To be sure, the intellectuals in these groups held varying degrees of belief in and commitments to official Church versions of history and theology, but most understood their involvement to be constructive, particularly early on. Church leaders, however, were not convinced, and became all the more concerned in the 1970s with the thriving new generation of independent historians more willing to posit revisionist models of Mormon history.

By the 1980s, the polarization between the correlation and dialogical movements was increasing exponentially, making it difficult for a Church member to participate in dialogical forums *and* retain the institutional Church's acceptance. This polarization stifled many intellectuals and triggered strong reactions from those worried about the consequences of aspiring to doctrinal purity. In this way, dialogical projects and forums found a significant niche for themselves in intellectual culture, countered in turn by Church leaders who spoke aggressively against member participation. This conflict exacerbated until tensions reached critical mass in 1992 and 1993 and culminated in the discipline of the September Six.

The September Six

The September Six came to epitomize the dialogical movement. They were precise in their research, unremitting in their devotion to open inquiry and dialogue, and wary of the negative effects that correlated orthodoxy could have on the future of intellectual debate. These characteristics placed Church leaders, and particularly local stake presidents and bishops, in a difficult position. Intellectual public discourse on Mormonism was viewed by LDS leaders as threatening to the Church and the faith of its members, even when well intended. As a result, six intellectuals were held accountable in September 1993.

During my interviews with members of the September Six, I discovered that they were not expelled for having personal concerns or scholarly disagreements, but for sharing them in public. Consequently, with every article, presentation, book, and interview, the September Six further incriminated themselves in the eyes of many Church leaders. A brief reference to the interviews is poignantly illustrative here.

Lynne Kanavel Whitesides, a feminist and former president of the Mormon Women's Forum, was disfellowshipped immediately following a television interview that she gave on feminist issues. In her interview with me, she declared, "I think the Church insisting on everybody keeping what's on their mind to themselves, to hide it, is a really evil thing to do." When I then asked her, "Can you believe whatever you want and still be a member of the Mormon Church?" She responded, "They have that! All over the place, people believe whatever they want and they're still members of the Church." Likewise, Paul Toscano, a Salt Lake City lawyer, recalled telling his local Church authority, "For you it's just about keeping us quiet."

Feminist theologian Maxine Hanks reflected on how she knew that continuing to speak about feminism "could 'jeopardize' my membership."[11] D. Michael Quinn, a distinguished Mormon historian and former professor at BYU, reported that Church leaders had commanded him to stop publishing work on Mormonism. When he protested that all of his research came from publicly available records, his dean replied, "I know, but Church leaders still don't want *you* to publish it."

As I was conducting the final interview with Lavina Fielding Anderson in December of 2004, I had a telling correspondence with Grant Palmer—a career LDS Institute teacher and chaplain at the Salt Lake County Jail. On December 12, 2004, Palmer was disfellowshipped following the publication of his revisionist book, *An Insider's View of Mormon Origins* (Salt Lake City: Signature Books, 2002). I spoke with Palmer by telephone the day after his disfellowshipment, and we agreed to meet later that week. The following day, Palmer cancelled stating in an email, "I feel that I am to[o] emotionally close to my trial to talk about it. I also think doing so would cause me harm in the eyes of the church at this time."[12] Palmer had clearly become aware of the deeply negative effects publicity can have on one's ability to remain in good standing in the eyes of Church leaders. Indeed, Palmer and the September Six had learned the same lesson: The Church insists upon keeping divergent views quiet. This policy is best demonstrated in the case of Avraham Gileadi, also excommunicated in September 1993. A conservative biblical scholar, Gileadi consistently refused to speak to the press following his excommunication, and he remains the only member of the September Six to be rebaptized and admitted back into the fold. In keeping with precedent, Gileadi did not respond to my interview request for this volume. Gileadi had conformed.

As former Prophet and President Gordon B. Hinckley has stated, "People think in a very critical way before they come into this church. When they come into this church they're expected to conform."[13] This position is adamantly confirmed by Donald Jessee in this volume, and is reminiscent of Joseph Smith's late (Nauvoo) views on authority, which identified some members' disagreement with the hierarchy as being "in the high road to apostasy."[14]

In the LDS Church, public dissent can be akin to a public expression of apostasy. In such cases, a concern for the image and welfare of the community dictates silence. This can be seen not only today, but long ago in a compelling statement by nineteenth-century Apostle Orson Hyde: "President Young told me in 1850 that my views on the Baby resurrection was not true, that I might Believe what I pleased if I would not Preach fals doctrin."[15] Young's desire to maintain the *appearance* of doctrinal unity implied that silence procures acceptance. This view partially resulted from the severe persecution experienced by the early LDS community.

From External Persecution to Internal Discipline

The LDS Church grew up in a milieu deeply hostile to its communal and theological ideals.[16] Terryl L. Givens notes, "Mormonism was erected on the premise of radical difference,"[17] and this premise naturally proved acerbic within the increasingly individualistic American society. Yet, despite persecution and humble beginnings with just six members in 1830, Mormonism grew like wildfire out of New York's burned-over district. By 1840, membership had reached thirty thousand, then doubled within ten years, and has continued to double approximately every nineteen years since.[18]

The persecution plaguing the burgeoning LDS community climaxed with its founder's murder by a raging mob. Early followers then fled from the Midwest into the desolate Salt Lake Valley of Utah, were invaded by the U.S. Army in 1857, and were pressured for forty years by the federal government due to its practice of plural marriage.[19] The LDS Church managed to endure these remarkable hardships through its devotion to seeing the Lord's will through to completion. However, it also developed a strong sense of exteriority, an exophobic mentality, in the process. This made internal critique, however minute, a sensitive enterprise, and swift discipline from the Church became a common response. As Brigham Young described the Kirtland period (1831–38), "We had High Council upon High Council, Bishop's trial upon Bishop's trial; and labor and toil constantly to settle difficulties and get our minds instructed in principle and doctrine, and in power that we had to contend with."[20]

Joseph Smith prompted Church leaders to punish and banish "corrupt" individuals to protect the Church from being "contaminated,"[21] and even some minor transgressions resulted in excommunication. For example, Sylvester Smith, who was a member of the Kirtland High Council, was excommunicated in 1838 after numerous arguments with Joseph Smith on the Zion's Camp march, which became heated when Sylvester refused to share his bread, threatened Joseph's dog, and accused him of stealing a quilt.[22] Lyman Wight, who was named an apostle in 1841, was threatened with excommunication if he did not repent for being drunk in public.[23] Burr Riggs was excommunicated in 1833 for borrowing a copy of the Book of Mormon and selling it, but was rebaptized in 1834.[24]

As exemplified in Riggs's case, excommunication and subsequent rebaptism were not rare in early Mormonism. Some of the earlier Mormons like Francis Bishop were excommunicated and readmitted three or more times. In fact, by the time of Joseph Smith's murder in 1844, more than 60 percent of the apostles who had been appointed under his direction had been excommunicated. In 1838, Smith even allowed the excommunications of Oliver Cowdery, the first scribe of the Book of Mormon, and Martin Harris, who had mortgaged his farm to pay for the book's first printing. Both were eventually rebaptized.

While many excommunicants like Cowdery and Harris were happily readmitted, others were deeply disillusioned and turned to violent opposition. Examples include the alienated members who published the *Nauvoo Expositor* in 1844, the estranged Mormons who helped tar and feather Joseph Smith and beat Sidney Rigdon in 1832, and Robert D. Foster and Joseph H. Jackson who reportedly participated in the mob that murdered Joseph Smith and his brother Hyrum in 1844. The embitterment of such excommunicants strongly contributed to the rise of what is now over a hundred Mormon splinter groups, many of whom trace their origins back to early disputes over prophetic succession and, most of all, authority.

Authority and Silence

Authority is a pillar of the Mormon faith, which Joseph Smith himself erected. Smith claimed direct apostolic authority from Peter, James, and John, and authority from God the Father and Jesus Christ to reject Christendom in favor of a restored Christianity. Ever since, the Church's prophet-president and other General Authorities have been divinely called, ordained, and sustained, and members generally revere this God-given authority exercised by Church leaders.

One of the most concise and hotly contested expressions of ecclesiastical authority is found in the 1945 message for ward teachers (now home teachers), which was printed by the Church-sponsored *Improvement Era*:

> Any Latter-day Saint who denounces or opposes, whether actively or otherwise, any plan or doctrine advocated by the "prophets, seers, and revelators" of the Church is cultivating the spirit of apostasy. One cannot speak evil of the Lord's anointed and retain the Holy Spirit in his heart. . . . When our leaders speak, the thinking has been done. When they propose a plan—it is God's plan. When they point the way, there is no other which is safe. When they give direction, it should mark the end of controversy. God works in no other way. To think otherwise, without immediate repentance, may cost one his faith, may destroy his testimony, and leave him a stranger to the kingdom of God.[25]

Whether members today agree with the unflinching obedience to authority described above, these sentiments have certainly been echoed in more recent teachings of Church leaders.

First Counselor N. Eldon Tanner said in 1979, "When the prophet speaks, the debate is over."[26] On February 26, 1980, Ezra Taft Benson, then president of the Quorum of the Twelve (and, in 1985, Church president), outlined "Fourteen Fundamentals in Following the Prophet," declaring that to abide by these was to ensure salvation.[27] In a similar fashion, Apostle Dallin H. Oaks stressed in 1986 that one should beware of questioning the leadership.

> A different principle applies in our Church, where the selection of leaders is based on revelation, subject to the sustaining vote of the membership. In our system of Church government, evil speaking and criticism of leaders by members is always negative. Whether the criticism is true or not, as Elder George F. Richards explained, it tends to impair the leaders' influence and usefulness, thus working against the Lord and his cause.[28]

Oaks also taught, "Truth should be disciplined by other values. . . . When truth is constrained by other virtues, the outcome is not falsehood but silence for a season."[29] Elder Charles Didier of the Seventy was even more explicit when he said in 1991, "Know by asking your Heavenly Father in the name of his Son Jesus Christ. Do not turn to public discussions and forums."[30]

The issue being discussed here is not one of truth, but of public expression. This notion necessitates that members first consider the effects of their public remarks on the community and remain silent where speaking is deemed harmful. Indeed, Apostles Bruce R. McConkie and Russell M. Nelson have explicitly stated the importance of silent disagreement. In the much-publicized 1981 correspondence between Apostle McConkie and member Eugene England, co-founder of *Dialogue*, McConkie told England, "It is my province to teach to the Church what the doctrine is. It is your province to echo what I say or to remain silent. You do not have a divine commission to correct me or any of the Brethren. The Lord does not operate that way."[31] Five years later, Apostle Nelson remarked,

"In some instances, the merciful companion to truth is silence. Some truths are best left unsaid."[32]

In contrast to these sentiments by Church officials, the dialogical movement feels that public expression is vital to honestly engaging with the issues and questions facing the faithful. The beliefs of the dialogical movement could be said to echo statements made by LDS leaders themselves, with Joseph Smith attesting, "By proving contraries truth is made manifest,"[33] and the statement of former President/Prophet John Taylor: "I think a full, free talk is frequently of great use; we want nothing secret nor underhanded, and I for one want no association with things that cannot be talked about and will not bear investigation."[34]

Without dialogue, doubt and disbelief fester, generally leading to one of two courses of action. The most common response in the LDS Church is to refrain from public expression until concerns are tempered or abolished. This is the approach advocated by Church leaders and is, in fact, the position consistently recommended by Public Affairs official Donald Jessee in this volume. The member may consult with friends or a local Church leader, but if his or her concerns persist, then they should not escape the confines of this safe, small network.

The September Six, with the notable exception of Avraham Gileadi, took a different approach that characterizes a different form of response—public discourse. They struggled for change, spoke out and published, all in order to inspire dialogue in the community to which they had devoted significant portions of their lives. To be sure, all of them had spent vast amounts of time in their respective Church communities, had either studied, taught, or worked at Church-operated Brigham Young University, and still have difficulty identifying as anything but Mormon. Theirs was not a passing interest in the faith, and they did not necessarily seek, as was more generally claimed by John Sillito and Susan Staker, "to differentiate his or her view of the Mormon experience from that of the Church leaders and from the overwhelming majority of Church members as well."[35] The September Six publicly expressed their divergent opinions simply to bring about honest and intellectual inquiries into concepts intrinsic to Mormonism.

To be sure, frustration felt by the September Six is not universal. Members in Utah may feel free to question or express doubt in the local ward building, while members living farther away from Utah might exercise even more liberty to question, doubt, or disbelieve. However, it remains the case that the moment a public discourse is engendered, the moment the LDS Church's public image or the faith of its members is endangered, or the moment *the appearance* of doctrinal unity is under threat, then discipline may well ensue.

As such, the tension between the Church and its intellectuals does not principally result from a concern to maintain doctrinal purity, but rather from the former seeking to ensure innocuous and irenic expressions of disagreement.[36] Comments by LDS sociologist Armand Mauss, who spent his adult career outside Utah, elaborate on this point:

> Even the most careful and diplomatic comments will not be much appreciated by many Church leaders, perhaps most Church leaders, whether general or local. We have to understand that much going in. Do not expect to appear on the short list for bishop or Relief Society president if you have been regularly commenting on local or general Church matters. If prominent Church positions are important to you, keep quiet. If you're going to speak up, whether in oral or written media, first cultivate a thick skin, then abandon your aspiration for important Church callings; you shouldn't have them anyway. Finally, don't whine when you're passed over or looked upon with some suspicion.[37]

Mauss acknowledges the freedom to publicly dissent, but only at the right times, in the right places, and in the right ways. He also indicates that regularly engaging in public dialogue precludes holding prominent Church positions and may well invite suspicion and derision. The September Six were not aspiring to such leadership positions when they were excommunicated, but they did seek to facilitate dialogue, and were duly expelled.

In his interview for this volume, LDS official Donald Jessee affirmed, "You can believe whatever you want as long as you keep it to yourself" and reiterated in his concluding remarks that members "can do what they want, they can think anything they want, and they can believe anything they want, so long as they keep it to themselves." The interview clearly demonstrates the Church's principal interest in the public nature of disagreement as expressed by one of its prominent and long-time employees. It is not the case, as former *Dialogue* editor Allen Roberts claims, that Joseph Smith's remark, "I teach the people correct principles and they govern themselves"[38] should be translated for today's Church as "We teach them what to believe and punish them if they question it."[39] Mormons have every freedom to question quietly, but not in the public sphere without threat of reprisal. This has resulted in an ideological vacuum that excludes acknowledgement of diverse opinions in the Church.

Yet, diversity on doctrinal, theological, political, and cultural issues is nothing new to Mormonism.[40] For example, after noting that the biblical apostles disagreed on doctrine, Brigham Young pointed out that an apostle in his own quorum did not believe in a personage called God, another apostle believed in a form of resurrection whereby infants are inhabited by the souls of those who formerly lived on earth, and yet another denied the atonement and had been preaching for fifteen years that Jesus was just a good man.[41] But times have changed. Church leaders now aim to keep the doctrinal diversity of the minority to a faint murmur for the majority.

Of course, the ability of the Church to monitor the public exchanges of its members has been radically complicated by the explosion of internet discussions, which are immediately public and largely immune to censorship. Comments that could have warranted discipline in 1993 are now commonplace on various blogs and forums, and are often anonymous and untraceable. The Church has yet to design a calculated response.

And Mormonism is not alone in its desire to censor. Most Christian traditions—Orthodox, Catholic, and Protestant alike—have a long history of disciplining vocal dissent,[42] which is a practice supported by a rather strong biblical basis.[43] The LDS Church, however, is different in that its leaders actively discipline select members in order to sustain the appearance of doctrinal purity for the sake of the Church's integrity and public image.⁴⁴ The dialogic movement, rather, wants to develop explorations of difference, but the ever-increasing polarization of the correlation and dialogical movements has resulted in an over-compensatory reaction by the former, placing in question the future of public debate in Mormonism.

There are promising developments, though, which include the rapid growth of Mormon discussions on the internet and the increasing presence of Mormon studies in the academy, as represented by new courses about Mormonism, a series of Ivy League conferences on Mormon studies, the establishment of the Howard W. Hunter Chair in Mormon Studies at the Claremont Graduate University School of Religion, and the founding of the Leonard J. Arrington Chair in Mormon History and Culture at Utah State University in Logan. It now remains to be seen whether the increasing acceptance of Mormon studies in the academy will be fully embraced by LDS leaders and ultimately reconcile the Church with the vibrant scholarship being produced within its own walls.

Currently, the dialogical movement and the work it produces is too far removed from the mainstream to be embraced by the Church, and those faithfully engaging in dialogue continue to experience a sense of alienation from their own tradition, as conveyed by the often heart-wrenching interviews in this volume. For members loyal to both their ward and Sunstone, for example, a ruptured identity of split allegiances is not uncommon.⁴⁵

In 1992, Paul Toscano and fellow Mormon Alliance members sought dialogue with the Church when they wrote a series of letters to Church leaders asking to discuss problematic issues regarding Church policy and the dominion of its leaders. These requests were denied, and Toscano felt so betrayed, particularly after being excommunicated, that he later described his expulsion to me as analogous to "being gang-raped by the Care Bears." Lynne Whitesides felt similarly rebuffed, noting in her interview, "If [Church leaders] would have just called me in, put their arm around me and said, 'Hey, Lynne, let's talk,' then things could have been a whole lot different."⁴⁶ While Givens is correct in noting that "efforts to enforce doctrinal conformity within a community of believers are, to some extent, common to most religious groups,"[47] there are often severe emotional and cultural repercussions, as evidenced by Whitesides, Toscano, and other contributors in this volume. If such members can ultimately find a home in the LDS Church, then the future of the institution looks bright as one that thrives in the midst of secularism.[48]

While much of the Christian mainstream continues to battle postmodern relativism and indifference, the LDS Church has succeeded in using the wayward world as a foil against the spiritual refuge it aims to provide. Part of maintaining this refuge, though, involves vigilance in caring for how the Church is publicly perceived, both *ad extra* and *ad intra*; and as the cultural horizons of the global LDS community continue to expand, leaders and members alike will be increasingly tested by more diverse perspectives. They will thus be compelled to continually redefine the extent to which LDS intellectual discourse is permissible, and that stance will crucially affect the precarious relationship between the Church and the more vocal and erudite portions of its membership. Perhaps one day, the ecclesiastical Church will decide that enforcing doctrinal conformity in public restricts from coming forth the vibrant spiritual community to which it aspires. Perhaps not.

Notes

[1] See also George D. Smith, ed., *Religion, Feminism, and Freedom of Conscience: A Mormon/Humanist Dialogue* (Salt Lake City: Signature Books, 1994). This work collects a number of essays primarily emerging from a three-day conference attended by both secular humanists and Mormons (or those affiliated with Mormonism), but emphasizes academic freedom and the role of conscience more than the nature and effects of LDS disciplinary procedures.

² "LDS Church Leaders State Their Position," *Salt Lake Tribune*, October 17, 1993, A23.

³ Relevant figures here would include Justin Martyr (ca. 100–165), Irenaeus (ca. 140–202), Tertullian (ca. 160–220), Hippolytus (ca. 170–235), and Origen (ca. 185–254).

⁴ Save to a certain extent for Judaism, early Christianity distinguished itself in the Greco-Roman world by emphasizing proper belief over behavior. Only orthodoxy could lead to orthopraxy. Consequently, eradicating heresy became a primary concern. For a more detailed discussion, see Bart Ehrman, *After the New Testament: A Reader in Early Christianity* (New York: Oxford University Press, 1999), esp. 194–95 and chap. 6.

⁵ The 1998 edition of the *General Handbook of Instructions* that took effect in 1999 included a new statement concerning symposia that reads: "The Church warns its members against symposia and other similar gatherings that include presentations that (1) disparage, ridicule, make light of, or are otherwise inappropriate in their treatment of sacred matters or (2) could injure the Church, detract from its mission, or jeopardize its members' well-being. Members should not allow their position or standing in the Church to be used to promote or imply endorsement of such gatherings." *Church Handbook of Instructions: Book 1* (Salt Lake City: Church of Jesus Christ of Latter-day Saints, 1998), 153. The handbook in effect at the time of the September Six expulsions, the 1989 edition, did not include this statement.

⁶ Dallin H. Oaks, "Alternate Voices," *Ensign*, May 1989, 27.

⁷ Boyd K. Packer, "Talk to the All-Church Coordinating Council," May 18, 1993, photocopy of typescript in my possession.

⁸ Frank O. May Jr., "Correlation of the Church: Administration," *Encyclopedia of Mormonism*, 4 vols. (New York: Macmillan, 1992), 1: 324. "In 1907, the First Presidency appointed the Committee of Correlation and Adjustments; in 1908, the Correlation Committee and the General Priesthood Committee on Outlines; in 1916, the Social Advisory Committee (combined with the Correlation Committee in 1920); in 1939, the Committee of Correlation and Coordination; and in 1940, the Union Board of the Auxiliaries. Relying on the mandates found in latter-day scripture, these groups were to correlate Church organizations in their structures, curricula, activities, and meetings."

⁹ An essential facet of Church monitoring takes place via the Strengthening Church Members Committee, which Apostle Dallin H. Oaks has identified as a "clipping service" that "pores over newspapers and other publications and identifies

members accused of crimes, preaching false doctrine, criticizing leadership or other problems. That information is forwarded on to the person's bishop or stake president, who is charged with helping them overcome problems and stay active in the Church." Quoted in "Six Intellectuals Disciplined for the Apostasy," *Sunstone* 92 (November 1993): 69. The First Presidency further clarified the nature and history of the Strengthening the Members Committee when it stated, "This committee serves as a resource to priesthood leaders throughout the world who may desire assistance on a wide variety of topics. It is a General Authority committee, currently comprised of Elder James E. Faust and Elder Russell M. Nelson of the Quorum of the Twelve Apostles. They work through established priesthood channels, and neither impose nor direct Church disciplinary action." Quoted in "Church Defends Keeping Files on Members," *Sunstone* 88 (August 1992): 63.

[10] In 1954 when University of Utah Professor McMurrin was threatened with excommunication for allegedly holding liberal theological views, especially regarding human evolution, McKay told McMurrin, "Sterling, you just think and believe as you please," and volunteered to appear as a character witness. The scheduled court was never held. McMurrin followed McKay's advice and, in addition to serving as U.S. Commissioner of Education during the Kennedy administration, taught in either the philosophy or history department at the University of Utah until his retirement in 1988. L. Jackson Newell, "Sterling Moss McMurrin: A Philosopher in Action," *Dialogue: A Journal of Mormon Thought* 28, no. 1 (Spring 1995): 6.

[11] In her interview, Maxine also notes that her membership was threatened due to the explicitly *public* expression of her views. See pg. 57 and the wider text of Chapter Three.

[12] Grant Palmer, email to Philip Lindholm, December 14, 2004.

[13] Hinckley was being interviewed on Compass (ABC), which aired on November 9, 1997. For a complete transcript of the interview, see http://www.abc.net.au/compass/intervs/hinckley.htm (accessed October 25, 2009).

[14] Joseph Fielding Smith, comp. and ed., *Teachings of the Prophet Joseph Smith* (Salt Lake City: Deseret Book, 1976), 157. This is not to say, however, that Joseph Smith was closed to dialogue and debate. Among some instances in which he encouraged a more liberal approach, he stopped a proposed disciplinary trial against one Mormon, Pelatiah Brown, for his interpretation of a verse in the book of Revelation: "I never thought it was right to call up a man and try him because he erred in doctrine, it looks too much like methodism and not like Latter day

Saintism. Methodists have creeds which a man must believe or be kicked out of their church. I want the liberty of believing as I please, it feels so good not to be trammeled. It don't prove that a man is not a good man, because he errs in doctrine." Andrew Ehat and Lyndon W. Cook, eds., *The Words of Joseph Smith: The Contemporary Accounts of the Nauvoo Discourses of the Prophet Joseph* (Provo, Utah: BYU Religious Studies Center, 1980), 183–84. A trammel is, as Frederick S. Buchanan relates, "something which everybody in 1842 was familiar with: a hobble or shackle used to make a horse amble instead of run—a means of impeding the horse's freedom and keeping it from straying. Smith wanted the freedom to 'lengthen his stride' in all areas of life [which] is impossible if we're forced to wear a trammel, no matter how comfortable it might be." Frederick S. Buchanan, "Academic Freedom Forever; However . . . " In *Religion, Feminism, and Freedom of Conscience*, 77–78.

[15] Orson Hyde, quoted in Scott G. Kenney, ed., *Wilford Woodruff's Journal, 1833–1898*, typescript, (Midvale, Utah: Signature Books, 1983–85), 6:363.

[16] George D. Smith comments that Thomas Ford, Illinois governor when Joseph Smith was assassinated, identified the following points of incitement regarding the early LDS community: "violations of freedom of the press, general religious views, polygamy, military strength, rumors of intent to destroy a nearby newspaper, Mormon alliance with native Americans, alleged coronation of Joseph Smith, vigilante bands, assertions that God has consecrated neighbors' property to Mormons, and bloc voting which made Mormon approval necessary for politicians." Quoted in Introduction, *Religion, Feminism, and Freedom of Conscience*, xii.

[17] Terryl L. Givens, *The Viper on the Hearth: Mormons, Myths, and the Construction of Heresy* (New York: Oxford University Press, 1997), 61.

[18] Tim B. Heaton, "Vital Statistics" in *Latter-day Saint Social Life*, edited by James T. Duke (Provo, Utah: Brigham Young University, 1998), 107. Such remarkable gradations provided the foundational data for Rodney Stark's projections that membership could swell to over 265 million by 2080, which would proportionately boost the missionary effort from 60,000 currently to 1.45 million. Rodney Stark, "The Rise of a New World Faith," in ibid., 15–17.

[19] Wilford Woodruff, "Official Declaration—1," in current (1981) edition of the LDS Doctrine and Covenants. First issued in 1890 as a press release and later canonized, the Woodruff Manifesto signaled the first retreat from plural marriage, which is now an excommunicable offense.

[20] Brigham Young, November 15, 1864, *Journal of Discourses* (London and Liverpool: LDS Booksellers Depot, 1855–86), 11:7.

[21] "If one member becomes corrupt, and you know it, you must immediately put it away, or it will either injure or destroy the whole body. The sympathies of the heads of the Church have induced them to bear a long time with those who were corrupt until they are obliged to cut them off, lest all become contaminated." Joseph Fielding Smith, *Teachings of the Prophet Joseph Smith*, 226.

[22] Young, *Journal of Discourses*, 11:7.

[23] Donald Q. Cannon and Lyndon W. Cook, eds., *Far West Record: Minutes of the Church of Jesus Christ of Latter-day Saints, 1830–1844* (Salt Lake City: Deseret Book, 1983), 196.

[24] Ibid.

[25] Lee A. Palmer, "Sustaining the General Authorities of the Church," *Improvement Era*, June 1945, 354.

[26] N. Eldon Tanner, "The Debate Is Over," *Ensign*, August 1979, 2–3. As recently as July 2008, the BYU student newspaper editorialized in favor of the First Presidency's support of a proposed amendment to the California constitution that would restrict marriage to a man and a woman. The editorial quoted Tanner without attributing the statement to him: "Active Mormons know that when the prophet speaks, the debate is over." The editorial continued: "This position is not robbing Church members of free-thinking. . . . No seminary graduate or gospel doctrine teacher can recite a story in any of the standard works where contradicting the Prophet turned out to be a good idea." "Follow the Prophet: Church Statement against Gay Marriage" (editorial), *Daily Universe*, July 8, 2008, 4.

[27] Ezra Taft Benson, "Fourteen Fundamentals in Following the Prophets," 1–7; all-capitalization of words and underlining eliminated. See also David Briscoe, "Benson Speech Stirs Speculation on LDS Changes," *Ogden Standard-Examiner*, March 2, 1980; "Interpretation of Speech Not Correct, Church Says," *Ogden Standard-Examiner*, February 27, 1980. The fourteen fundamentals were: "1. The prophet is the only man who speaks for the Lord in everything. 2. The living prophet is more vital to us than the standard works. 3. The living prophet is more important to us than a dead prophet. 4. The prophet will never lead the church astray. 5. The prophet is not required to have any particular earthly training or credentials to speak on any subject or act on any matter at any time. 6. The prophet does not have to say 'Thus Saith the Lord' to give us scripture. 7. The prophet tells us what we need to know, not always what we want to know. 8. The prophet is not limited by men's rea-

soning. 9. The prophet can receive revelation on any matter—temporal or spiritual; 10. The prophet may be involved in civic matters; 11. The two groups who have the greatest difficulty in following the prophet are the proud who are learned and the proud who are rich. 12. The prophet will not necessarily be popular with the world or the worldly. 13. The prophet and his counselors make up the First Presidency—the Highest Quorum in the Church. 14. Follow them and be blessed—reject them and suffer." Don LeFevre, Public Communications spokesman, responding to press inquiries, agreed that "Benson's speech accurately portrayed the Church's position that a prophet can receive revelations from God on any matter—temporal or spiritual," and that "the prophet's word is scripture, as far as the Church is concerned, and the living prophet's words take precedence in interpreting the written scripture as it applies to the present." However, he denied a newspaper report which said the president of the Church "is God's prophet and his word is law on all issues—including politics." That is "simply not true and contrary to a basic tenet of the religion," LeFevre was quoted as saying.

[28] Dallin H. Oaks, "Criticism," *Ensign*, February 1987, 68. He delivered this address in May 1986 at an LDS Student Association fireside, and it was published nine months later.

[29] Ibid.

[30] Charles Didier, "Statement," *Deseret News*, August 31,1991, B1.

[31] Bruce R. McConkie, Letter to Eugene England, February 19, 1981, quoted in Mark S. Gustavson, "Scriptural Horror and the Divine Will," *Dialogue: A Journal of Mormon Thought* 21, no. 1 (Spring 1988): 70.

[32] Russell M. Nelson, "Truth—and More," *Ensign*, January 1986, 69, quoted in Oaks, "Criticism."

[33] Joseph Smith Jr. et al., *History of the Church of Jesus Christ of Latter-day Saints*, edited by B. H. Roberts, 2d ed. rev. (6 vols., 1902–12, Vol. 7, 1932; rpt., Salt Lake City: Deseret Book, 1980 printing): 6:428.

[34] John Taylor, March 2,1879, *Journal of Discourses*, 20:264.

[35] John Sillito and Susan Staker, eds. *Mormon Mavericks* (Salt Lake City: Signature Books, 2002), ix.

[36] This is illustrated by the fact that inactive members, and even those who openly participate in other faith communities, can remain members in good standing in the LDS Church. The 2006 edition of the *Church Handbook of Instructions* includes, as a new provision to the previous three definitions of apostasy: "Formally join another church." Evidence of apostasy is one of the "transgressions" for which

"a disciplinary council is mandatory." *Church Handbook of Instructions* (Salt Lake City: Church of Jesus Christ of Latter-day Saints, 2006), 110.

[37] Armand L. Mauss, "A New 'Lost' Generation: The Future of Mormon Scholarship," Session 131, 2001 Sunstone Symposium, Salt Lake City.

[38] Young, *Journal of Discourses*, 10:57–58.

[39] Roberts, "Academic Freedom at Brigham Young University: Free Inquiry in Religious Context," in *Religion, Feminism, and Freedom of Conscience*, 55. The Joseph Smith quotation was recalled by John Taylor, May 18, 1862, *Journal of Discourses*, 10:57–58.

[40] Fifty-seven percent of Mormons remark that some doctrines are hard for them to accept and 66 percent do not agree with all the standards of the Church. Marie Cornwall and others, "The Dimensions of Religiosity: A Conceptual Model with an Empirical Test." In *Latter-day Saint Social Life*, 222.

[41] Brigham Young, June 23, 1867, *Journal of Discourses*, 12:66.

[42] Perhaps the strongest parallel to the way in which discipline is carried out in the LDS Church is found in Roman Catholicism. While leaders in the former are lay and the latter are professional, the hierarchical structures are often constructed in a similarly vertical fashion. With respect to disciplining vocal questioning or divergence, the cases of Hans Küng and Charles Curran are the most prominent Roman Catholic examples in the last half of the twentieth century. After publicly criticizing aspects of papal authority, especially the doctrine of infallibility, Küng lost his license to teach as a Roman Catholic theologian in 1979. Curran was removed from the Catholic University of America in 1986 for seeking to retain the right of vocal dissent on teachings not made *ex cathedra*. He now teaches at Southern Methodist University. However, while Küng and Curran were both forbidden to officially teach in the name of the Roman Catholic Church, neither was excommunicated. Anthony J. Figueiredo, *The Magistcrium-Theology Relationship: Contemporary Theological Conceptions in the Light of Universal Church Teaching since 1835 and the Pronouncements of the Bishops of the United States* (Rome: Gregorian University Press, 2001); *Instruction on the Ecclesial Vocation of the Theologian* (London: Catholic Truth Society, 1990); C. Curran, *Faithful Dissent* (Kansas City, KS: Sheed and Ward, 1986).

[43] Both the Old and the New Testaments warn the people of God against false prophets and teachers (e.g., Deut. 13:1–5; 1 Kgs. 22:5–23; Jer. 5:13, 31; 6:13; Mark 13:22–23; Acts 20:30; 2 Pe. 2:1). And indeed, Paul advocated handing blasphemers over to Satan (1 Tim. 1:20) and expelling incestuous Corinthians (1 Cor. 5:5), so that

both the transgressor and the community might be cleansed. Christian communities are to appreciate that "a little leaven leaveneth the whole lump." The righteous should "purge out therefore the old leaven, that ye may be a new lump, as ye are unleavened" (1 Cor. 5:6-7). Moreover, the New Testament stresses that Christians should not be deceived (Matt. 24:4) nor accept a different gospel (Gal. 1:8). This does not, however, mean that debate and dialogue were not prized in early Christianity. Jesus discussed and taught in the temple daily (Matt. 26:55), and Paul reasoned from the scriptures and engaged in disputations (Acts 7:2, 17:17, 18:4, 19:8), which is how "all they which dwelt in Asia heard the word of the Lord Jesus, both Jews and Greeks" (Acts 19:10). Common passages cited from the Book of Mormon in discussions of disciplinary action include 3 Nephi 18:31, Mosiah 26:36, and Alma 5:59.

[44] *The General Handbook of Instructions* (1998) 1:91, notes, "Transgressions that significantly impair the good name or moral influence of the Church may require the action of a disciplinary council."

[45] Armand Mauss, *The Angel and the Beehive* (Urbana: University of Illinois Press, 1994), xii-xiii, stated: "I have come to feel increasingly marginal to the Mormon community during my adult life, at least in a social and intellectual sense, despite my continuing and conscientious participation in church activity (including leadership) and despite my own deep personal faith in the religion itself."

[46] It is also worth noting that "DNA Mormons," those with lineages reaching far back into Mormon history, generally experience a different sense of longing and separation than do converts. In this volume, for example, one does not come across remorse in the interviews of converts Lynne Whitesides and Paul Toscano *in the same way* as that found with Margaret Toscano, her sister Janice Allred, or D. Michael Quinn, each of whom has deep, familial roots in Mormon history. I am indebted to Jan Shipps for pointing out this factor to me. She has also written: "If members are 'birthright' members of a religious community or members of very long standing, they not only are connected to the group through the continuing affirmation of its religious claims that regular and wholehearted participation in public and private worship signifies but also are tied to it ethnically and culturally, thus unifying the ascribed and the achieved dimensions of their personal identities within the framework of the faith community. Even if, at some point in their lives, members reject the theological and doctrinal underpinnings of the community's institutional structure and make a conscious decision to disclose this, they do not so easily shed the ethnic and cultural dimension of their identity. As a result, much of its meaning-

making and value-imparting structure stays with them." Shipps, *Sojourner in the Promised Land: Forty Years among the Mormons* (Urbana: University of Illinois Press, 2000), 178–79.

[47] Givens, *The Viper on the Hearth*, 77.

[48] Stark, "The Rise of a New World Faith," 18.

Acknowledgments

In a collaborative work such as this, the greatest and most sincere thanks are due the contributors, without whom the project would not have been possible. They were uniformly gracious and open in recounting their pasts, for which I will be forever grateful. Furthermore, Lavina Fielding Anderson was an editor of remarkable sensitivity and acumen, and Maxine Hanks's thoughts helped shape my own. Greg Kofford admirably oversaw a project encumbered with obstacles, and the manuscript benefitted greatly from feedback offered by Jan Shipps, Juli Geiger, Mattijs Kronmeyer, Cameron Neblett, Lita Lindholm, Dustin Wood, and Jessica Lindholm-Wood.

Funding from Squire and Marriott and the University of Oxford facilitated extended periods of research in Salt Lake City, and access to the LDS Church History Library proved invaluable.

Finally, thanks are due to Professor Frank Wilson, whose passion for the LDS Church initiated my own spiritual and scholarly journey into a tradition not my own; J for Santa Barbara, and L for making the future bright.

Chapter 1
Lynne Kanavel Whitesides

Feminist, president of the Mormon Women's Forum, disfellowshipped September 14, 1993.

Lynne Kanavel Whitesides was the second of two children, born in January of 1952 in Philadelphia, Pennsylvania. Soon thereafter her parents, Violet and Edward Kanavel, moved the family to Levittown, Pennsylvania. Subsequent moves, including to St. Pete, Florida, meant that Lynne attended different schools for eighth, ninth, tenth, and eleventh grades. In the eleventh grade, she began to investigate the LDS Church, though admittedly more out of intrigue and loneliness than from any aspiration to convert. Constantly moving had deeply troubled Lynne, and she grew frustrated with making friends only to leave them. Her decision to investigate Mormonism was an outgrowth of this frustration, for Mormonism offered a reliable community that promised to be close, no matter where she might move in the future.

Lynne's decision to seek companionship in Mormonism appalled her devout Lutheran parents. Then, when Lynne was a high school senior, they all received a shock when their Lutheran minister and close family friend passed away. This death further dissipated Lynne's already tenuous ties to Lutheranism and gave her the freedom to investigate Mormonism with newfound vigor. Vigor bred perseverance and culminated in conviction. Lynne chose to be baptized into the LDS Church a week after her eighteenth birthday. Begrudgingly, her parents attended the baptism and, to everyone's surprise, had a profound spiritual experience that resulted in their own baptism the following spring. Violet and Edward shared their faith with the rest of the family and helped convert thirty of Lynne's relatives to Mormonism, including aunts, cousins, uncles, and grandparents.

In September of 1970, Lynne entered the center of Mormon academic thought—Brigham Young University (BYU) in Provo, Utah. Upon her arrival, both she and the conservative campus experienced culture shock. The outspoken and budding feminist from Pennsylvania encountered a deeply traditional culture reluctant to tolerate her sharp criticism of conventional theological and cultural views. Lynne failed to fully integrate into the mainstream Mormon community throughout her time at BYU and eventually stopped trying.

In 1977, Lynne fell in love with Alan Whitesides, a Mormon and aspiring doctor, and they married on January 20, 1978, in the Provo Temple. The newlyweds then moved to Guadalajara, Mexico, where Lynne baked seventy pies a week and sold them on the street to support Alan through medical school. After his graduation, they moved into an extremely liberal ward in Chicago near Northwestern University before settling down in Salt Lake City in 1985.

In Salt Lake City, while raising their three children, Lynne's budding feminism blossomed. She began chairing the symposia sponsored by *Sunstone*—a left-of-center periodical that also hosts an annual symposium in Salt Lake City in late summer and sometimes regional symposia as well. Lynne's lively programming started to bring in feminist sessions that attracted standing-room-only crowds. Then, in 1990, she took graduate classes at the University of Utah, which allowed her to delve into the literature of twentieth-century French feminists. During this time she also chaired the B. H. Roberts Society, a group founded in 1980 to discuss "timely issues in Mormonism." These affiliations, in conjunction with her election as president of the controversial Mormon Women's Forum in 1992, proved perilous. Church leaders disapproved of such organizations that were willing to question every aspect of the faith, especially the authority of the Church hierarchy. A television interview with local news anchor Chris Vanocur in the summer of 1992 sealed Lynne's fate in Mormonism.

I sat down with Lynne in a restaurant two blocks away from the BYU campus in Provo, Utah, on Saturday, July 12, 2003. She entered the restaurant in jeans and a white T-shirt. She smiled warmly and often, maintaining an upbeat attitude throughout our three-hour interview, despite being asked to recall some of the most traumatic events of her life.

The Excommunication

Philip: Going into the Chris Vanocur show,[1] did you have any idea of the repercussions that you would incur as a result?

Lynne: No! I was shocked when they sent me a summons letter to appear before a Church court at the end of August. On the TV show I was saying anything I wanted to and knew the Church was getting upset, but not that upset. I wasn't going to church regularly. My bishop wasn't telling me to knock it off, and we hadn't even met since May of 1993, which is when I told him that I didn't feel comfortable in my ward.

In May when my bishop called me to come in to talk, I thought, "Wow . . . this is so great. Maybe the system does work. Maybe this church really is a place where I can get comfortable." I was very excited. I left early from my feminism class up at the University of Utah to meet with him. When I walked in, he was with his two counselors, all in suits, and I'm thinking, "Wow, they really want me back at church. This is great! This is so great!" I sat down, and Virgil Merrill, the bishop, said, "Elder Loren C. Dunn has asked us to meet with you to see if we need to take any ecclesiastical action against you."

I started to laugh and couldn't stop. "Give me a minute," I said, "I thought you called me in here because you cared about me. Let me just have a quick moment to adjust." Their faces . . . you could see that what I had said shocked them, but then we had a lovely talk. It was not confrontational at all; it was amazing. At the end, Virgil said he was going to tell Dunn that I was fine. So, when I received the summons letter I was shocked.

Philip: Your bishop gave you no warning at all that you were going to be tried by a church court?

Lynne: No, nothing. When I found out, I called Lavina [Fielding Anderson] immediately, whom I had met back in 1985 and just adored. She showed up with homemade bread and jam, and then got on the phone. We also wrote a letter to the bishop saying that if he went through with the Church court, then we were going to let the media know. Virgil wrote back saying that he wanted to hold it. He didn't realize what he was getting into. He didn't realize how much press coverage it was going to get. We heard through the grapevine that he was getting pressure from [Boyd K.] Packer[2] and other leaders to excommunicate me.

Philip: Can you elaborate on "the grapevine"?

Lynne: One of the bishopric counselors involved in my court was related to a reporter I knew. Both were at a barbeque once, and the counselor told the reporter, not thinking it would ever get back to me, that they were getting pressure from Church leaders to "do something" about Lynne Whitesides. Well, it did get back to me, and I knew this going into the trial.

Philip: How did you feel when you arrived for the trial?

Lynne: I was really nervous. There were about two hundred people outside holding a vigil, singing hymns, holding candles, and the TV stations and newspapers. . . . I was really surprised to see all the people and cameras. We had let the local media know, but somehow CNN and the *New York Times* found out and showed up. The story got on the front page of the *New York Times*. It was outrageous. All these people were getting kicked out, and apparently that was really interesting to people outside as well as inside the Church. In fact, as soon as the story hit, Connie Chung's people called to ask me if I would take a hidden camera into my court. I told them no. Integrity-wise, it was not something I wanted to do.

When I arrived at the church, the leaders said I couldn't have anybody with me inside, and I freaked out. My husband took me by the hand, looked at me, and said, "You can do this," and I went in. The bishop was shaking, because we had a letter-writing campaign going where everyone who knew me wrote in to tell him what a wonderful woman I was. He had a huge stack of papers in front of him. Then he looked at me and said, "It's not about whether you are a good person.

I get that you are a good person." I responded, "Are you getting pressure to excommunicate me?" He said, "No," and I knew he was lying. That really frustrated me. He could have at least told me the truth.

They started asking me a lot of questions. The bishop started by asking why I thought it was all right to pray to a female deity—a God who is not male. I said that people like my Chinese sister-in-law could not relate to a white, male God, which made the secretary mad. He yelled, "We know what God looks like. Joseph Smith told us." I just looked at him and said, "Which one of his accounts are you talking about? Which one do you choose?" The bishop got him to quiet down, and it was the only time anyone got angry.

We then brought in my six witnesses, which was kind of pathetic now that I think about it. One was Margaret [Merrill Toscano], and another was Lavina, both of whom would later endure the same thing I did. The problem was that all my friends were on the fringe. After they testified, we were all sent out so they could deliberate.

Philip: The trial started at 8:00 P.M. and finished at midnight, correct?

Lynne: It was five hours from start to finish, because they deliberated for an hour, from midnight till 1:00. After deliberating, I was asked to come into the bishop's office. He told me, "You've been disfellowshipped." As I slowly walked out of the building, the reporters came and yelled questions at me.

Philip: How did it feel to emerge from the bishop's office knowing that you had been disfellowshipped?

Lynne: I was—tired. I felt that being disfellowshipped was fine, but they might as well have excommunicated me, because now I would be seen as an enemy of the Church. Even if I had still wanted to be active, my experience from books about Juanita Brooks[3] and others who have spoken out on something the Church didn't like was that, once you did what I did, there's no getting back in. They don't want you back. "At least I'm still sealed to my husband and kids," I thought to myself.

Philip: What exactly did the Church charge you with?

Lynne: Apostasy.

Philip: Can you be more specific? There are three official definitions of apostasy.[4]

Lynne: Not really. They did tell me what the conditions were for me to come back into the Church. One was that I could no longer speak evil of the Lord's anointed by saying anything derogatory about the Church or its leaders. Also, I was not allowed to talk about Mother in Heaven or how women should hold the priesthood. They had all kinds of information on me, files of things I'd said. They even had transcripts of interviews I gave underlined in yellow.

Philip: So they had been tracking you for a while.

Lynne: Oh, yeah. There is a Strengthening Church Members Committee that we didn't know about at the time, a Gestapo-like group which press-clipped everything anyone said who might be considered an enemy of the Church, meaning one who disagrees with Church policy.

Philip: Why do you think you were disfellowshipped when the other members of the September Six were excommunicated? Did you avoid the more drastic punishment because you were the first one?

Lynne: Partly, though a week after the disfellowshipment a wife of one of the counselors in the bishopric came over to my house and said, "I need to tell you something. They were told to excommunicate you; but when you walked into the room, every one of them thought, 'We cannot excommunicate this woman.' That's why you were disfellowshipped." That was really nice. It was all very difficult for the bishop. They'll probably never allow him to be a bishop again.

Philip: Because he didn't excommunicate you?

Lynne: Yeah. That probably made them mad, especially someone like Packer.

The Church Hierarchy/Authority

Philip: In 1993, before your excommunication, you declared on public television that Christ was not to be found in a speech recently given by Elder Boyd K. Packer.[5] Do you feel that Church leaders generally speak of Christ to the degree that they should?

Lynne: No. I don't think they even have the slightest understanding. That may be arrogant of me, but that is my experience. The

Church is so much about works that the few people who would actually like to talk about Christ and the amazing gift that Christ is have been silenced. It can only come from my experience, Philip, and my experience of God since I left the Church is one so different than anything I could have ever imagined. It feels so narrow in there when they talk about Christ, when they talk about hierarchy, when they talk about who God is. It's almost like God is a general ordering people around. I've worked with Native American traditions a lot since leaving the Church and one particular Native American medicine man for five years. So, my experience is a little different.

When I hear them speak about Christ in the Church, it's always about how much you have to do to be saved. There is so much you have to do to be saved! But in my experience of Christ, you are already saved through the grace of God. Done. All you have to do is open your heart. I don't feel like they ever embrace that awe of it all. I never feel awe when I hear them talk. I never hear from them that feeling when you just get it—"Oh my God, thank you." I don't hear that, and I wish I did.

Philip: Did you *ever* feel that when you were in the Church?

Lynne: No, I didn't even know it was possible to feel that. I had no idea.

Philip: The LDS Church claims to be thoroughly founded upon revelation and the authority God bestows on leaders to guide the Church. You questioned this authority repeatedly. Wouldn't that qualify as apostasy in LDS terms?

Lynne: Why would disagreeing be apostasy? Of course not. To disagree and to disobey are two very different things. I wasn't smoking, drinking, or having sex with people I shouldn't be having sex with. None of the behavioral code was broken. The fact that I was thinking does not seem like apostasy to me. The fact that I was saying, "I don't agree with this," and still going to church, paying tithing, and doing all those things does not seem like apostasy to me. And you know, if they would have just called me in, put their arm around me, and said, "Hey, Lynne, let's talk," then things could have been a whole lot different.

Philip: But you didn't trust in the authority of Church leaders.

Lynne: There has to be a mutual trusting. As far as I can tell about authority, the people who claim it have to warrant it. They have to be who they say they are. They have to come across as people I can trust. As much as Church leaders said how things were, *I* still had to know. I couldn't just go by what they said.

My grandfather was German and left Germany in 1920. The idea to just trust your leader. . . . My family was very aware of what happened in Nazi Germany when people had just obeyed their leader, so for me to just trust some guy or some group of guys without feeling it myself was not going to happen. Most people wouldn't just trust unless they grew up in the Church. Who would just say, "You're my leader" and go by that?

Philip: Well, the Church *would* advocate that each member obtain their own personal witness to what the prophet tells them.

Lynne: Yeah, except half of the time the prophet is comatose. If you have that kind of gerontocracy going on, you don't have a leg to stand on when you're trying to claim authority. When I was living in Chicago, President Kimball's grandson was in our ward, and we all knew very well that the Prophet wasn't making any decisions. Yet we were raising our arm to the square and sustaining him as the prophet of God. It's not true! We have this history with Benson, Kimball, and McKay who became so old and comatose,[6] and we just kept them alive . . . it doesn't make any sense to me. Let's tell the truth! That would be a refreshing thing in the Church.

Philip: So General Authorities—prophets—are lying?

Lynne: They lie all the time! Are you kidding? Oh my gosh! They lie all the time. I think that's why so many women are taking Prozac and leaving the Church. They can't find the truth anywhere and it doesn't feel good. That's exactly what is going on.

President Benson once gave a talk to women in the Church saying that we should stay at home, make beds, and clean the house.[7] That's where we would get our biggest joy from. We should all come home from the typewriter. That talk motivated most of us to do what we did! It was so demeaning and untrue. There is overt and covert lying, and women's place in this Church has always been a covert lie.

They put women on a pedestal in the Church like they're great, and yet there is this patriarchal hierarchy.

I don't even want to go into this because it's such a moot point for me now. . . . When I became a member of the Church, girls were being told to shine the shoes of their brothers so they could make it to priesthood meeting on time. Then there were corresponding lessons during "Standards Night" where girls were told to squish up tinfoil, pin it around a mirror, and tell themselves that they were beautiful, while the boys learned how to orient themselves on a compass. Girls also had a lesson with a chewed-up piece of gum and were asked, "Do you want to be a chewed-up piece of gum?" referring to sexual sin, and when the boys had this lesson they were asked, "Would you want a girl who was a chewed-up piece of gum?"

There's always this subtle message that women and girls are just in a box—they can't move. They have to live up to a standard. When I left there was little truth-telling about the sadness of women in the Church. They felt tied down, overworked, and only their nine or ten kids were allowed to reflect how they were doing. My feeling was that women in the Church were going to die out if something didn't change.

One time, somebody from the Relief Society general presidency came to my house and talked to a group of women about what we needed to do to make some changes in the Church. She had been in the presidency for five years at that point and asked us, "How many times do you think the prophet and the Relief Society president meet?" Now, I think most members of the Church would think that at least once a month the head of the Church and the head of the women's organization would meet, but within five years they had not met—even once! Even Mrs. America got a moment with the prophet!

The fact is that the Relief Society general presidency is under the auspices of the priesthood and the General Authorities. They can't do anything for the women on their own. They have no access to get anything done, and when those kinds of things come to light . . . you ask me if they lie? They don't lie overtly, but there is a covert thing going on. I was pissed when I saw that what women were being handed by the Church was never about being a woman. It was how not to be a man.

I wrote a letter to the General Authorities two years after I was disfellowshipped saying, "I'm really sorry. I thought you could give me something I already had. I put it on you. I got angry at you, and I'm really sorry because I wanted you to give me power as a woman. You could not give me what I already possessed." That was a big development for me. They just wrote back and said, "Come back to the Church."

Philip: Do you think the average member should have a larger role in establishing the doctrines and practices of the Church?

Lynne: Well, in a perfect Church, you'd actually have a prophet who was talking to God and God was talking to the prophet, but I think every single person can have that. Every single one of us has access to God. It doesn't have to be through some church. Unfortunately though, every church becomes dogmatic, and it becomes difficult for one to have an idea of the living, amazing God.

So, do I think members should have a larger role in the Church? I don't know. I think people should find their own inner path and go that way, and if you keep putting it on someone else to find God for you, then you'll be lost forever.

Philip: President Wilford Woodruff and others have said that each member of the Church is a prophet, but he did differentiate between the type of revelation received by a General Authority and that of the average member: The former receives guidance on how to guide the Church whereas the latter does not. Do you take the opposite position that average members are given revelation that dictates how the Church should be run?

Lynne: I understand that Woodruff is making a distinction by saying that prophetic revelation somehow has the wheel of the boat, but I just don't know if church in general is the place to find God, especially this Church. I guess if you really want to be part of this community, then you would hope that leaders are receiving revelation, and you pray to receive your own personal revelation. It would be pretty perfect if that was happening. I don't believe that's happening. I believe that if this Church was actually receiving revelation, then it would open its doors to homeless people, single moms, and people who are in pain. It would become an actual hospital. As Paul Toscano says, the Church should stop being a social club and start being a hospital. It would stop being a business, stop earning money like it does, stop spending money like it does, stop proselytizing like it does, and go help people instead. I don't know how or even if it's possible to fix this Church. In every neighborhood in Utah, there should not be one homeless person, one person in pain, and that's not happening. So what is this Church about?

Philip: Where in the hierarchy does the Church fail?

Lynne: It fails at the top, because it's at the top that they're making those money decisions. But if you think about it, Philip, why aren't people at the bottom, in the wards, saying, "Oh my gosh. Harry Jones is sitting out in Pioneer Park strung out on heroin. We should help him"? The Church would change if people would open their hearts and actually share their goods, knowledge, and comforting thoughts. There's something clearly not right about the way it's set up. The Church has a welfare program, but there are all these rules surrounding it, and it's usually only for Mormons. Aren't we all God's children?

Philip: Wait, the LDS Church is one of the world's greatest benefactors, providing humanitarian relief worldwide to Mormons and non-Mormons alike.

Lynne: That's true, but from what I understand there are often strings attached. Right here at home they could be doing so much. Can you imagine if people actually gave comfort to homeless people, or if there was a really good drug rehab place for people to go, get clean, and feel better? What would that do for membership numbers in the Church? If you really want to increase numbers, go out there and take care of the people who are in pain. It's not that hard. Mother Teresa did it over and over.

Belief and Doctrine

Philip: At what point is one an apostate in Mormonism? Are there particular beliefs you must hold to be Mormon, and if so, what are they?

Lynne: I think the Church insisting on everybody keeping what's on their mind to themselves, to hide it, is a really evil thing to do. That feels like an apostate act to me. To not encourage people to actually speak about what is troubling them is going to blow up in their face, and that's a huge problem. That's more of an apostate act than someone pointing out issues and asking to talk about them.

Philip: Can you believe whatever you want and still be a member of the LDS Church?

Lynne: They *have* that! All over the place, people believe whatever they want and they're still members of the Church, and if they think that people who come from Mozambique don't have a different view of the Church . . . just like how I came into the Church with a Catholic/Lutheran lens. I am aware that the words others speak and the words I speak may be the same but still have different meanings. I've seen it in South America. When I lived in Mexico I saw that Mexican Mormons, because it is so Catholic down there, have a very different idea of what it means to be Mormon than a ward up here. Everyone believes different things, but somehow a balance is found. It's when you tip that balance that you're suddenly an apostate.

Philip: Does the balance consist of believing in the distinguishing tenets of Mormonism, like the prophethood of Joseph Smith or the veracity of the Book of Mormon? If you compromise on those, are you compromising your good standing in the Church?

Lynne: Yeah. If you want to be an active Mormon those are the types of things that you probably want to believe in.

The Status of Women in Mormonism

Philip: You have advocated in the past that women should officially have the priesthood—why? And if the prophet says they shouldn't, then shouldn't you acknowledge that there could be a divine reason of which you are not aware?

Lynne: Absolutely, but what does priesthood mean? Priesthood is the power to act with the authority of God. There should be equality in that. To bless someone I shouldn't have to have the priesthood. Sure there could be something I don't understand, that's always a possibility, but withholding the priesthood from women just doesn't make sense to me. Maybe ordinances are important, but . . .

Philip: You've been baptized, and baptism is an ordinance. Isn't baptism important?

Lynne: I was baptized twice—Lutheran and Mormon—and it's just a symbol. I don't know. The New Testament says it's important. Christ himself did it, and I'll go along with that, but who does the baptizing is not important. It's just presenting someone to God.

Philip: But in Mormon thought there is a literal cleansing of sins when one is baptized.

Lynne: Yeah? What—you go under the water, come up, and there's a literal cleansing? Baptism just presents who you are in a conscious way to God, and the water is part of the symbol. I was baptized by Elder Paul Ek when I was eighteen years old, and he immediately left the Church afterwards. Was that holy? Did his holding the priesthood really matter?

Philip: Concerning the priesthood, some Mormon leaders have charged feminists with trying to create a competition between men and women that goes against God's will—they are to complement rather than compete against one another. How do you react to that sentiment?

Lynne: I actually agree with that, but what they are thinking probably differs from what I'm thinking. I think competition in a personal relationship is always a problem, and that's not what Christ was talking about. Men and women do different things.

Unfortunately, it's very difficult in this day and age to get equality, and certain things would have to arise to make that happen: equal pay, equal vote, and equal roles in making decisions. Those types of complementary things don't mean you have to compete, but rather just that my vote is as important as yours, my point of view is as important as your point of view.

They are probably not giving any thought to what it took for women to get what they have. The fact that women couldn't vote until 1920 never gets talked about. It never gets talked about that women after 1945, when they finally realized they *could* do more than just stay at home and have babies, were *sent* home, and that's when the huge depression of women began. They make it too easy, but the heart of what he's saying is true. Men and women do different things, but he doesn't take into consideration why he has to say that. It has been so inequitable and unlivable for women that of course we now have to compete in order to be heard.

Philip: So if there was equality in the first place, then there would be no need for competition today?

Lynne: Exactly.

Philip: In your response to Janice Allred's excommunication in 1995, you declared that the LDS Church treats its female intellectuals as if this were a medieval witch hunt. You then prescribed a rather hyperbolic solution to the witch hunt: "When women come to the waters of baptism from now on, we could add one step: See if they float, then we can save all of us a lot of time and heartache."[8] Aren't there women who don't feel hunted by Church leaders and don't aspire for change? Are they wrong?

Lynne: Many women are perfectly happy in the Church. I don't disagree with that, but there are women who are miserable in the Church. It might have changed since 1993; but if you were a female intellectual Mormon then and had something to say, you might as well have been a witch in the Middle Ages. We would have been burned, those of us who were doing what we did back then. That's what I was trying to say. If you disagreed or you said what you felt, then you might as well just hit the road.

Philip: So it's all right for Mormon women to not have the issues you do?

Lynne: Yes, but if women do have those issues is it wrong for them to say how they feel? Of course not. If someone is happy in the place provided for women in the Church, then fine, but if you aren't, then you have to be able to do something about it or you will just get depressed and die.

Philip: The *New York Times* quoted you on October 2, 1993, as saying, "If you excommunicate one of us there will be 10 more to step up and take her place. Excommunicate those 10 and there will be 100 to take their places" (p. 7). Nothing of the scale of the September Six has transpired since 1993. This manifold group that you anticipated has yet to step up. Were you wrong?

Lynne: I think I was right, not so much that women are getting excommunicated by the tens of hundreds, but rather that women are leaving. I don't know what the stats are, but I think they're pretty high and especially for young women leaving the Church.

Reflection

Philip: In retrospect, how have your thoughts and feelings changed over the last ten years toward both the Church and the events that transpired?

Lynne: Actually they've changed quite a bit. I was so pissed off when I left, and then my marriage fell apart right after that. Everything in my life crumbled. But out of having everything fall apart, I was able to find myself in a way that I hadn't before. I never could have found Native American spirituality without having gone to the Mormon Church first. I don't think I would have been so desperate to find something that could bring me some peace. I'm now in love with Rumi and the poetry of Islam that is so beautiful, and I don't know if I would have looked for it had I not been so sad that this Church wasn't what I had thought it was going to be. I've now found different sources that give life.

I'm surprised at how I feel about the Church now. I can now drive past the temple and the Church Office Building and not want to flip it off. I can live in Salt Lake City and not notice whether someone is Mormon or not anymore—I just don't care. That's been a really nice place to be in, and I didn't expect that. It has really been an amazing ten years for me.

Philip: Are you upset about what happened?

Lynne: No. I was, but when I look back I just wonder what I should have expected. I was baiting the Church in order to get its attention and make some changes, but there was no way they would hear someone saying, "Listen to me!" Of course they were going to discipline me. Look at what I wrote about Janice Allred . . . it's a very funny piece! It's hilarious that I wrote that, that I was so pissed off, but not anymore. It feels okay now.

Philip: You never hesitated to publicly address controversial issues in the Church, such as Heavenly Mother or the fact that only men can have the priesthood. Didn't you ever think these inquiries could result in disciplinary action that might include excommunication?

Lynne: No. Isn't that funny? If I was paying attention I would have, but I wasn't raised Mormon so maybe that's why. I guess I counted on the fact that people generally liked me, and I just didn't think excommunication would ever happen to me. You know, all of this stuff was to help people stay in the Church! *Sunstone*, B. H. Roberts, Mormon Women's Forum—these were all places where people could go and talk about the things they couldn't talk about at church. Most of these people were very active in the Church. They went every Sunday, paid their tithing, all that stuff. For them it was such a relief to find a forum where you could talk about things that were bothering you and work them out. If the Church had just left all of them alone, then most of them would have worked through these issues and, mostly, been able to stay in the Church.

Philip: Did you deserve to be disfellowshipped?

Lynne: I don't think anybody *deserves* to be excommunicated or disfellowshipped. I don't think anyone deserves that. If this was a church of love, then there would be another way to entreat people to come back into the fold. You can wear your garments, pay your tithing, but you can't speak in Church or sing in choir . . . they have all these rules.

No, I didn't deserve to be disfellowshipped. Yet I'm really glad. I wouldn't have been able to leave the Church if they had put their arm around me and said, "Lynne, you're having a hard time. Let's talk about it." Things would have been a whole lot different. And do I think that Paul, Margaret, Maxine [Hanks], Mike [D. Michael Quinn], and Lavina should have been excommunicated? No. And Janice? Absolutely not. Aside from Paul, who converted, Mormonism was in all of their DNA with roots going to the beginnings of Mormonism. I think that Boyd Packer is a bully. He's a mean guy.

There's a piece in Dostoyevsky's *The Brothers Karamazov* where the monk says that the state has to exact justice, and the church is there for mercy, like a mother with arms open wide (Pt. 1, bk 2, chap. 5).

Therefore, when your church excommunicates you, then where do you go for mercy? I'll tell you where a lot of people go—they just throw it all out. God's gone, all of it's gone. We need to find a way to love people. Neither murder, nor rape, nor child abuse deserves excommunication.

Philip: But the LDS Church claims that excommunication is out of love. It allows you to humble yourself and come back into full fellowship.

Lynne: Isn't that sweet? That is so sweet. I don't believe that. I'll tell you a quick story. I had a friend from California who had nine children, did everything the Church ever asked, and was about to crack. Her husband was an emotionally absent kind of guy. Then she had a one-night stand with someone and confessed to her bishop, who quickly excommunicated her and didn't offer much help afterwards. She killed herself and left her nine children. A court of love? I don't think so. I don't think you take a woman who has devoted her life to being a model Mormon and then excommunicate her when she had a moment of falling apart. It's insane. She's dead!

Philip: Have you attended any church since your excommunication?

Lynne: No. I do ceremonies with a Native American medicine man, but church? No.

Philip: Was Joseph Smith a prophet?

Lynne: I don't know anymore. He surely was charismatic and had a way about him. I think he was amazing and had an experience that he wanted to share. I like that about him. I think, like a lot of people, perhaps polygamy was a little off, but most people will have an experience and never share it. Not him.

Philip: Are you Mormon?

Lynne: . . . No. It's a hard question, but no. Not at all. Maybe a little. The lens is there, and I can't remove it because I was Mormon for twenty years, but I don't feel Mormon.

Philip: So Mormonism for you now is only an aspect of your perspective with which you can look at the world?

Lynne: Yeah. It's not my life. I don't believe in my heart of hearts that Gordon B. Hinckley is a prophet of God.

Philip: As you see Mormonism today, do you want it to flourish?

Lynne: You know, I don't care. I wish if it were to flourish that it would do so in a way that was all-inclusive, loving, and could tell the truth about its shadow. I guess I wish it well, but to flourish means to be alive and full of life, and it doesn't feel full of life to me at this point. It feels very burdened.

Philip: Do you have any regrets?

Lynne: No. I mean, I wish I wouldn't have been so angry, because maybe they would have heard me if I wasn't so angry. But I have no regrets, really. I'm glad for every minute of it. It was a kick. It was really fun. Doing radio shows with the BBC in England on the phone was hilarious to me. I'd be lying on my bed drinking a diet Coke, and they would come a-callin'.

I am so grateful for the Mormon Church and have no regrets about being Mormon nor for leaving the Church. It gave me so much. It gave me a community, a feel for God that I hadn't had before, and it also gave me the ability to question. It was so ludicrous that it was easy to question.

On some level, Mormonism made sense to me because it is very simple. A lot of the Christian religions like Lutheranism and especially Catholicism have more of a mystical side to them, but there is not a lot of mysticism about the Mormon Church as it is given to the people. God has a body, parts, and passions, and that appealed to me. It was something that made sense to me as an eighteen-year-old, something I could grasp, though another part of it was that I was a lonely high school senior who didn't have any friends because we kept moving. When I converted, there were things they didn't tell me, and some of it turned out to be ludicrous, but I'm really glad I joined. I don't blame the leaders for anything. They're actually doing the best job they know how.

Philip: Do you miss the LDS Church at all?

Lynne: Not. One. Bit. Not one bit.

Notes

1. The program aired on KXVX, Channel 4, in Salt Lake City.

2. Boyd K. Packer, an apostle since 1970, became Acting President of the Quorum of the Twelve in 1994. He is now (2010) president of the Twelve.

3. Juanita Brooks (1898–1989), a graduate of BYU and Columbia University, wrote controversial books on Mormon history, including *Mountain Meadows Massacre* (1950). Though threatened with excommunication, Brooks constantly fought for the right to publish her historical research, against the will of Church leaders. See Levi S. Peterson, *Juanita Brooks: Mormon Woman Historian* (Salt Lake City: University of Utah Press, 1988).

4. *The General Handbook of Instructions* is the official guide for church leaders. It outlines the administrative rules and regulations of the Church. It defines an apostate as someone who "(1) Repeatedly acts in clear, open, and deliberate public opposition to the Church or its leaders. (2) Persists in teaching as Church doctrine information that is not Church doctrine after they have been corrected by their bishops or higher authority. (3) Continues to follow the teachings of apostate sects (such as those that advocate plural marriage) after being corrected by their bishop or higher authority." It goes on to say that "excommunication may be necessary if repentance is not evident after counseling and encouragement." *Church Handbook of Instructions*, Book 1: Stake Presidencies and Bishoprics (Salt Lake City: The Church of Jesus Christ of Latter-day Saints, 1998). Although this current edition postdates the 1993 disciplinary councils, the definitions of apostasy were essentially the same in the then-operational 1989 *Handbook*.

5. "Verdict in Trials of 6 LDS Scholars: Guilty in Each Case," *Salt Lake Tribune*, October 2, 1993, Religion section.

6. All three prophets mentioned served in the second half of the twentieth century. David O. McKay was prophet until his death at ninety-six, Spencer W. Kimball until age ninety, and Ezra Taft Benson until ninety-four. Despite ceremonial appearances and publicity, Benson and Kimball suffered strokes and other brain trauma that left them essentially nonfunctional for the last three or four years of their presidency.

7. See Benson, "To the Mothers in Zion," a fireside for parents, February 22, 1987, published in pamphlet form and distributed to all homes by the home teachers. Benson declared, "My dear mothers, knowing of your divine role to bear and rear

children and bring them back to Him, how will you accomplish this in the Lord's way? I say the Lord's way, because it is different from the world's way. The Lord clearly defined the roles of mothers and fathers in providing for and rearing a righteous posterity. In the beginning, Adam—not Eve—was instructed to earn the bread by the sweat of his brow. Contrary to conventional wisdom, a mother's calling is in the home, not in the market place. . . . This is the divine right of a wife and mother. She cares for and nourishes her children at home. Her husband earns the living for the family, which makes this nourishing possible. With that claim on their husbands for their financial support, the counsel of the Church has always been for mothers to spend their full time in the home in rearing and caring for their children. We realize also that some of our choice sisters are widowed and divorced and that others find themselves in unusual circumstances where, out of necessity, they are required to work for a period of time. But these instances are the exception, not the rule. In a home where there is an able-bodied husband, he is expected to be the breadwinner. Sometimes we hear of husbands who, because of economic conditions, have lost their jobs and expect their wives to go out of the home and work even though the husband is still capable of providing for his family. In these cases, we urge the husband to do all in his power to allow his wife to remain in the home caring for the children while he continues to provide for his family the best he can."

President Benson then quoted his immediate predecessor, President Spencer W. Kimball: "I beg of you, you who could and should be bearing and rearing a family: Wives, come home from the typewriter, the laundry, the nursing, come home from the factory, the cafe. No career approaches in importance that of wife, homemaker, mother—cooking meals, washing dishes, making beds for one's precious husband and children. Come home, wives, to your husbands. Make home a heaven for them. Come home, wives, to your children, born and unborn. Wrap the motherly cloak about you and, unembarrassed, help in a major role to create the bodies for the immortal souls who anxiously await. When you have fully complemented your husband in home life and borne the children, growing up full of faith, integrity, responsibility, and goodness, then you have achieved your accomplishment supreme, without peer, and you will be the envy [of all] through time and eternity." Spencer W. Kimball, San Antonio Fireside, December 3, 1977, 11–12.

8. Lynne Kanavel Whitesides, quoted in "Time and Heartache," *Salt Lake Tribune*, May 19, 1995.

Chapter 2
Paul James Toscano

Lawyer and author, excommunicated from the LDS Church on September 19, 1993.

Paul James Toscano was born May 24, 1945, in Brooklyn, New York, the oldest of four boys. Paul grew up in a Catholic home speaking both Sicilian and English. In 1951 when he was six, his parents, Sam and Rose Toscano, moved the family to southern California, where Paul converted to Mormonism ten years later. However, the sixteen-year-old was not immediately baptized, because the LDS Church could not secure the consent of Paul's Catholic parents, who strongly opposed his conversion. It was not until just before his eighteenth birthday, at which point Paul could have acted on his own behalf, that his parents finally gave their permission. He was baptized on March 15, 1963.

Paul describes his conversion as one of destiny, a path he was compelled to follow. He found himself in agreement with much of Mormon theology, especially the belief that God continues to speak to his people through prophets to this day, and he felt a sense of belonging in Mormonism. In the fall of 1963, he enrolled at Brigham Young University to study literature and immersed himself in the LDS community. Though Paul's parents were pleased with his decision to be the first in his family to attend college, they were not so thrilled that he chose to attend the Mormon-owned and -operated university.

Once at BYU, Paul began his lifelong, deep exploration into Mormon theology with the valuable assistance of his religion professor, Hyrum Andrus. He accepted a mission call to Italy in 1966, serving as part of the first Mormon missionary pair to officially proselyte in Rome. On his mission, Paul was both Church historian and branch president, which entailed approving baptisms, performing ordinations to the priesthood, and preliminarily approving temple wedding ceremonies. Paul says he was transformed by the mission for it was here that he fell in love with Jesus Christ.

After returning from his mission, Paul taught Italian to other Mormon missionaries yet to embark for the mission field. He also reinitiated his studies in literature at BYU and completed a B.A. and M.A. in 1970 and 1972, respectively. After graduation, he worked for two BYU departments and for the Church-sponsored magazine, the *Ensign*.

Paul decided to enter law school in 1975, graduated in 1978, and married his long-time friend, Margaret Ann Merrill, on September 23, 1978. They eventually had four daughters. Paul practiced law in Utah County and Salt Lake County. In 1980, trouble began.

Paul became involved in a series of controversies with Church leaders who disapproved of his outspokenness and increasing involvement with the free-thinking Sunstone Symposia. Paul's relationship with Church leaders further deteriorated when he helped found the Mormon Alliance with fifteen other members on July 4, 1992. For a short but intense period in 1992, these individuals met to draft a single, important, carefully worded letter to the First Presidency and Council of the Twelve, outlining cases of "spiritual abuse" by Church leaders who had intimidated or manipulated Church members. The letter asked for top-level meetings to discuss and resolve these issues, but to no avail. Then, in 1993, the Toscanos' stake president threatened disciplinary action against Margaret but rapidly switched his attentions to an outraged Paul. Margaret was excommunicated seven years later. (See chap. 7.)

On July 5, 2003, I sat down with Paul Toscano and his family in their suburban Salt Lake City home amid books piled from floor to ceiling. He relaxed in his living room recliner, rocking back and forth. A clean-cut, middle-aged man wearing black-rimmed glasses, a short-sleeved black shirt, and green warm-up pants, Paul's relaxed demeanor hid the vibrancy I would soon discover in the course of the discussion to follow.

The Excommunication

Philip: Is it true that the disciplinary process that would culminate in your excommunication began on July 11, 1993, when your stake president, Kerry M. Heinz, demanded that you and your wife, Margaret, stop writing, speaking, and publishing about the Church?

Paul: Yes, but I don't think it had anything to do with me at that time. The focus of the disciplinary action Kerry was going to carry out at that time was intended for Margaret.

Philip: But the Church's inquiry must have evolved to include you by August 5, 1993, when both of you met with President Heinz and Bishop Wilson Martin to discuss your upcoming Sunstone presentations. Can you describe the events leading up to this meeting?

Paul: We had been investigated a couple times in the past, and I knew by then that my records had been tagged, because a General Authority looked them up and told me so. This meant that I could never hold a leadership position in the Church. I began to have strong, negative feelings about some abusive Church leaders; paraphrasing Mark Twain in *Life on the Mississippi*, I felt that "the partiality of Providence for these undeserving reptiles had reached a point where it was open to criticism."[1]

By 1993, I was fed up with the authoritarianism in Mormonism and with dictatorial leaders, and I was upset at Kerry. I called him by his first name rather than "President Heinz," and I admit that I was disrespectful and somewhat insulting. I said to him: "Kerry, what do you know about the scripture? You're a real estate agent. They made you a stake president—so what!? You don't care about this religion. For you it's just about keeping us quiet and kissing up to your friend Boyd K. Packer. It's insulting that you're sitting across from us questioning our theology. What's *your* theology? It's a vacant lot! Anything could tramp through there. It's a traveling freak show. You'd believe in anything a Church leader told you. You don't have any fixed religion. You're sitting here, talking to my wife as if you're superior? She knows a thousand times more than you do about this religion!"

He just fumed. I confess that I peppered him with ad hominem attacks because, in my mind, Church leaders were engaged in ad hominem attacks against Margaret, my friends, and me. In spite of our requests for meetings and dialogue, there was never any attempt on the part of Church leaders on a General Authority level to seriously look at what we'd said and compare it to the scriptures. There was never a discussion. So, because I saw Kerry as a bull chasing my wife across a field, I decided to run through waving a red flag to distract him, since I was a convert to the Church and Margaret has relatives in the Church going back to 1830. They were there at the Kirtland Temple. I, on the other hand, was expendable, and it was a supremely successful plot because as soon as I started to insult him, he lost all sight of Margaret and the original mandate from Apostle Boyd K. Packer to oust her.

Philip: After the meeting you gave a provocative paper at the Sunstone Symposium. How did President Heinz react when he heard the tape of your Sunstone presentation?

Paul: He felt my speech was bad—that I did a bad thing by mocking them, ridiculing them. That was the worst thing I did. When I met with him and he said he was going to take action against me, I said, "Fine. Do what you have to do."

He said, "You must learn to obey."

I said, "I am not going to obey you when I think you're wrong."

He said, "It's like parents and children."

I responded, "But Kerry, you're not like my parent. We're practically the same age. You certainly don't have the competence to deal with this kind of stuff. This is not like a confession of sexual transgression. These are disputes over the doctrine of the Church of which you know nothing. Don't go on with this!"

Then he said, "You have to learn to obey the prophet."

I said, "Kerry, *you* don't obey the prophet."

"What do you mean?" he asked, incensed.

I said, "There's a deer's head on the wall of your study. You shot it. How long ago was it that Spencer Kimball, the president of the

Church, announced in priesthood meeting that we shouldn't be shooting animals—'hurt not the little birds.'"[2]

Kerry said, "It's not a deer. It's an elk."

"All right, an elk. The point is you shot this elk! The president of the Church said don't shoot animals and you shot this elk. How can you believe that you are in compliance with what the living prophets teach? You're disobedient."

He said, "Yeah, well, that's not controversial now."

I told him, "It's impossible talking with you. You have no sense of principle. You don't believe in principle. You believe in following whatever you're told right now and that's it. Can you imagine the kind of religion that would create, following anything that anybody says without respect for the tradition, the past, the scriptures? It would turn Mormonism into a hodgepodge."

He said, "We have to follow the living prophets. The prophet would never ask us to sin."

He kept saying this like it was a mantra, and I responded, "He's asking you to sin if he's asking you to abdicate your judgment in favor of somebody else's. What's the good of the last judgment if, in fact, all we did was follow some leader's judgment? God would then just judge the leader alone and the rest of us accordingly. That would be the end of it. There can be no last judgment unless I judge, and my judgment depends on doing what I think is right rather than what you think is right."

He said, "Well then, you must take the consequences."

"I am willing to take the consequences if our dispute was about the content of my beliefs rather than about whether I was obedient. You're making this a test of loyalty. You want to excommunicate me because I didn't obey you, not because of the truth or sincerity of what I said."

"Well, I think what you said was wrong," he insisted.

"Fine," I said.

Philip: What was the stated reason that you were being called into a disciplinary council?

Paul: That changed. It was different in the letter they sent me from what they said in the tribunal from what they finally stated they excommunicated me for. It was first for teaching false doctrine, then for leading people astray, and then for not being sufficiently obedient and respectful of Church leaders. Generally it was for being obstreperous and insubordinate.

Philip: How did you feel the morning of your excommunication?

Paul: That's a story in itself. . . . I was served with the summons to my excommunication hearing on the 12th of September, a Sunday. That morning, which was back when I could sleep through the night (which I can't do anymore), I woke up at 4:00 A.M. and sat up in bed. I had what seemed like a remnant of a dream of four individuals standing at the foot of my bed, two males and two females, who were dressed peculiarly. They reminded me of the figures on the eastern portals of the Chartres Cathedral: elongated, very graceful, and elegant-looking beings, but not human. They gave me a message, and I woke up Margaret and told her, "I'm going to be excommunicated, and I'm going to receive my summons today. It will be soon, but I'm not supposed to worry about it because everything will be all right." That day they served me with the summons for a disciplinary council to be held the very next week, Sunday, September 19.

I knew then, on the 12th, that my case wouldn't be a matter of evidence. It was a closed question. It was a scripted result. So, when I went in on the morning of the 19th of September I knew that was it . . . the end of my life in Mormonism. I was going to go in and they were going to behead me, spiritually.

Philip: Can you explain what happened at the trial?

Paul: A lot of time was spent on preliminaries. When I went in I had to shake everybody's hand, and there were fifteen men. Then Kerry explained to everybody why I was there and what I was charged with. That took half an hour. It took another half hour to divide up the twelve high council members into the six members who would make sure no injury was done to the Church and six who would ensure that there is no injury done to the accused—me. They then spent a long time handing out my most recent Sunstone Symposium speech,[3] which somebody had gone through the trouble of transcribing. I would have been more than happy to give them a copy had anybody asked me for one, and I had to correct parts of it because they had it wrong, possibly because the transcriber had a hard time hearing the tape recording of what I had said.

They played the tape of my presentation, too, which they had purchased at Sunstone. The off-hand quips I made during the speech, though funny at Sunstone, weren't funny in the high council meeting—I'll tell you that. I was hitting on some hard questions in that speech, because doctrine in Mormonism has always been open; and if you start peeling back what people really believe, you never get identical feelings or beliefs about certain questions. The joke or two I made at the expenses of top Church leaders was taken very ill by the high council trying my case. They felt I was very disrespectful.

One offensive joke related to a comment made by Elder Russell M. Nelson in the April 1993 priesthood session at general conference, in which he basically laid down a rule that when an apostle enters a room we, the members, should all stand up. That infuriated me. When Jesus was on earth, he washed the apostles' feet and said don't call each other master. I thought, "What the hell are they talking about? Whenever one of them walks in we all stand up?" So, I said in my speech, "Maybe we should all stand up and leave!" Then I said that, just as the Lord said to Moses, "Take the shoes off thy feet,"[4] maybe we should just take off. These jokes irritated them. I was sticking it to this old geezer [Elder Nelson] who had the nerve to call himself an apostle while uttering words directly repugnant to the teachings of Jesus Christ when he was on earth. I couldn't tolerate it.

Proscribed Christianity is dead Christianity. As soon as you make a rule you kill the spirit. The spirit giveth life but the letter killeth.[5] Who cares whether or not we stand up? What are you worried about that for? If you were a real apostle, that would never enter your mind. You should be trying to preach the message of Jesus Christ, his death, and the meaning of the atonement and resurrection, of justice and mercy. The high council couldn't deal with the whole speech or even its theme. There were a couple of things they underlined particularly . . .

Philip: There were eleven parts in total.

Paul: Yes, there were eleven points, and they focused on three or four. So, in my trial we heard the taped speech for about forty-five minutes, and then they asked me questions for another hour. The next two hours were spent listening to my character witnesses. Margaret came in first, then Lavina, then Jeff Hawker, and then a written statement from Fred Voros, who is my best friend and a member of the high council who happened to be out of town that day. After all that, at about noon or 1:00, they said, "That's it," and wanted me to leave so they could deliberate. I went out and found there had been a vigil,[6] which I never saw because I was not there when the crowd had gathered that morning. By that time, the people had dwindled away to those who waited as the high council and stake presidency deliberated.

I didn't doubt the outcome. The only thing I doubted was what I would say when they announced it. I wrote down what I wanted to say in response ahead of time, because I was afraid that in the emotional moment of being excommunicated I would be shaken in mind and unable to say anything. I didn't want that to happen. I didn't want them to think "Aha! The heretic has been confounded."

At about 3:00 P.M. they called me back in, but I had forgotten the paper with my notes. I sat down and Kerry said, "We have deliberated and determined to excommunicate you." It was like a wrecking ball hit me in the chest. Even though I knew they were going to say this, when they uttered those words, it hurt, and I knew then that I had expected some miracle would happen, that maybe they would do something less. Then they asked me if I had anything to say. I nodded. What I wanted to say was, "Look. I know that I'm an irritant to you. I know I say things that are chastening and insulting and in some ways you think of me as vulgar or disrespectful, and all those things may be true, but they are not excommunicable. We may have a difference of doctrine, but we've always had differences of doctrine in the Church, and Joseph Smith said we shouldn't excommunicate one another for that. We may not always like each other. Love fails. Even though St. Paul says the love of God doesn't fail,[7] the love that we humans have for each other sometimes does because we have hurt feelings. I know I do. Doctrine fails because it's hard to interpret. What binds us together are ordinances: We've all been baptized, confirmed, endowed, and accepted the gospel through the metaphors given to Joseph Smith. That should make us one. We're in this together. Don't excommunicate me. Think of the damage it would do to my daughters, to my wife. Why do that? Chasten me, disfellowship me, publicly rebuke me. I deserve it because I *was* disrespectful, but you have to understand that I've been very angry because I left my culture and family to join the house of Israel under the promise that I would be treated as an equal. Don't excommunicate me."

I didn't say that. Instead, I reeled from this wrecking ball announcement and my short-term memory collapsed. I stammered, dry-mouthed, without my notes which I had forgotten to take back into the council room with me. So I just said, "I don't know what to say except that I think it would be a mistake to excommunicate me merely for being insolent when I was sincere. Don't excommunicate me for that." But they did.

Philip: Of the eleven points that you outlined in your speech, they focused specifically on four areas: disrespect for Church leaders, assertions that Church leaders abuse priesthood authority, claims that the Holy Ghost is a female, and damage to the faith of Church members. In the trial, did you specifically respond to each of these?

Paul: Yes, I did.

Philip: How so?

Paul: I said yes, I have been disrespectful to Church leaders, and that's because Church leaders are sometimes disrespectful to the Saints, to me. They plot, and they connive—what am I supposed to do? Respect is something that shouldn't be accorded because somebody has an office but because they earn the respect, and you earn respect by giving respect. It's a two-way street.

Philip: That then relates to the second area, which is the assertion that Church leaders abuse their priesthood authority.

Paul: There is a line in the speech where I say they are abusive, but certainly it's a checkered experience. Some people have bishops and stake presidents and encounters with General Authorities that are benign and wonderful. My experience, rather, has been a long litany of abuse on the part of leaders.

I'm not saying that all leaders are this way, have to be, or that this is a policy of the Church. I'm just saying that it happens. If it didn't happen why would there be such a big deal in the 121st section of the

Doctrine and Covenants where it says that when men get a little authority they begin to practice unrighteous dominion?[8] Why would that be there if authority wasn't a constant temptation? I'm saying it's not just a temptation—it actually happens. I've seen it.

Philip: How did you address the third area that claims you asserted the Holy Spirit was feminine?

Paul: I said I don't know if the Holy Ghost is a female, but I think the Holy Ghost probably is. Otherwise, there wouldn't be a female in the godhead; and without a female in the godhead, women have no hope. I don't want my daughters to grow up in a Church where the godhead excludes their gender. I certainly may be wrong, but I don't see any harm in thinking that. Also, I said this at Sunstone. I certainly wouldn't speak like this in church, because church is a place where people feel like they have to come; and if they have to come, I'm not going to take advantage of the situation by telling them stuff the Church doesn't teach. But it was at Sunstone, a theological symposium comprised of explorations in theology. I wasn't claiming to be the revelator of the Church. It was speculation, and I proposed a different hermeneutic, and there's only one member of the godhead that we haven't assigned a sex to. So, if we're going to assign one, I suggest it be to the Holy Ghost and that we call her a her.

This Church is not friendly to women, and women have got to see that they have always been excluded from official positions of power. It can't be that we're tacking them on here at the end of the twentieth century just because we got nervous about our treatment of them. If the Church is divine, and women have always been of equal status with men, then you've got to be able to see that's true in the existing theological structures. A female divinity is indispensable.

Philip: How did you address the claim that you damaged the faith of Church members?

Paul: I said that I would be willing to put my body count against the body count of the Twelve Apostles any day of the week. I can't imagine more damage done to the Church than by the leaders of the current Church. They're the ones who have influence. Who hears me? I'm speaking to 400 people at Sunstone, and Boyd Packer speaks to thousands and thousands, millions of people. Who do you think is going to destroy more people's faith just on the random particle theory? Go find someone who will come in here and testify under oath that I destroyed their faith.

Philip: Do you believe your excommunication was instigated at the ecclesiastical level as opposed to the congregational level?

Paul: Oh, absolutely. There is no question in my mind that it was instigated by Boyd Packer. Seven years later when Margaret was excommunicated, in 2000, that was also instigated by him. Kerry Heinz admitted that to me. I asked him, "Kerry, did Boyd Packer tell you to excommunicate me?" He said no. I said, "Kerry . . . was the fair implication of his statement to you that I should be excommunicated"? And Kerry said yes. And I said, "Well, then I have no hope."

Philip: Is it true that you received letters of support from a few General Authorities during and after your excommunication?

Paul: That's true.

Philip: Which ones?

Paul: I never said which authorities because they're still there and I don't want to get them in trouble. . . . I will tell one. In April of 1995, my friend Fred Voros had a private interview with Howard W. Hunter, then president of the Quorum of the Twelve and who later, for a short period, served as president of the Church.

Fred had written a letter complimenting President Hunter on a speech he gave that was very christocentric, a very good speech about spirituality and the relationship to Christ we should have. Fred was then invited up to the Church Office Building and met with Howard Hunter, who was sitting in a wheelchair looking a bit frail but very clear. He called Fred over, shook his hand and sat him down. Howard Hunter, a wonderful and very friendly man, asked Fred about his family, his sons, and all this. They didn't talk about my excommunication.

When Fred gets up to leave, Howard Hunter grabs him by the hand with a very firm grip. He didn't say anything. He just held Fred's hand. Then President Hunter said, "Tell Brother Toscano that I think highly of him and that we will make amends." That was nice.

The Church Hierarchy/Authority

Philip: In your book of collected essays, *The Sanctity of Dissent* (1994), you wrote that you "underwent a paradigm shift" and came to believe that "rebellion to tyrants is obedience to God."[9] You also claim in *Sanctity* that having Church leaders "contradicts Jesus' teachings."[10] Assuming you didn't feel this way when you converted, what eventually bred such mistrust of authority?

Paul: Well, it gradually exacerbated over time. First I wanted to believe that the authoritarianism wasn't happening. Then I wanted to believe that it was happening, but only to a few people. I gradually began to realize that Church leaders were largely indifferent to the history and the context of Mormonism and that they were primarily interested in controlling people and letting the tithing funds roll in. I began to eliminate the various possibilities of what could be the problem and came to the conclusion that the biggest problem was them.

What convinced me was law school. Friedrich Augustus Von Hayek in *The Road to Serfdom* says that in any closed political system, the ruthless always rise to the top, because only the most ruthless would be willing to do the things necessary to rise.[11] In Mormonism, it is the most manipulative who rise to the top.

Philip: As indicated by former president Heber J. Grant and others, it is generally understood in the Church that leaders receive revelation and are given authority "from God direct, to act in their callings and to enjoy the gifts and powers of the gospel."[12] Since you challenged the authority of Church leaders, weren't you undermining one of the foundational tenets of Mormonism?

Paul: I don't think so. Many people have told me, "Paul, your problem is that you don't understand that the Brethren are human." I *do* understand that. It's the Brethren who don't understand it. They're the ones who seem to be in denial about their imperfections. If they get revelation they should say so, which they don't. And if they don't get revelation, they should say so. Since continuing revelation is one of the principal pillars of Mormonism and the reason that we give our allegiance to the leaders of the Church, they should be quite clear on whether they're getting it, but they're not. They're deliberately evasive on whether they get revelation, but you can tell they're not talking to God because what they say is pablum, nonsensical, contradictory, and mediocre.

It's no sin to be a mediocre prophet if you just tell the people, "We pray, we keep the commandments, we sit up here and wash each other's feet, we pass the sacrament, we pray some more, and all we can tell you is God isn't talking to us clearly. So, all we can do is hold the line on what we know, and that's what we're doing. We don't think the Church is untrue. Israel has suffered moments of silence. It's a probationary state, could be a test, let's keep going."

I don't blame them for not getting revelation. I blame them for not being honest about it. It's not their fault God doesn't talk to them. It might be, but I doubt it. But if they lay claim to the obedience of the Saints on the basis that they talk to God, they'd better be talking to Him. Otherwise they'd better relax their demand for obedience, because their revelation is no better than ours and Mormonism has just become Presbyterianism with goofy doctrine. The problem is they want everyone to obey them as if they talk to God, but they try to evade the question of whether they do or not. That's what irritates me.

It's like Gordon B. Hinckley has a lot to say about body piercings, but absolutely nothing to say about the atonement. Search! Search through the speeches of Gordon B. Hinckley and see if you can find one single illuminating statement about the atonement. You can't!

Jesus said the greatest of all is the least of all.[13] Apostles should be washing other peoples' feet, making themselves lower than other people, and not worrying about forcing others to show respect. They should be giving up power so that other people can feel empowered, but they don't because they're not looking to Christ, who is their avatar. They're making it up as they go. It's a lie! You don't tell people whether or not to get tattoos or to use the missionary position. Those are idiotic things. It's not soul work; it's just crap! It's the Republican Party! What they should be doing is preaching Christ, and him crucified, and the Spirit of God will then lead them to truth—but no. What they do is list off a bunch of things that personally offend them because they're old. These old men are geriatrics who have forgotten the last time they touched their wives' breasts.

I don't want to offend you because you're a very good person, and I'm raising my voice, but I'm so mad because there's a very simple way this continuing revelation question could be solved. Sign it. Sign the revelation. Joseph Smith wrote revelations down and said, "Thus saith the Lord." He was very specific not only as to the fact that it was a revelation, but the manner by which he got it. He would say, "Given by a seer stone on such-and-such a date." All they can say is "Had a good feeling on May 16th," which, if the Saints saw it in writing, they would be shocked.

Have them sign it. Our current Church leaders should write their revelations down and sign them. They won't, because they know better. They know it's not revelation. They know it's a lie and would be afraid because, no matter how many problems they have, they're still afraid of God . . . a little bit. It's like a client sitting across the table telling me things in my law office. In that context they can say anything. When it comes down to signing the oath on an affidavit that says they are testifying under penalty of perjury that it is true, they say, "Well, I'd better tell you the truth, the whole truth, and nothing but the truth." The leaders need to write it down and sign it.

Everything has been said from the pulpit. You go back in the last 150 years of general conference, and there is not a thing they haven't said, most of which is bullshit, because it changes: it's a sin to practice birth control, it's not a sin to practice birth control, you have to do this to be saved, you've got to do that to be saved—that's not continuing revelation. That's continuing chaos, which results from them not being afraid to advance these things in the name of the Father, the Son, and the Holy Ghost. Yet, if you hauled them to the line and said, "Sign it. Write it down on this piece of paper," they would retreat. Some General Authorities don't even write their own speeches! It's not even written by an apostle!

Philip: Do you feel that the guidance of the Holy Spirit allowed you to assess whether or not Church authorities were receiving revelation?

Paul: I don't claim revelation. I wasn't assessing their words as a matter of my personal revelation. I was assessing their words as a matter of conscience. There is the Book of Mormon, the Doctrine and Covenants, and the Pearl of Great Price. . . . Joseph Smith had an obvious outpouring of spiritual gifts. You could question whether these things are fraudulent, question them as to whether they make any sense, but you couldn't question that they exist. The content of these books can be assessed as a matter of conscience. We can assess whether they contain ideas that are good or bad. We can assess whether they contain words that are spiritual or prophetic.

What has Gordon B. Hinckley ever said that's been prophetic? He's built a couple of beautiful buildings and restored the Nauvoo Temple, and I say hats off to him, but architecture isn't revelation. Gordon B. Hinckley's article in the *Ensign* isn't revelation—good advice, maybe? I can tell the difference because I'm a literary man. I can read the Book of Mormon and see there is something there. I can read St. Paul's letters and see there's something there that is not just ordinary. I can use my brain and conclude that in these words there is said something extraordinary. But Hinckley is boring! People go to Church, are bored to death, and are happy about it. They're happy because they're not being challenged. Nobody's pushing the envelope.

No questioner, you included, will ever get me to say that I believe anything I did was inspired. I have never claimed to be inspired. If I'm inspired, I don't know it. That's a judgment people will have to make. My opinion about it makes no difference at all. If it was inspired, and I don't know it, it doesn't make it any less inspired.

Philip: But if you knew that you were inspired, then that would be relevant.

Paul: If I knew that I was inspired, I would tell you. But I don't know. If I were inspired, then that inspiration came because I was unable to tolerate the hypocrisy of someone claiming to speak to God who didn't. Hypocrisy is essentially a lie! I certainly am not going to advance something I don't think is true. I was convicted that what I said was truth. I cannot say if Church leaders do or don't get revelation for certain. I can only say that it doesn't sound like revelation to me. It doesn't compare to the revelations of Joseph Smith. I can only say that Church leaders claiming revelation have the obligation to say when they are getting revelation and when they are not—and not to pretend that their personal voices are the voice of God. This is an example of how power corrupts and absolute power corrupts absolutely. A prophet can become corrupt.

I said this to Dallin Oaks, one of the Twelve Apostles, in a private interview years ago. I had been his research assistant briefly at BYU when he was the president of the university,[14] so I got in to see him more easily than others. He wondered why I was so angry.

I said, "I'm angry because it is wrong for Apostles to pretend like you get revelation when you don't. Can't you see that's immoral? People believe that you meet with Christ once a week when you have your Thursday meetings!"

He said, "No, people can't believe that."

I said, "Well, go to my ward and put a bag over your head and tell them you don't believe that and see how long you last. I'm not saying that you're not apostles, but just that you're the worst apostles we've ever had in the history of Christianity, because you're stuck on yourselves. Why don't you just get out of Salt Lake and go get crucified upside down in China? Do something for the Lord instead of hanging around here bothering people like me."

He asked, "Is it one of us you don't like, or all of us?"

I said, "Dallin, every one of you is a better man than I am. You're more temperate, better spoken. You probably endure pain better than I do. You certainly have a greater tolerance than I do. In all those things you're better men—individually. But as a group you stink because you group-think and checkmate each other's best spiritual instincts. You line up in seniority order just to go the urinal. What kind of people are you?"

It's the group authoritarianism that I don't like and what I consider a gross misrepresentation of their connection to God. It's not that I don't believe in continuing revelation. I just think that revelation comes to Balaam's ass.[15] Revelation comes to a little girl in Nazareth, and her cousin Elisabeth (Luke 1:36). And through this little girl everything changes. Who would expect that? Don't act like Pharisees, like God can't trick you. That's one of God's main occupations—to be a trickster. He's always setting it up to look this way, and then He does it that way, the unexpected way. Doesn't anybody read this stuff? You read it but you don't believe. You think He's going to work through you. Well, fine, I'm sure He does work through you, but don't be surprised when He works through somebody else. It may even be someone you don't approve of. Look at King David—this half-naked little Jewish boy with a slingshot (1 Sam. 17)—nobody would have believed it. The Bible and Book of Mormon are full of things that happen outside the envelope.

Philip: In "A Plea to the Leadership of the Church," you make the point that Church authorities are contentious, in part, because they have "divided the Church into leaders and followers."[16] However, it was originally Joseph Smith who established this division. Was Joseph Smith being contentious? Was he wrong?

Paul: Yes.

Philip: On both counts?

Paul: Yes. It was his greatest failing. He was an insecure, uneducated, frontier hick, who was so pretentious as to run for president of the United States when he was too uneducated to do so.[17] He should have been told this, but he was not able to be told because people who are insecure cannot tolerate criticism of their insecurity, and they lash back. He received punishment for this, more than he deserved, but his problem was not the failure to get revelation, but insecurity from being disrespected, hounded, and persecuted. I can't seriously fault him for this; I only point it out. Most of us are frontier hicks.

Jesus Christ did not die on the cross to perpetuate the class system. Jesus Christ did not shed His blood so we could have a Mormon elite. The reason Jesus Christ, who was God, descended to earth as a Jew and got nailed to a piece of wood as a traitor and then buried in a borrowed tomb was to show that we have to give up power so that other people can be empowered. A class structure is dedicated to the opposite principle—getting power by disempowering, in other words, killing to get gain. So yes, I think Joseph Smith was quite wrong to allow to grow, for his personal security or comfort, a class system. Devotion in Mormonism is now basically defined as loyalty to the leadership of the Church. That's wrong because it's idolatrous.

Philip: You wrote in that same essay that your anger toward Church authorities was fueled by "grief, sorrow, depression, helplessness."[18] How helpless were you really? Do you feel that any of your speeches ever had a positive effect?

Paul: No, they had no positive effect. Leaders hear but they hearken not. I felt helpless because I couldn't get Church leaders to sit down with me. I do not doubt that they have concerns about Mormonism. I do not doubt that they love the Saints. I do not doubt that they have given their lives in service to the Saints. I just doubt that they believe that anybody has done it as well as they have. I just doubt their view that you can't be called of God without their permission.

It isn't that I think they're not apostles; it's just that they're arrogant. I suppose it's not their fault because anyone who has contact with God always comes away feeling like God loves them best. That's one of the problems with the divine. That's God's problem. He makes everybody feel special, and it takes years and years to realize He's doing this to everybody.

Philip: Is everybody special?

Paul: I suppose so, from God's perspective. They aren't from mine. I'm much more cynical than God. He loves them all. I'm not sure I have the capacity to feel that way, but he does make everyone feel special. Some people don't realize that for them to feel that way about themselves is quite different than for God to feel that way about them.

Philip: In his review of *The Sanctity of Dissent*, William J. Hamblin said, "Many of Toscano's theological dogmas are supported by neither scripture, prophetic teaching, nor argumentation; they are simply asserted on his own authority."[19] Do you agree?

Paul: Yes.

Philip: Do you think that's a problem?

Paul: Yes, I do rely on my own authority, and it is a problem. But everybody does, even those who quote scripture. God relies on his own authority. Jesus spoke on his own authority. St. Paul changed the Jewish religion on the basis of his own authority. Everybody acts on their own authority. The question is not whether you act on your own authority. The question is if what you're saying makes any sense.

Philip: St. Paul spoke about being given the authority to preach the gospel.

Paul: I suppose, but anybody who feels the Spirit of God has the authority to preach the gospel. I'm not so sure people have authority to establish churches or tear them down. I wasn't trying to do either. I was introducing a different hermeneutic into a discussion that was becoming more and more closed.

Belief and Doctrine

Philip: You wrote an article published on October 20, 1993, in the *Salt Lake Tribune* stating, "There exists no revelation that allows Church leaders to excommunicate Church members to preserve 'doctrinal purity.'"[20] Also, in *Strangers in Paradox*, you and Margaret stress that your views are subjective and sometimes depart from official Church teachings.[21] At what point do beliefs diverge enough to be called apostate? Are there certain tenets Mormons must hold; and if so, what are they?

Paul: I don't think anyone should be excommunicated for beliefs, unless it can be shown that they present an immediate physical danger to the membership or property of the Church. To excommunicate someone from the body of Christ should be an agonizing decision—like the decision to amputate your own leg. You never sever body parts lightly. You might do it under very extreme cases where you're going to die if you don't, but you don't normally amputate. Dentists don't even pull a tooth nowadays if the procedure can be avoided.

But the Church excommunicates like it was nothing because the people doing it are never in danger of it happening to them. If we all stood in the same danger of excommunication, it wouldn't happen so much. I can think of a couple of instances where people have done horrible things and might likely do them again, so that member must be excommunicated to protect the Church, but that should be rare and certainly should not turn upon a question of doctrine. There is no purity of doctrine. In a church of continuing revelation the doctrine is never settled. It is never pure.

Philip: In almost a prophetic fashion, you stated in "The Call of Mormon Feminism" that hopefully "as a Church and a people we will neither forbid nor discourage either the worship or prayerful invocation of God the Mother, said in the name of Jesus Christ."[22] This essay, dated September 7, 1991, was only about three weeks before Prophet Gordon B. Hinckley stated in the Relief Society meeting preceding general conference that no member should pray to the Heavenly Mother and no Church president, "from Joseph Smith to Ezra Taft Benson, has offered a prayer to 'our Mother in Heaven.'"[23] Were many people advocating praying to Heavenly Mother, a situation which might have inspired Hinckley's response?

Paul: He was responding to the fact that some men and women were praying to Heavenly Father and Mother, but we've been doing that for years in the hymn "O My Father." One of the verses goes: "Father, Mother, may I greet you / in your royal courts on high?" Sounds like a prayer to me, and people have been singing that since the days of Eliza Snow.[24] There is a precedent, but in a patriarchal structure, God is male. I think, however, that we should promote prayer. After all, "It's the evil spirit that teacheth not to pray," reads the scripture.[25]

Some women can't pray to a Father in Heaven because their father on earth had sex with them, but they can pray to a Heavenly Mother. I don't think it makes any difference. If God is male, he certainly must be above the ego that comes with that. If one of his children accidentally calls him "mommy" by accident, I don't think it's going to make any difference to him. There is a revelation to Joseph Smith with Zebedee Coltrin and maybe Oliver Cowdery out in the woods where they lie down, a vision opens, and they see the Father and the Mother.[26] That should have settled the issue of the Heavenly Mother.

Philip: But the existence of Heavenly Mother was not questioned—just the practice of members praying to her.

Paul: If She's a divinity, I don't understand why you can't pray to her. It's an attempt to keep the feminine out of the divine. It's fear. It doesn't change the Christian religion to believe in a Heavenly Father and Heavenly Mother. It's just another set of metaphors you've got to figure out. It doesn't change that redemption comes through Jesus Christ.

Philip: Should the priesthood be opened up to women?

Paul: It was opened up to women in 1842 by Joseph Smith,[27] and I don't think we can close that door. He was the one who anointed women as priestesses and conferred the fullness of the priesthood on the man and woman jointly. Since then men have backed off on that because they didn't like it; but in the temple, women are clothed in the robes of the priesthood, and they're told that with the robe on the right shoulder they can officiate in all the ordinances of the Melchizedek Priesthood. It's said to them at the same time it's said to the man. So, if it means nothing to the women, then it means nothing to the men. If it means something to the men, then it means exactly the same thing to the women.

Philip: Is it possible that subsequent prophets were inspired to repeal Joseph Smith's endowment of the priesthood on women?

Paul: There was no revelation that ever repealed anything. They have never admitted to such a revelation. You can't repeal what you won't admit. Besides, how can you undo what Joseph Smith said? He's the founding prophet of the Church. Either you accept his revelations as true or you don't.

Philip: What about polygamy?

Paul: What about it?

Philip: It was repealed in 1890.

Paul: It never should have been repealed. It should never have been advanced, because that wasn't the revelation. The revelation wasn't about polygyny, one man and many women. It was about polygamy—multiple marriages among adults. The problem that Joseph Smith attempted to solve was how to allow adults to have sex with more than one adult in their lifetime or in the hereafter without destroying the notion of the family as a protected environment for children.

Marriage creates a series of mounting, layered problems if you believe in the resurrection from the dead, if you believe that the gender of men and women continues, and if you believe in eternal marriage and that people are going to last for all eternity. In such an eternal, physicalized existence, marrying one person to another person forever and ever and ever is hell. Human desire is to have contact with other people, and humans are obviously capable of having love relationships with more than one person, though they can't sustain them very well in mortality. So, how do you create a situation in the resurrected state where people can have multiple sexual partners but still be faithful and love one another? How do you ground these relationships not just in lust but in the desire for the well-being of the other person? That's one of the problems that Joseph Smith's concept of multiple marriages was trying to solve, and his solution was unsuccessful. It was not only unsuccessful, it was disastrously unsuccessful. But just because disastrous things happen does not mean they don't come from God.

I don't like the polygamy concept because what evolved in the Church was polygyny—one man and many women, an arrangement that insinuates that it takes many women to equal the value of one man. That's absurd. I don't think that's what was happening in Nauvoo when this practice was first instituted. Some of the women there had multiple husbands; some men had multiple wives. It seemed like chaos. Brigham Young was not going to let that continue. So, as soon as Joseph Smith died, he put the kibosh on that, and it became a patriarchal structure where men could have multiple wives, but women could not exercise their prerogative of having multiple husbands.

Philip: Polygyny.

Paul: Yes. It became polygyny rather than polygamy. What was the meaning of all that? I don't know—probably to illuminate the complex nature of human sexuality and, I think, to institute in the Church a practice that would keep the Church from crawling back into Protestantism. In my view, polygamy, polygyny, and polyandry (one woman married to many men) at least addressed serious issues and were more likely the subject of divine revelation than, for example, the introduction into the Church of the Boy Scout program.

Reflection

Philip: Ten years have elapsed since your excommunication. In retrospect, how have your thoughts and feelings toward the Church and the events that occurred changed or developed during that time?

Paul: I've lost my faith. Losing your faith is not like denying what you knew once. That's how most people interpret losing your faith. It's like losing your sense of sight or smell. I used to be able to taste Jesus in my mouth. I can't now. I can remember thinking that he was as real as you sitting there, or my daughter or my wife. Now it's very difficult.

I used to be able to feel like Jesus was there. Many young people feel this way, and that's good. Many people carry this feeling through life. I'm not sure that's so good, because I don't know if they ever come to understand what it's like to have an existential crisis. I certainly don't fault them for not having that sense of crisis, but I myself have it—in spades. I wish I could say that I believe Jesus is the Christ. All I can say is I hope he's the Christ. I hope it's true. I have grave doubts.

I remember C. S. Lewis's statement that people go out and look at the sky on a cloudless night, see the stars, and feel terrified because the universe is so huge and beyond comprehension. It's even more incomprehensible now than when C. S. Lewis was alive. Now we know that, in only one small square of the sky, there are hundreds of millions of galaxies. But Lewis said we could go out and look at the sky and feel that it's a cozy place with just the right number of stars all in place. We can feel at home. It's the same point that Shakespeare makes: "There is nothing good or bad, but thinking makes it so."[28]

I'm afraid that, as my life has progressed and I have seen a lot of hopes and aspirations fail, I'm terrified that the universe might be one horrible, relentless plane of indifferent molecules. That's a frightening thought. I don't believe that, but I do worry about it even though I can't do anything about it.

Philip: Some of those in the Church might point to your excommunication—your no longer being involved in the Church—as the reason that you have difficulty feeling the presence of Christ. How would you react to that?

Paul: It's a perfectly rational and disturbingly frightening observation, because they can say: "You were excommunicated, you lost the spirit of God, you lost your faith, and it all comes from your disobedience." What can I say except that I think that what I've experienced happens to people who are quite faithful as well? I think it's possible that my excommunication is a punishment for my arrogance, and I *am* arrogant because I don't simply comply with Church leaders' judgment. But what am I to judge with except my own judgment? I don't know what else to do. I could submit to the judgment of others, but it seems like lying, like bribing God, by denying the very essence of my personhood, which is to judge with my own judgment.

Philip: Do you attend any church?

Paul: No church for me.

Philip: Did you at any point after your excommunication?

Paul: No.

Philip: Are your children members of the Church?

Paul: No . . . well, technically they're members, but they don't identify with Mormonism. They are on the records of the Church and I'm sure they are counted among the eleven million faithful.

Philip: In 1990 before your excommunication, you and Margaret wrote, "We love and admire" Joseph Smith.[29] What are your feelings toward him now?

Paul: He's not a hero of mine like he was at one time, but I've never been a detractor of Joseph Smith. To me, only simple creatures can read his life and not see that it was an extraordinary religious life that cannot be weighed against an ordinary life. Joseph Smith is a difficult person. He claims to see God, he gets revelations, there are books he writes, he makes big mistakes, he makes extraordinary statements that are profoundly important. How do you judge a man like this? I don't know. But I never was a detractor, and I'm not now.

Philip: Did you deserve your excommunication?

Paul: Yes.

Philip: For the reasons the Church authorities outlined?

Paul: Yes, particularly for those reasons. I was disrespectful, I was impertinent, I was angry, I was all of the things that they said. Excommunication was the price I had to pay.

Philip: Are you still Mormon?

Paul: I suppose I'll always be Mormon on some level. I'm not a Mormon in the sense of being a member of the Church, and I'm not a Saint in exile as I said I was back in 1993 when I thought of myself as standing outside the official structure of the Church waiting for some miracle to allow me to come back in triumphantly. I don't believe in triumph. I'm a Mormon in the sense that I'm imbued with Mormon ideas.

In one discussion I had with Kerry Heinz in December of 1993 after my excommunication, I asked him: "Kerry, do you believe that my excommunication has separated me from Christ, nullified my baptism, revoked my remission of sins, broken the sealings to my wife and my family that were set upon me in the temple, taken away my priesthood, and basically eliminated any possibility while I'm an excommunicant of being in the presence of God?"

He said, "Yes, absolutely."

"And all this for a quip?" I said. "Then why didn't you just shoot me. Wouldn't it have been more merciful to have just destroyed my body rather than my soul?"

"Well," he said, "you can come back into the Church on certain conditions." The conditions were that I must admit that I was wrong about everything—that my doctrine was wrong, my attitude was wrong, everything I did was wrong, and that Kerry and Boyd were right. If I were to admit this, then I could come back in—maybe. But I couldn't admit those things, not truthfully.

I said to Kerry, "Look, I will get up, and I will say that I may very well have been wrong and apologize. I will apologize for the offense that I've given, and I will be more than happy to submit myself to the leadership. But the leadership would have to say that it, too, may very well have been wrong to try and control my thinking. To the extent that I was offensive and I hurt people's feelings, I will apologize for all of that openly. I will say that I was angry and irritated and shouldn't have said some things. It was disrespectful. I may have been wrong. But you have to get up and apologize for hurting my feelings. You, too, must say you're sorry for putting me into a position where I felt like nobody was listening to me and frustrating me nearly to distraction. You must be sorry about that."

Then we would both get up there, shake hands, and bury the hatchet. But I couldn't say that I was wrong about everything and

Kerry and Boyd were right, because I don't believe it. I won't lie. Kerry's response to this was that it would never happen.

The irritating thing about being an excommunicant is that you get lumped in with sex offenders, molesters, and serial killers. People who betray their country get excommunicated. People who chop up cats get excommunicated. Margaret and I are in the same class with them. There's no distinction. One punishment fits all—excommunication. So, when they talk about the apostates and all of the evil people who have been excommunicated, we're lumped in with bipolars who murder with boning knives. It's really just too much.

Philip: The nature of excommunication is such that you can still attend church. Is that even an option?

Paul: No. My daughters are not interested, and my wife has been excommunicated. I don't feel like it's a welcoming place. I don't think that Church leaders have changed their attitude about people like me. They don't want apostates like me back.

Philip: Change their attitude how?

Paul: I don't think they're welcoming of people who question them, who have a theological interest, who are suspicious of authority, who feel like they have to be more forthcoming about their relationship with God before they can get people to obey them.

Philip: In this Church, as Joseph F. Smith said, nearly everything depends on authority.[30]

Paul: Yeah, in this Church nearly everything does, I'm afraid. I'm very distrustful of authority. I don't see great men here. I see ordinary men. I'm an ordinary man. I wouldn't want people to hang upon my words. I wouldn't want to tell people how to live their lives. I wouldn't want to substitute my judgment for their judgment. I can't understand why these men want to do that. I certainly would want to have a say, to be an influence, to have my words considered. Mutual respect was what I wanted. I wanted them to love me as much as I loved them. I wanted them to be willing to give me the same dignity that they wanted me to accord to them. If they wanted me to treat them as apostles, I wanted them to at least treat me as an ordinary Saint. I felt that was a deep betrayal, not just of me, but of the fundamental basis of Christianity. Jesus said, "As you have done it unto the least of these you have done it unto me" (Matt. 25:40). Even with all my barbs, I never treated them differently than I expected to be treated. It should not be considered rudeness when people are impassioned or in pain and they're lashing out. That's human nature.

Philip: Can you contrast your earlier belief just after your conversion with that held immediately before your excommunication?

Paul: My early belief was that I had a destiny in Mormonism, that my place was in Mormonism and that I was going to significantly participate in the rolling forth of the kingdom of God. I didn't believe at the time that I would ever be excommunicated.

Philip: In 1992, a year before your excommunication, you wrote "I love Mormonism and want to see it flourish,"[31] which was echoed in your letter to the *Salt Lake Tribune* on October 20, 1993, after your excommunication.[32] Has this sentiment changed in the last ten years?

Paul: I think so. I hate Mormonism and I love Mormonism, because Mormonism isn't one single thing. Mormonism has many manifestations. Are we talking about the Mormonism of the 1820s based upon magic, or the Mormonism of the 1830s based upon more traditional Christian principles, or the Mormonism of the 1840s based upon the idea of the temple, or the Mormonism of the pioneer era that was much more practical and based upon survival out in the West? There are too many to love or hate. You love some of them, you hate others.

Philip: As you see Mormonism today, do you want it to flourish?

Paul: I don't want George Bush to be reelected. I don't want to see or hear much from Boyd K. Packer. I don't want to see or hear much from the people who want simplicity over complexity. No, I don't want that. But on the other hand, I see that underneath its ugly surface dying for a makeover, Mormonism is a religion full of paradox and of extraordinary riches of the mind and the spirit. I don't want to see that destroyed. I want to see that come forth.

Philip: Last question: you declared in "All Is Not Well in Zion," the Sunstone presentation that served as the primary impetus for your excommunication, that "we must not fear excommunication."

Do you ever wish that you had feared excommunication, that you had been more careful?

Paul: I'm a bit old-fashioned in one respect. I believe slavery is worse than death, and I think slavery is also worse than excommunication. But the pain of my excommunication did turn out to be greater, different, and prolonged, and it seeped into me more deeply that I thought it would have. Excommunication is terrifying. Not at the moment it happens, because you're still in the glow of thinking that you're doing the right thing, but afterwards when there is a reckoning. It works. It has an effect. It alienates. It alienates your family who has to make a choice: Are they going to be with you or stay with the Church? My daughters have been very supportive of Margaret and me, but it has alienated them from the community. Those are things I didn't think clearly about.

It's like saying to a guy who went to World War I and got his legs blown off in the trenches, "Would you have been so patriotic had you known what was going to happen to you?" Naturally, the answer is probably not. Had I known I would be excommunicated, I probably wouldn't have sounded so triumphant. Was it worth getting my legs blown off? I don't know. My legs are gone, and it has changed my life. But my choice wasn't made with foreknowledge. I made my decision and suffered the consequences. Would I do it again? Yes, given the same circumstances, I would do the same thing. Would I do it over again had I known what was going to follow? Probably not. I'm not that courageous. An element of courage is a certain ignorance or perhaps denial about what's to come.

Notes

1. Mark Twain, *Life on the Mississippi* (New York: Harper and Brothers, 1917), 36.

2. Spencer W. Kimball addressed this theme in two separate general conferences: "Strengthening the Family: The Basic Unit of the Church," *Ensign*, May 1978, 45; and "Fundamental Principles to Ponder and Live," *Ensign*, November 1978, 43.

3. "All Is Not Well in Zion: False Teachings of the True Church," Sunstone Symposium, August 12, 1993, Salt Lake City.

4. "And he said, Draw not nigh hither: put off thy shoes from off thy feet, for the place whereon thou standest is holy ground" (Ex. 3:5).

5. "Who also hath made us able ministers of the new testament; not of the letter, but of the spirit: for the letter killeth, but the spirit giveth life" (2 Cor. 3:6).

6. More than eighty people attended the vigil.

7. "Charity never faileth: but whether there be prophecies, they shall fail; whether there be tongues, they shall cease; whether there be knowledge, it shall vanish away" (1 Cor. 13:8).

8. "We have learned by sad experience that it is the nature and disposition of almost all men, as soon as they get a little authority as they suppose, they will immediately begin to exercise unrighteous dominion" (D&C 121:39).

9. Paul James Toscano, "Beyond Tyranny, Beyond Arrogance," in *The Sanctity of Dissent* (Salt Lake City: Signature Books, 1994), 23.

10. Introduction, in ibid., xii.

11. This is a paraphrase of Friedrich Augustus Von Hayek, *The Road to Serfdom* (Chicago, Ill.: University of Chicago Press, 1994), 165-66: "To be a useful assistant in the running of a totalitarian state, it is not enough that a man should be prepared to accept specious justification of vile deeds; he must himself be prepared actively to break every moral rule he has ever known if this seems necessary to achieve the end set for him. Since it is the supreme leader who alone determines the ends, his instruments must have no moral convictions of their own. They must, above all, be unreservedly committed to the person of the leader; but next to this the most important thing is that they should be completely unprincipled and literally capable of everything. They must have no ideals of their own which they want to realize; no ideas about right or wrong which might interfere with the intentions of the leader . . . while there is little that is likely to induce men who are good by our standards to aspire to leading positions in the totalitarian machine, and much to deter them, there will be special opportunities for the ruthless and unscrupulous."

12. Heber J. Grant, *Gospel Standards*, compiled by G. Homer Durham (Salt Lake City: Improvement Era, 1943), 17.

13. "And Jesus, perceiving the thought of their heart, took a child, and set him by him, And said unto them, Whosoever shall receive this child in my name receiveth me: and whosoever shall receive me receiveth him that sent me: for he that is least among you all, the same shall be great" (Luke 9:47–48).

14. Dallin H. Oaks was president of BYU (1971–80) and has been an apostle since 1984.

15. Numbers 22:21–41 records the story of Balaam who is, in part, rebuked when the Lord speaks to him through his donkey.

16. Paul James Toscano, "A Plea to the Leadership of the Church," in *The Sanctity of Dissent*, 60.

17. As mayor of Nauvoo, Illinois, Joseph Smith decided to run for president of the United States in the spring of 1844, but his campaign was cut short when he was assassinated in jail later that year.

18. Toscano, "A Plea to the Leadership of the Church," 72.

19. William J. Hamblin, "Review, Paul J. Toscano: *The Sanctity of Dissent*," *FARMS Review of Books* 7, no. 1 (Provo, Utah: Foundation for Ancient Research and Mormon Studies, 1995), 301.

20. Paul James Toscano, "Mormon Dissident Answers Leaders," Letter, *Salt Lake Tribune*, October 20, 1993, editorial page.

21. Margaret and Paul Toscano, *Strangers in Paradox: Explorations in Mormon Theology* (Salt Lake City: Signature Books, 1990), xi.

22. Paul James Toscano, "The Call of Mormon Feminism," in *The Sanctity of Dissent*, 97.

23. Gordon B. Hinckley, "Daughters of God," *Ensign*, November 1991, 97.

24. Eliza R. Snow (1804–87), who married both Joseph Smith and his successor Brigham Young, was baptized in the spring of 1835 and served as the secretary to the Relief Society after it was organized on March 17, 1842. She penned the hymn "O My Father" in 1845.

25. "And now, my beloved brethren, I perceive that ye ponder still in your hearts; and it grieveth me that I must speak concerning this thing. For if ye would hearken unto the Spirit which teacheth a man to pray ye would know that ye must pray; for the evil spirit teacheth not a man to pray, but teacheth him that he must not pray" (2 Ne. 32:8).

26. This joint vision occurred April, 19, 1834: "Once after returning from a mission, he [Zebedee Coltrin] met Bro. Joseph in Kirtland, who asked him if he did not wish to go with him to a conference at New Portage. The party consisted of Prests.

Joseph Smith, Sidney Rigdon, Oliver Cowdery and myself. Next morning at New Portage, he noticed that Joseph seemed to have a far off look in his eyes, or was looking at a distance, and presently he, Joseph, stepped between Brothers Cowdery, and Coltrin and taking them by the arm, said, 'lets take a walk.' They went to a place where there was some beautiful grass, and grapevines and swampbeech interlaced. President Joseph Smith then said, 'let us pray.' They all three prayed in turn—Joseph, Oliver and Zebedee. Bro. Joseph then said, 'now brethren we will see some visions.' Joseph lay down on the ground on his back and stretched out his arms and the two brethren lay on them. The heavens gradually opened, and they saw a golden throne, on a circular foundation, something like a light house, and on the throne were two aged personages, having white hair, and clothed in white garments. They were the two most beautiful and perfect specimens of mankind he ever saw. Joseph said, They are our first parents, Adam and Eve. Adam was a large broad-shouldered man, and Eve as a woman, was as large in proportion." The Minutes of the Salt Lake School of the Prophets on October 11, 1883, 67–70, LDS Church History Library, Salt Lake City.

27. For perhaps the most representative argument on this topic, see D. Michael Quinn, "Mormon Women Have Had the Priesthood Since 1843," in *Women and Authority*, edited by Maxine Hanks (Salt Lake City: Signature Books, 1992), 365–409.

28. William Shakespeare, *Hamlet*, Act 2, scene 2.

29. Toscano and Toscano, *Strangers in Paradox*, xi.

30. Joseph F. Smith, *Gospel Doctrine* (Salt Lake City: Deseret Book, 1939), 102.

31. Paul James Toscano, "Dealing with Spiritual Abuse" in *The Sanctity of Dissent*, 113.

32. "I love Mormonism. I accept the gospel of Jesus Christ and the truth of the restoration. I am committed to the LDS Church. I am not an apostate by any definition." Toscano, "Mormon Dissident Answers Leaders."

Chapter 3
Maxine Hanks

Feminist theologian, excommunicated from the LDS Church on September 19, 1993.

Maxine Hanks was born on Christmas day, 1955, in Idaho Falls, Idaho. She grew up in a strong Mormon household and was baptized at the age of eight (the first year of eligibility for LDS children). That same year, the family moved to Walla Walla, Washington, and then to Yakima, Washington, where Maxine's father, D. Max Hanks, began his own small-scale commercial flying business.

It was in Washington that Maxine commenced her lifelong journey to understand the divine and her relationship thereto. In this respect, Mormonism was most appealing because it had explanations for the profound spiritual experiences she was having. Yet as her affection and loyalty for the Church grew, so did a sense of being stifled as a woman. Maxine yearned for God and the highest forms of spirituality possible, but the prohibition against women holding the LDS priesthood, for example, grew frustrating, and an inner dichotomy developed that posed devotion to the Church against deep frustration with it.

To compensate for not having the priesthood, Maxine pursued every leadership role available to her including president of the youth program, vice-president of seminary class, and teacher of the Gospel Doctrine class in Sunday School. Maxine also felt drawn to other faiths and spiritual traditions during this time and graduated from high school in 1974 with a yearning to delve deeper into the wider intellectual dimensions of religious faith and practice.

After high school, Maxine envisioned her life path as an academic and earned her way through LDS colleges via scholarships and side jobs. She studied humanities at Ricks College (now BYU-Idaho) (1975–77) while working as a teaching and research assistant for Dr. Ruth Barrus, and then self-funded her LDS mission (1978–80), hoping that missionary work would be a surrogate "priestly role" for her. Instead, the mission awoke Maxine to what she calls the "utterly male machine" of the LDS hierarchy, and she returned disillusioned from her mission in April 1980. Nevertheless, she chose to continue her studies at Church-run Brigham Young University in Provo, Utah, from 1980 to 1983.

Maxine chose to study English at BYU while working as a teacher at the LDS Missionary Training Center (MTC), preparing missionaries for the field. She also explored Mormon theology and history further as a trustee and staff member of the independent student paper, *Seventh East Press*. However, at this time of tension between LDS intellectuals and the Church, the more liberal *Seventh East Press* was banned from the BYU campus in 1973 and Maxine was simultaneously released from the MTC. So she moved on.

From 1983 to 1986, Maxine worked for BYU's College of Humanities as a full-time manuscript editor and publishing assistant, and was a teaching assistant for Dr. Arthur Henry King. Thereafter, Maxine underwent a serious existential crisis that set her adrift from Mormonism, and she started to channel her former passion for the Church into the social causes of feminism, humanism, and pacifism.

In 1986, Maxine commenced studies in philosophy and history at the University of Utah and the LDS Church Archives before working as a full-time editor/writer for the university from 1988 to 1991. In 1992, Maxine's work culminated in the publication of her edited anthology *Women and Authority: Re-emerging Mormon Feminism* (Salt Lake City: Signature Books, 1992), which caused tension between Maxine and her local LDS leaders that ultimately resulted in her excommunication from the Church in September 1993.

Maxine ultimately continued graduate studies in religion, including a fellowship at Harvard Divinity School, and found a spiritual home in Gnosticism, which affords equal opportunity to women seeking leadership roles. She was baptized in 1998, entered clergy orders in 1999, and has served as Gnostic clergy ever since.

I sat down with Maxine in August 2003 at a small diner in the suburbs of Provo, Utah. Dressed in a long black dress and with a piercing gaze, Maxine graciously related her past. This is her story.

The Excommunication

Philip: Why did you undertake the book project *Women and Authority* if you knew it would likely get you into trouble with the Church?

Maxine: When I began the project in 1989, I didn't know it would bring Church reaction. I only knew that Mormon women were afraid to discuss feminism in public. Church objections came later, after I'd discussed Mormon feminism in public. However, my purpose was not to engage or provoke the LDS Church, but to create a textbook for a women's studies course. *Women and Authority* was not intended as an appeal to the LDS Church, as I explained in the Foreword. It was an anthology about Mormon women, intended for students, scholars, and the public.

This was the error in my excommunication. *Women and Authority* was a scholarly project, not a personal statement. Church leaders misunderstood my work, although I heard that the Relief Society general presidency appreciated the book.

There's a difference between academic work and personal dissent. I was a teaching assistant in women's studies at the University of Utah for a course on "Women in Mormon Culture," taught by Dr. Vella Evans, and I created *Women and Authority* as a text for that course. It wasn't critical of Mormonism. It was a compilation of discourse by Mormon feminists. It was apologetic because it valued and validated Mormon women's voices, history, heritage, and authority. It didn't venture outside of Mormon precedent nor impose secular feminism onto Mormonism. It revealed feminism within the faith. It may have appeared to veer outside of Mormonism, because Mormon feminism had not been recognized. *Women and Authority* was a watershed moment that legitimized Mormon feminism.

Philip: Why were Mormon women afraid to talk about feminism in public?

Maxine: Feminism had a negative stigma after Sonia Johnson's excommunication in 1979 and fears still lingered fresh in feminist memory. People even avoided the word. So I wanted to educate readers about feminism and correct misconceptions by letting feminism speak for itself through many voices and generations. I used "feminism" in the title and included feminist voices or examples from both the nineteenth and twentieth centuries, in order to put different Mormon feminisms into context and document a feminist tradition in Mormon history.

Jan Tyler told me the book "vindicated Sonia." I think it vindicated feminism as a whole. This is why a scholarly approach was necessary. Defining and identifying feminism in Mormon history, culture, and theology require feminist theory and women's studies, which recognize feminism within religion. Mormon feminism deserved serious scholarly treatment.

I'd been researching Mormonism since 1975 and had noticed a persistence of feminist voices in LDS culture, history, and discourse. I was surprised by how much feminism pervaded Mormonism. I found enough material for several books. A women's studies program was the appropriate place to address Mormon feminism, yet I found myself facing intrusion from the Church.

Philip: How did the Church intrude?

Maxine: The Church monitored my public speaking and writing, then directed local leaders to interview me. Between 1989 and 1993 as I worked on the book, I was questioned by a Church security officer, a stake president, the area president, two bishops, and several male defenders of the faith—all warning me that my research was dangerous or wrong. It was creepy, being summoned by Church leaders for questions about my college studies. It felt like bad *film noir*. I should have simply refused, but I submitted to pointless meetings that tried to impose church onto university. I discussed my work with them as a scholar, not as a member.

The stake president was a nice man, in fact a distant cousin of mine. Church leaders who interviewed me liked my research on Ephraim Hanks, yet they warned me about work on feminism. So my rum-drinking Danite ancestor who disposed of "apostates" for Brigham Young was an approved topic, but feminism was dangerous. I was told that if I didn't stop speaking about feminism in public, it could "jeopardize" my Church membership. If I had been sharing my secular work in the Church, then they'd have been justified in asking me to stop, but they were imposing ecclesiastical control on public discourse and using my membership to leverage silence, which was censorship.

I endured interrogations and threats for five years. It was draining. It gave me headaches. I didn't feel the "spirit of God" in that process. By 1992, I wondered which would happen first—publication or excommunication. As it turned out, the minute *Women and Authority* came off the press in December 1992, LDS Church leaders took action to counter the book.

Philip: How do you know?

Maxine: Well, first, the timing of the Church's reaction was obvious: *Women and Authority* hit bookstores in January 1993 and the Associated Press ran a story about the book that highlighted Mike Quinn's essay.[1] Then, on the first Sunday in February 1993, both Mike and I were contacted by the stake president regarding *Women and Authority*. (We lived in the same stake on Capitol Hill in Salt Lake City.) I doubt that the stake president was browsing brand-new feminist books fresh off the press, barely on store shelves. The LDS Church monitors press about Mormonism and sends it to local Church leaders, so the AP article alerted Church leaders about my book.

Second, two LDS leaders told me—one in May and one in August—about high-level Church reaction to my work.

Third, the apostles discussed my book in their meeting on February 4, 1993. At that meeting, one apostle voiced serious concerns, which were relayed to the stake president.

Philip: Who was that apostle?

Maxine: Well, I learned this third hand, so I can't give names. Reportedly one apostle expressed concern that *Women and*

Authority was "harmful to the Church," and specifically mentioned Mike's essay on women's priesthood. He felt that Mike's writings showed an "intent to hurt the Church," so "something needs to be done." Mike is a professional historian who documented that Mormon women received the Melchizedek Priesthood in 1843,[2] and that the modern Church had suppressed this knowledge. Mike was also an LDS priesthood holder. So the brethren saw his work as a betrayal.

I was stunned by this, because Mike's intent was never to "harm the Church." Mike is a Yale-trained PhD whose work and objectivity are impeccable. And my intent certainly was not to harm anyone but to compile scholarship on Mormon women and make it available to the public. The fears didn't match the reality. The problem wasn't *intent*, it was *content*—new research about Mormon women's history, including ways that women received religious authority and priesthood. I think Church leaders were unsure how to deal with the topic. It was complex and required scholarly work on historical and theological issues.

Philip: Why do Church issues require scholarly work?

Maxine: The study of religion requires scholarship. Historical issues need historians, theological issues need theologians, gender issues need gender theorists. Evaluating women's status in religion is a task of gender studies. Mormon women are a complex topic, located in religious texts and history. It takes decades to grasp Mormon studies, which include many hundreds of articles, publications, books, papers, archive collections, and conferences.

Women and Authority explored women's relationship to religious authority, including priesthood. The book discussed historical evidence and precedence for women's authority and how Church policy changed over time. When scholarship differs with Church policy, it puts Church leaders in a bind. Yet scholarship isn't binding on Church members. It has no religious authority. It's secular discourse. So refuting or punishing scholars is unnecessary. Unfortunately, the Church excommunicated scholars with specific skills for complex Mormon historical, theological, and gender topics.

Philip: How did the Church deal with the issues of feminism that you brought up?

Maxine: They denounced feminism and scholarship in public and privately directed Church discipline our way. A couple of apostles had kindled warnings about scholarship for years, so when *Women and Authority* appeared in January, it fanned a smoldering fire, igniting the purge of 1993. Apostolic concern was conveyed down the line to stake presidents and bishops who summoned scholars and feminists for questioning. By May, the purge was well underway: Elder Packer publicly denounced "relatively new" feminism and "so-called scholars or intellectuals" as "dangers" making "major invasions into church membership."[3] Liberal Mormon BYU professors, David C. Knowlton and Cecilia Konchar Farr, were notified that they were losing their jobs, and Mike Quinn was summoned for discipline.

I was alarmed, so I approached the LDS Salt Lake Area President, Elder Loren C. Dunn, hoping to explain my book and alleviate tensions. He confirmed apostolic indigestion, saying that my "book gave us heartburn" and insisted that "the brethren have no interest in feminist ideas." I explained the purpose of feminist scholarship, but he told me to cease feminist work, because "it serves no purpose."

They assumed my book was directed at the Church, as dissent. It wasn't. It was a women's studies text. They never understood that. So they initiated disciplinary action against me in February, which culminated in my excommunication in September.

Philip: Why didn't you attend your disciplinary council?

Maxine: It was nonsensical—they were calling me "contrary to the laws and order of the Church" for publishing women's studies scholarship. Talk about a non sequitur. The Church was holding a court on a textbook?

And my summons, dated September 11, was spooky, sudden. The stake president had been interviewing me for two years. He knew my work, intent, sincerity, and good will. Out of the blue, he convened a Church court for me in a hurry. I asked if we could talk about it, but he refused. I asked for time to prepare. He declined. I insisted. He relented, giving me until September 19. He clearly had been given an ultimatum from leaders higher up.

Although I was flattered to merit a high priests' council of twelve rather than a bishop's court of three, I declined to enter that room.

These were churchmen whom I'd never met, judging my scholarly work which they'd either not read or understood. The apostles didn't even know me, nor did the high council who got the job of disciplining me, because the bishop had never met or even heard of me.

Also, their only intent was to make me recant and submit to their authority, which had no bearing on my work. Disciplinary councils are not positive meetings. At best, I'd achieve a migraine headache. I'd had enough of Church interviews. My only intent was to end their disciplinary process. The cost of membership was too high.

Philip: So you wrote a statement instead of attending the council?

Maxine: Yes, I responded to their charge of being "contrary to the laws and order of the Church." I was tempted to write a satire, but the mood was too serious for humor. So I quoted "Prophetess" Eliza R. Snow defining the Relief Society as "a self-governing organization."[4] I let Eliza refute the disciplinary process. And I said the Church couldn't judge me.

That would have been the end, but the press was covering each excommunication, calling for live comment "on the scene" either at the church or my home, an impossible choice. So I met them in front of a chapel I'd never entered with a statement I'd faxed the day before. The whole thing was surreal. I stood amid a mass of cameras and microphones like a movie set or a strange play. I kept thinking, "Why does everyone take this so seriously?"

It reminded me of the *Acts of John*, where Jesus views the crucifixion from a distance telling John, "I am not that. . . . What I am I alone know."[5] Public image is illusion. Personal reality is something else. The Church and the media defined me and my excommunication, yet neither knew me. The Church portrayed me as an enemy, and the media portrayed me as a victim. I was neither.

Scholars know what they're doing. We weren't enemies or victims. We were experts. The real story was that we were misjudged; we were something other than what Church leaders feared. I tried to explain this to the Church, but they wanted the enemy story. I tried to explain it to the media, but they wanted the victim story. So the Church told the enemy story and the press told the victim story, and it was all over the evening news.

Philip: How would you describe your religious beliefs immediately before your excommunication?

Maxine: Well originally, God was very Mormon, a loving Father in Heaven whose presence was real in my life along with Jesus. I had a personal witness of Mormonism, specifically that aspects of early Christianity were revived in the LDS Church.

Then I had an existential crisis of faith in 1983, ten years before the purge. After that, God was more archetypal than anthropic, more Jungian.[6] Theology was real, but it resided in the transcendent realm, the mythic. The masculine and feminine Mormon Gods were powerful archetypes. Yet the feminine had been obscured and diminished, which affected Mormon identity. I saw how the Mormon God both shaped and reflected the Mormon psyche.

Curiously, when *Women and Authority* was published, my sense of God shifted again—from mythic to essential, transcendent to immanent. It was a new aspect or level of God, an encounter with God-mind—beyond archetype, beyond gender, beyond all forms. God simply let me know that I was known and that God was known by me. In that moment, I became Gnostic.

Philip: And that was the faith you had going into your excommunication trial?

Maxine: Yes. I had an epiphany in January 1993, coincidentally during Epiphany week, one month before the disciplinary process began in February. Rather than lose my faith, I encountered a deeper knowledge of God, a new sense of God—not faith or belief, but *gnosis*. This sustained me through the entire year. I also had a dream of a divine feminine figure who conveyed pure wisdom.

Philip: It sounds like the Hebrew *Hokmah*.

Maxine: Yes, it was Sophia.[7] She appeared in a series of dreams that year, a continuing presence like the Paraclete. Dreams are important in my life. I listen to them. Sophia brought clarity about events, concerns, and priorities all that year, throughout the disciplinary process, and its aftermath. For example, I had a Gethsemane moment that summer; I saw what was coming and longed to avoid it, so I prayed about resigning from the Church to bypass the ordeal. The answer was clear—that I would be excommunicated and needed to go through that because it would serve a purpose.

Ironically, I wound up requesting a last-minute resignation just days before my disciplinary council—not to bypass the ordeal but to ensure that the council would excommunicate me, rather than drag out the process for months as they'd done with Mike Quinn.

Philip: Do you still feel that divine presence of Sophia today?

Maxine: Yes, though not as intensely as in 1993. I've always felt a spiritual presence in my life. I'm prone to metaphysical experience—dreams and glimpses, intuitive senses of intangible things, not visible, but vivid impressions and insights. For me, spirituality is primary, originary, while scholarship is secondary, yet both are equally important in acquiring knowledge. I use both scholarly and spiritual approaches to learning. I'd say the mantle is as great as the intellect, or perhaps *only* as great as the intellect.[8]

Philip: Was excommunication the only or best option for the Church?

Maxine: No, not the only option. We could have talked, found understanding. We didn't deserve excommunication. The book wasn't apostate; the sin was scholarship. Excommunication is a category for criminals, child abusers, rapists, murderers. It stigmatized our reputations.

The excommunication was based on fear, not reality. The purge was about the Mormon "shadow" or fear of the unknown self. Scholarly work is shadow work. The Mormon shadow was made visible through us. The real conflict was within the religious personality of Mormonism.

The apostles' role in the purge seemed evident at the October 1993 LDS conference. Many talks responded to the sins of the scholars. President Hinckley—he was in the First Presidency then—denounced "critics within." Elder Faust charged bishops with keeping the Church pure from a "loyal opposition." Elder Maxwell faulted intellectual tradition and "accommodating revealed theology to conventional wisdom." Elder Scott urged spiritual knowledge over secular. Elder Packer urged separate gender roles: motherhood for women, and "priesthood entrusted to men since the beginning."

Elder Oaks defined gender and separate gender roles. Elder Ballard specified motherhood for women and priesthood for men and caution in "gospel scholarship." Elder Nelson defined priesthood as "carefully controlled through the lineage of fathers." Elder Poelman said "Church discipline" was "not punishment" but was "intended to heal and renew." Elder Busche questioned "so-called intellect" in a "war" between learning versus truth.[9] In 1994, the brethren continued to denounce "dissidents."

I forgave the apostles for misjudging me, and I forgave myself for publishing feminist theology before the Church was ready for it. But it was terribly ironic that the Church punished us for scholarly Mormon studies in 1993, then embraced scholarly Mormon studies by 2001.[10] Also, I noticed that Church rhetoric become more feminist about women's contributions, identity, education, and careers between 1993 and 2003. Some leaders even began using the word "feminist." Elder Bruce R. Hafen has talked about feminism and even women's theology.[11] If *Women and Authority* were published today, we wouldn't be punished, we'd be quoted.

The Status of Women in Mormonism

Philip: In *Women and Authority*, you stated, "Feminist theology is a revisionist theology—it seeks to install the feminine into our view of God and our relationship to God."[12] What do you mean by installing a feminist view? That may make women more comfortable, but what if it's not reality?

Maxine: "Revisionist" means to correct, make accurate, include what is present but unseen. By "install" I meant reveal the feminine as inherent in Mormon theology. Gender is always present in theology; feminine and masculine aspects coexist in religion from its origins. How they're expressed or repressed is what makes a religion unique. Feminist theology excavates how gender is embedded in religious ideas and texts, how it's constructed, positioned, valued. It reveals how religion shapes gender, how gender shapes religion, and the values that shape gender in religion, including cultural and political values.

God is gendered in Mormonism, a dual-gendered deity of male and female gods with divine equality, who are both "gods, because they have all power" (D&C 132:20). So gender is balanced in Mormon theology, but imbalanced in Church discourse, which focuses on the male over the female, distorting their equality. This approach translates into imbalanced attitudes about women and affects how women view themselves.

Philip: I appreciate that you want to balance the power between men and women, but what if you are creating a false image that misconstrues reality and the will of God? What if God wants a patriarchal structure and, in fact, you are bringing women away from that proper perspective?

Maxine: Scholars don't try to balance Mormonism. We reveal its balance or imbalances, its constructs. Feminist theologians don't impose gender on religion; we examine how religion is gendered. Joseph Smith envisioned gendered gods, male and female, of equal power and glory. Sure, there are contradictions, tensions, within Mormon theology, between equality and patriarchy. For example, gods are equal, yet some are polygamous. These tensions haven't been fully explored.

Mormon theology is interesting for its complexity and unfinished nature. Joseph established a church led by men and women, each endowed with the Melchizedek Priesthood. He organized Mormon women as "a kingdom of Priests" who "should move according to the ancient Priesthood."[13] A patriarchal church seems contrary to the ways that Joseph envisioned gender operating in theology. Even polygamy was based on polyandry as much as on polygyny.

Philip: Because women do not hold General Authority-level positions in the Church, they do not formally participate in the establishment of doctrine. Do you feel that average members should have a more active role in establishing doctrine, which would then give women more of a say?

Maxine: Women *do* hold General Authority-level positions in the Church—via the Relief Society. Joseph did "ordain them to preside over the society, and let them preside just as the Presidency presides over the church."[14] Joseph intended the Relief Society as a parallel organization to the First Presidency and apostles, with a line of authority from the president down to the ward level, just like the male priesthood hierarchy. Eliza R. Snow reiterated this parallel in 1884.[15]

Rather than being a ladies' aid society or a mechanism for keeping women silent about polygamy, the Relief Society was more like a female Masonic order, an extension of male privilege to women. The Church organization gave Mormon women separate but equal standing, from top to bottom. Male leaders may not fully recognize that. Women have filled General Authority *roles*, and they have participated in establishing theology and doctrine. I believe that historical evidence suggests that Lucy Mack Smith influenced Joseph's early visions and revelations and that Emma Smith helped Joseph obtain and bring forth the Book of Mormon, and influenced some sections of the Doctrine and Covenants. I believe that Lucy and Emma were co-founders with Joseph, not unlike Oliver Cowdery or Martin Harris.

The Church structure already gives women equality at all levels, but women might be more active at all levels if they were valued equally.

Philip: Yet, Mormonism fundamentally diverges from that construct. The male prophet receives revelation from God as to how the Church should be run. One male *does* have insight into the mind of God with respect to leadership. So why would he ever need to consult with women?

Maxine: Well, the prophet does consult with leaders and members about decisions—sometimes including his own wife and family. Joseph told the women if they "wanted to carry out the designs of the Institution, let them be appointed and act apart, as Deacons, Teachers &c., are among us."[16] He defined the Church as operating via the spiritual gifts of each member contributing to the whole (D&C 46). Also many ideas that have shaped Mormon theology, doctrine, or policy have come from women, including ideas about the Mother God, the Word of Wisdom, storing grain, women's leadership and titles, women's ordinations, blessings, prayers, programs, and publications.

Philip: You once wrote, "It makes sense that Mormon women would be feminists: within male-centered religion and discourse, feminism and feminist theology are necessary."[17] Many in the Church would respond that Mormonism is not necessarily male-focused. Just as the priesthood is given to men, motherhood is given to women. I'm sure you've heard this a thousand times before. Can one conflate the calling of motherhood with the priesthood callings?

Maxine: It's fallacious to equate them. Motherhood is a biological process that requires reproductive organs, while priesthood isn't. If motherhood is priesthood, that excludes many women, and it requires pregnancy. Meanwhile, Mormon women do have priesthood in several ways—priesthood roles, duties, and divine power. The question is not whether Mormon women have priesthood, but why it is denied or limited.

Philip: But with all due respect, if the priesthood was divinely bestowed upon men and men alone, what gives you the right to challenge God's will?

Maxine: Scholarship doesn't make claims about God's will for a religion. It studies the claims that religion makes, including claims about God and gender. It's not God that scholars question, but a religion's claims about God, theology, doctrine, history, and gender. Scholars study the discourse and texts of a religion; so if Mormon texts indicate that priesthood was given to women and Church leaders censor that information, scholars will still study and discuss it.

Philip: What if Mormon women don't want the priesthood? Does that mean there is something wrong with them?

Maxine: Of course not. Many women don't want priesthood. Feminist theology doesn't prescribe that women become priests. It analyzes gender and priesthood, and how religion shapes identity for women and men. It reveals how theology is constructed and written onto bodies, identities, and lives.

Philip: Some Church leaders charge feminists with trying to create a competition between men and women that goes against God's will. They posit that the genders are supposed to complement rather than compete against one another. Do you agree? How do you respond to such statements?

Maxine: It's projection, blaming feminists for competition when it's privilege that creates competition. Between equals there is no need to compete. It's sexism that erodes partnership and mutual empowerment. Members in patriarchal religions often voice a fear that "feminists want to replace patriarchy with matriarchy" or replace the male god with a female god. This projects a patriarchal fear of its own privilege, valuing masculine over feminine. Feminist scholarship doesn't advocate female privilege, dominance or hegemony, it deconstructs those very things. Feminist studies are inclusive, not exclusive. They value men and women equally, and recognize their diversity. Another common projection is the accusation that "feminists don't speak for the Church," which is nonsensical since feminists aren't trying to speak for the Church. The whole point is that they're trying to speak for themselves.

Joseph Smith and the Book of Mormon

Philip: Was Joseph Smith a prophet?

Maxine: Well, as he said, only he knows his history,[18] but yes, he functioned as a prophet in the biblical sense. He had visions of God and angels, received sacred texts, and spoke in a prophetic voice. Jan Shipps described it best—a prophet is a charismatic with followers who are involved together in a reflexive, mutually reinforcing relationship that creates a religious community.[19] That's Joseph Smith. He drew a devoted following and they had mutual religious experiences. Together they envisioned divine beings, produced new scripture, organized a new church, built a new society, and birthed a new religious tradition. Joseph's prophetic role was a collaboration with others—especially his family (his parents, Joseph Sr. and Lucy, his brothers Alvin and Hyrum, his wife, Emma, and his cousin Oliver Cowdery)—as well as neighbors and friends, Martin Harris and Sidney Rigdon.

Revelation is a rhetorical relationship that answers a need, a question, a situation.[20]

Harold Bloom said Joseph had a "genius" for "religion-making."[21] That's a prophet. Mike Quinn said Joseph was "divining" and "scrying" from age ten or eleven.[22] That's a seer.

What you're really asking is whether Joseph's revelations were human or divine. Believers view his revelations as divine, while nonbelievers view them as human. I think his revelations reveal both influences.

Joseph's revelations responded to human situations and needs in historical circumstances, yet divine presence inhabited the human beings, their process, and the resulting texts and religion. Visions and revelations are shaped by human perception, yet they're metaphysical by nature, transcendent. Spiritual experience transcends ordinary reality; the divine realms of God and angels are otherworldly, mystic. Believers and scholars can agree on that much. Revelation is both human and divine. The issue is how you define "divine"—whether from religious belief or a scholarly framework. Believers treat the divine as literal. Scholars treat the divine as mythic—beyond the literal where religion is real but mystic, not judged as true or false. Divine truths live in the mythic realm. So a prophet functions as a mythmaker.

Philip: You're using the definition of myth that is often used in literary studies of the Bible, which goes beyond assessing the "truth" of a work by its literal accuracy. So in that literary sense, is the Book of Mormon "true," if it has mythic qualities?

Maxine: Yes. It contains mythic truths, but "mythic" doesn't mean untrue or unreal. Mythic is transcendent, spiritual—whether we're talking about myth in literary criticism or religious studies or Jungian psychology. Visionaries from Pythagoras to Plato and Jesus to Jung viewed the mythic as more true or real than the physical. Any text that describes divine beings is mythic by nature. A religious story is an heroic epic, because mere historical reportage can't convey the workings of the divine in human lives and history. That requires mythic story where humans, gods, angels, and devils interact.

Jewish scriptures and Christian gospels blended mythic narrative with a spiritual witness of God's presence among humanity. Likewise, the Book of Mormon is scripture, a gospel. But is it ancient history? Believers say it's ancient. Critics say it's nineteenth century. I think it reflects qualities of both times. All scripture is couched in the culture of its time, shaped by its authors, editors, scribes, or transcribers; still, the human voice in the text doesn't negate the divine voice. Both voices are present in scripture.

The divinity of scripture doesn't come from its historicity. So it's a mistake to equate the two by claiming that scripture is divine because it's ancient, or because Moses, Mark, Paul, or Moroni wrote it. The divine value of the Book of Mormon isn't its literal depiction of historic times or places or events but its spiritual depictions of divinity in human life. It's the divine presence in the events and the divine voice in the story that make it sacred (Moro. 7:13). Divinity is determined by the soul. History is determined by scholarship. They're different endeavors.

A spiritual experience or story takes us beyond our mundane literal lives. Myth is better than literal history any day. The divine value of the Book of Mormon isn't its literal depiction of historic times or places or events but its spiritual depictions of divine interactions in human life. For example, viewing Mayans as Christians is problematic, but a vision of Christ in ancient America can be beautiful.

The divinity of scripture also isn't based on its *material*, whether parchment or metal plates, or its *process*, whether translation or inner vision. It's the quality of the message that matters—not the medium. Readers enter the story to find God or the divine, and encounter an inward, spiritual process more than an external, literal one.

Philip: So are you saying that Joseph Smith's mythical experiences of the divine motivated him to write about contentious South American Indians and that it's true because it was an inward process rather than drawing upon external sources?

Maxine: I'm saying that spiritual truth is transcendent more than historical, more mythic than literal. To understand Joseph, I think one has to enter the mythic realm oneself. Can we really talk about the mythic unless we experience it?

However, Joseph did draw upon both inner and external sources, including literary and biblical traditions. For example, the biblical tradition of "midrash"—where new scripture emerges from a theme in biblical texts to fill in and elaborate a missing story. The Book of Mormon is a midrash about refugees from Jerusalem in 600 BCE, a missing history about members of the tribes of Israel and their descendants. Joseph Smith himself became a kind of midrash of Joseph in the Bible, fleshing out that theme in his own life and work.

Another literary tradition that Joseph invoked is a national myth of origins—which gives a history to a people, origins that are pre-history and thus legendary in ancient times and places. Stories like the Gilgamesh epic, Genesis, Exodus, the Theogony, the *Iliad*, the *Odyssey*, the *Aeneid*, the Christian Gospels, *Beowulf*, and *Lord of the Rings* all envision cultural origins. A myth of origins is based on historical possibilities or legends, filled in with heroic myth.

One popular legend in early America was that the "Indians" were descendants of Israelites or the lost tribes of Israel. Another popular idea was the immanent restoration of "primitive" Christianity. The Book of Mormon answered both of these national longings with a Jewish/Christian bible story that revealed the ancient history of America as containing both an ancient Jewish history and a primitive Christianity. This story of origins also contained a precedent for restoring primitive Christianity and gathering Israel—in modern America. Joseph produced an American myth of origins.

Philip: He doesn't claim to be creating an American myth.

Maxine: He didn't use the term "myth," but he was an avid storyteller and visionary. He claimed to have a new vision of God, religion, society, and country. He claimed to restore ancient knowledge of a lost history, lost gospel, lost church. He claimed to translate a mysterious language[23] inscribed on ancient records "to come forth by the gift and power of God unto the interpretation thereof."[24] All of this requires mythic capacity, ability.

He did describe the divine beings and gold plates and ancient history as real—but did that mean visionary reality or literal reality? His process of receiving them was visionary, supernatural, metaphysical, mythic. He gazed into seer stones and saw images or words in vision, which his scribes recorded. Mormonism materialized from a spiritual realm. Joseph said that at times he couldn't tell whether he was "in the body or out."[25] This is mystic or mythic experience.

Anyway, Joseph's visions answered a national longing. I think he knew that he was bringing forth an American myth or religion. A mystic enters the mythic for personal solitary reasons, but a prophet enters the mythic for others, for many. Joseph's revelations and writings had mythic answers and power for an entire society.

Philip: Was he just giving people what they wanted to hear?

Maxine: No, Joseph entered the myth. Joseph entered the mythic fabric of the Bible and found himself within it—as did John the Baptist and Jesus.

There's a difference between a myth and a lie, as Tolkien told Lewis.[26] Myth contains spiritual truths, and myth-making discloses those truths. Joseph was immersed in visionary process with the transcendent. He entered the mythic dimensions of himself every day. He lived in myth, lived it out with others in every conversation. Joseph's capacity for myth was extraordinary.

Vision is always shaped by the seer, but a fraud doesn't believe in what he's doing. Joseph believed in what he was doing. He was a myth-maker, a religion-maker, not a fraud. Joseph was accessing the transcendent self, beyond self. Joseph's myth was real. The real question is, did he succeed? I don't know. Do any of us succeed? Joseph's legacy shows that he was trying to live out both his mythic and human lives. His work and life contain mythic patterns that indicate he was accessing the archetypal or spiritual. He dared to be fully himself, human and divine, flawed and enlightened, in front of others. That takes guts. Many believers don't know the human Joseph, while many nonbelievers don't know the mythic Joseph. I'm interested in the whole Joseph.

Philip: But what if he knew that what he claimed never happened?

Maxine: Did he? He claimed visionary experience, supernatural sight. Is a material of exterior experience more true than an interior or spiritual experience? Joseph said he saw God and Christ in vision, as did Moses and Paul. Does it matter whether divine beings are spirit, archetype, mythic, light, quantum, wave, particles, atoms, molecules, or fire? He envisioned beings not of this world. Joseph even described the gold plates in metaphysical terms, appearing and disappearing, given and taken by angelic means and beings.

The prophet versus fraud debate misses the point[27]—that religion-making is metaphysical process, rather than literally true or false. Vision and revelation may apply to literal reality, but they come from beyond it. We can't say that the metaphysical never happened. It happens beyond the physical world. We look for what happened in history and try to understand what happened for Joseph.

Also, Joseph may have doubted himself and overcompensated for it. Visionaries do wonder about themselves. If he questioned his visions or feared that others wouldn't believe him, he may have felt that he needed tangible evidence. Yet the literal aspects of his revelations are the problematic areas. Vision is transitory, amorphous, ambiguous. Visions are glimpses. Revelations are fragments. None is final or complete. A new vision always awaits. It makes sense that Joseph reported nine or more versions of the First Vision, because together they offer a more holistic picture. Also a vision is personal, subjective, therefore not incumbent upon other people. Limitations and problems of revelation can arise when followers accept a prophet's vision over their own knowing, as binding upon their lives.

Philip: Do you then see the Book of Mormon as valuable semiotically, for the symbolism it represents of Joseph's own personal mystical experience?

Maxine: Yes, for the symbolic, mythic images, the transcendent messages. It's also valuable for what it reveals about Joseph himself—his voice, personality, life, times, relationships, values. Joseph's presence within the narrative is not a flaw, or evidence of fraud, but proof of authenticity, proof that he was intimately involved in the story. He produced it rather than plagiarized it. Like the Stratfordian versus Oxfordian debate on Shakespeare authorship, I'm a Smithian, not Spauldian.[28] I think Joseph was the authentic storyteller, rather than Spaulding.

The Book of Mormon is valuable for its spiritual messages and resonance—sublime teachings or moments that speak to the soul and move the reader into holy experience. Spiritual experience is captured and recorded in the text, then reproduced in the reader, recreated anew. That's scripture.

Philip: So, because scripture is mythical and the Book of Mormon is scripture, then you believe one can access the divine through the Book of Mormon just as well as through the Bible?

Maxine: Yes, exactly. It's as divine as any other scripture. Yet the reverse also applies. The Book of Mormon is as human as other scripture—a product of people, times, places, and cultures. So it deserves the same scholarly analysis that is applied to other scripture. It requires historical, literary, language, rhetorical, biblical, and hermeneutic studies to reveal the human, cultural qualities of scripture. And it takes a mystical reading to reveal the divine spiritual qualities. Those who see only divine voice in scripture miss the human voice, and those who see only human voices miss the divine. Like all scripture, LDS scriptures show the presence of both voices. Critical hermeneutic studies of Mormon scripture is a field that is "white already to harvest" (John 4:35; D&C 4:4).

Philip: And what about the Tao Te Ching in Taoism, the Analects in Confucianism, or other texts held sacred?

Maxine: Yes, divine voice is present in all sacred texts, in moments of enlightenment and grace. The divine and the human coexist in text, as they do in human beings. I hear God's voice in the Tao, Homer, Plato, the Apocrypha, Nag Hammadi, Corpus Hermeticum, Shakespeare, Blake, and Yeats. All literary texts contain spiritual moments of divine resonance. I use scholarship to analyze a text, yet I also feel the spiritual presence or energy inhabiting a text.

Ancient Jews and Christians saw different levels of voice or teaching in scripture, from human to divine: a literal level or common teaching, a metaphorical level or hidden teaching, and a spiritual level or divine transmission. Jewish and Christian scripture attempted to convey those different levels. As Mark, Luke, and Matthew explain, "Unto you it is given to know the mystery of the kingdom of God: but unto them that are without, all these things are done in parables" (Mark 4:11, Luke 8:10, Matt. 13:11). Or as Thomas says, "These are the secret sayings which the living Jesus spoke ... Whoever finds the interpretation of these sayings will not experience death."[29]

Actually, all literature can be read or interpreted on different levels, including the literal, literary, allegorical, metaphorical, symbolic, mythic, psychological, philosophical, mystic, or spiritual. I realized this when I worked at BYU with Arthur Henry King[30] in 1983 on rhetorical analysis of Shakespeare—that different levels or types of knowing and interpretation coexist within a text, and that the spiritual level of interpretation is the most personal. The hermeneutics of mystery or mysticism is another field ready to harvest.

Reflection

Philip: In retrospect, how have your thoughts and feelings changed over the last ten years toward the Church and the events leading up to and including your excommunication?

Maxine: My intellectual approach to Mormonism hasn't changed in thirty or forty years. I research and write Mormon studies with an open mind, an honest and compassionate eye. I try to tell the truth, with respect, to help inform, not harm. For me, it was never about reforming Mormonism or changing the Church. It was about understanding it objectively. Yet, my relationship with the Church as a member has evolved from alienation to appreciation since 1993.

I'm both an outsider and insider, but I approach the LDS Church as an outsider now, with that respect. I study Mormonism academically. I appreciate it socially, as one of many faiths. I have transcended it personally. I don't mean I purged it. I have a transcendent perspective.

Philip: You have sometimes expressed a sense of lightness and joy in separating from a church which inflicts a restraining energy. Do you still feel that sense of joy?

Maxine: Yes, leaving the Church dissolved negative relationships, allowing me to heal. I wouldn't have found harmony with Mormonism by conforming to it, nor by reforming it, nor by rejecting it. I had to move beyond the Church to find peace with it. It's a paradox. "Leaving" doesn't mean walking away, in a horizontal move. "Leaving" is a vertical transition, within oneself, to a higher perspective or larger understanding. That's freedom. I didn't leave the battle. I left the war.

I'll never forget seeing the stake president a few months after the excommunication, while shopping. Instead of a dark blue suit, he was wearing a comfortable old tan sweater. We just smiled, looking at each other, lacking words, relating as human beings. Our humanity hovered above disciplinary action. We both shed a tear, then moved on.

Philip: Do you consider yourself Mormon?

Maxine: Sure, my past is still part of me. Decades of Mormon heritage didn't disappear with excommunication. My relationship to Mormon history and landscapes runs deep. My ancestors live in me, including my great-great-grandfather Eph Hanks and my fifth cousin Joseph Smith. My family on both sides is Mormon for seven generations; eighteen of my ancestors emigrated across the Atlantic Ocean and the American continent between 1847 and 1869 to homestead in Utah and Idaho. I've lived in the Mormon corridor for forty years. There's a Mormon corridor in my soul.

I'm genetically programmed to pioneer. The trek from LDS seminary president to feminist heretic to Gnostic chaplain is a personal emigration across ideological landscapes and paradigms. I learned to evolve. I moved beyond the purge in 1999 when I became clergy and began interfaith work. I don't identify as a September Six heretic. One finds the purpose in a negative role and fulfills it, then evolves into something new and positive.

I've moved beyond myself.

Philip: Do you still read the Book of Mormon?

Maxine: Yes, often. I find many passages alive with divine voice. As scripture, the Book of Mormon captures spiritual experience and recreates that divine resonance anew in the reader. Ether is still my favorite book.[31] I still enter the story, where God touches the white stones and illuminates them with divine light (Ether 3:6–16). I still lament my inadequacy along with Moroni and am reassured by God that "my grace is sufficient for all men that humble themselves . . . and have faith in me, then will I make weak things become strong unto them" (Ether 12:27). Likewise, the Doctrine and Covenants and Pearl of Great Price contain many passages that still resonate spiritually in me.

Philip: Is Gordon B. Hinckley a prophet of God?

Maxine: Yes, like Joseph Smith, he fits the biblical role of a charismatic visionary religious leader. He has a prophetic capacity for progress. He has helped the Church evolve beyond itself. For example, in 2001 the "Doctrine of Inclusion" counseled Church members to respect people of other faiths "regardless of the doctrines and philosophies which we may espouse" or because of "religious, political, or cultural differences."[32]

I honor President Hinckley's accomplishment. I comprehend the enormity of it. He reminds me of President Kimball in his capacity for change. I think he could do for women what President Kimball did for African Americans, if enough Church members asked. He's an extraordinary human being. His age and vigor alone are amazing. He's divinely blessed, a holy man. Yet, he doesn't describe himself in prophetic terms. I think he'd be the first to deny that image.

Philip: You think the prophet would be the first to deny the image of prophet?

Maxine: Well, yes. He's self-deprecating about his status or importance. He may entertain angels privately, but he downplays images of himself as a prophet or a seer. He's sensitive to other perspectives and nuances; he works on a subtle level.

Philip: Does he have the authority from God to guide the LDS Church?

Maxine: I think that's a personal question, for him. He certainly has the authority from the Church to guide the Church, which is the basis of religious authority. Community approval grants religious authority and ordination. Spiritual authority, though, is inner. Spiritual ordination can exist without social ordination, and vice versa, but, ideally, they ought to coincide, since that's the point of ministry. Yet Paul the apostle, and Mary Magdalene, and Joseph Smith all claimed spiritual authority—without social authority. Likewise, many women feel they have a spiritual calling without having the social authority.

Philip: Tell me about finding another community outside of Mormonism. Are you comfortable there?

Maxine: Yes, I am. But I've attended other churches since age five, so I feel at home in sanctuaries of all kinds. The Hagia Sophia in Istanbul is the major basilica of my faith. But what you're really asking is how can you leave the one, true, restored church of Christ? (D&C 1:30). An inner call to ministry pulled me beyond Mormonism. I was looking for a faith where inner and outer Christianity overlapped: "The kingdom of God is inside of you, and outside of you."[33] This led me to Gnosticism, because Mormonism left me nowhere else to go. Joseph Smith's restoration of "original" Christianity refuted Catholicism, Protestantism, and everything since. The only place left was early Christianity.

Philip: Did you find Joseph Smith there?

Maxine: Yes and no. Mormonism resembles early Christianity, yet they're dissimilar—very different times and cultures. It's difficult to define "original Christianity" or "original Mormonism." Scholars don't agree on Jesus or what he taught, nor do scholars agree about Joseph Smith and Mormonism. Was there an "original church" of Christ? Jesus was a Jew who preached about God, not himself. His disciples didn't become "apostles" until after his death when they morphed into witnesses, with Magdalene first. They preached independently, not as one church. Much of "primitive Christianity" was more Pauline than Jesus. It's hard to locate the original version of anything, including Mormonism.

From the moment the Jesus movement was born, it was searching for its authentic identity. The same is true of Mormonism. Both rapidly evolved, resulting in complex identities and divergent movements. Both declare the kingdom of God and its transformation of society. Both claim Jewish priesthood lineage. Both teach knowing God personally, and are compelled to spread the gospel. However, the Mormon emphasis on institutional authority and structure has moved away from the ecstatic, immanent "kingdom of God is at hand" (Mark 1:14–15; Matt. 4:17) or the democratic kingdom of God which is "within you" and spread out upon the earth" (Thomas 3, 113; Luke 17:21).[34] Also male-only priesthood refutes early Christian women's roles as deacons, bishops, priests, and prophets. Ultimately, all Christians have their own version of "original Christianity."

Philip: As you see Mormonism today, do you want it to flourish, to grow?

Maxine: I see true growth as spiritual progress rather than as increasing in numbers or size. Spiritual growth isn't easy—increasing one's light "brighter and brighter to the perfect day" (D&C 50:24) requires deeper and deeper shadow work. I'd like to see Mormonism mature. Joseph Smith facilitated a grand and complex religious system, which has yet to be comprehended, integrated, synthesized. I'd like to see that happen. Members, nonmembers, leaders, scholars, and media all contribute to that process.

Mormonism is a young faith. I don't think Mormonism knows itself yet. But then, does any faith? I'd like to see every religion find its own spiritual maturity or fulfillment. Mormonism is a former fundamentalist faith still in recovery, with remnants of fundamentalist thinking. I'd like to see Mormonism heal. But I'm more concerned about my own growth and healing. I haven't comprehended myself.

Philip: Do you have any regrets?

Maxine: Yes and no. I don't regret honesty or heresy, but I regret the costs. I regret the lack of belonging, the endless negativity, criticism, and stress. A feminist theologian is never loved in her own community. I'm amazed by how easily people can oppress each other without even realizing it. The heretic soul is refined by suffering, but the path is too hard.

Yet I find meaning in everything, including things I shouldn't. I work with the unworkable. I always thought that impossible circumstances without reward were normal. I still brace myself for every response, fearing a negative reaction. And I'm still surprised by positive replies. Scott Bartchy[35] once asked me why I've stayed in a hostile context for so many years. He said, "It seems perverse." I agreed. "It *is* perverse. I *am* perverse. That's the problem." The wrong context makes you perverse. If you belong, then you're no longer perverse. However, perverseness serves a purpose. It strengthens you. If you live authentically, then you pay a price, but if you're inauthentic, you're not free.

One has to defend individual freedom in any system, whether religious or unreligious, conservative or liberal, orthodox or heretic, fundamentalist or feminist. Being different in any system invites rejection, and it takes a heavy toll, removing support and limiting success. Finding clarity and speaking truth are necessary in any system, because freedom of religion and speech don't mean silencing difference.[36]

Philip: Do you miss being a member of the Church?

Maxine: I don't miss the limitations and impositions. I do miss the visible hugeness of the Mormon spiritual family, the hermetic power of so many spirits animating so much material life. I miss the acceptance that Mormonism offers, but that required religious plastic surgery.

I found a spiritual tradition that accepts me as I am and honors my freedom and my path. My religious life is richer now, especially my practice. I love Christian liturgy and serving in a sanctuary. Ten years of entering holy space has altered my being.

I see a spiritual family bigger than one church or theology—the invisible church of God that connects all souls, a transcendant oneness, a collective soul. I feel God's presence in Mormon testimony meeting and Catholic mass, in Jewish synagogue and Muslim call to prayer, in Buddhist chant and Quaker silence and Christian Science healing.

I saw the Salt Lake Tabernacle transformed by the ecstatic "spirit of God like a fire"[37] when Gladys Knight celebrated the 1978 revelation on priesthood—the crowds and choir were rapt with revival, the dome hovering. I love the annual LDS Christmas concert where the climactic crescendo of Tabernacle Choir and orchestra, lighting and decor are conducive to spiritual vision. I've seen the stage graced by supernatural radiance, heavenly glory resting on massive gold organ pipes resembling the throne of God, a majesty beyond material form, with myriad waves of angelic voices resonating in oceanic cosmic choir.

In both Gnostic chapel and LDS tabernacle, I've glimpsed the immensity of eternal dimension, the grandeur of divine being. If we could see the glory of our own soul, we would be speechless. God is immanent in the material world, in the spiritual communion of human beings. The kingdom of God is inside of you, and it is outside of you. The kingdom of the Father is spread out upon the earth, and we do not see it. The kingdom of God is at hand.

Notes

[1] See Chapter 5.

[2] D. Michael Quinn, "Mormon Women Have Had the Priesthood since 1843," in *Women and Authority: Re-emerging Mormon Feminism*, edited by Maxine Hanks (Salt Lake City: Signature Books, 1992), 365–409.

³ Boyd K. Packer, "Talk to the All-Church Coordinating Council," May 1993, photocopy of typescript in my possession.

⁴ Eliza R. Snow, "To the Branches of the Relief Society: Should Members of the Relief Society Go to the Bishop for Counsel?" *Woman's Exponent* 13 (September 15, 1884).

⁵ "The Acts of John," vv. 99–101, in *The Apocryphal New Testament*, translation and notes by M. R. James (Oxford, England: Clarendon Press, 1924); see also www.gnosis.org/library/actjohn.htm (accessed January 12, 2010).

⁶ C. G. Jung, *The Undiscovered Self*, translated by R. F. C. Hull (New York: Little, Brown, & Co., 1957–58), 90–91; Jung, *Psychology and Religion* (New Haven, Conn.: Yale University Press, 1938), 4, 6, 108, 113. Carl Jung (1875–1961) discussed myth and archetypes in the context of the shared "collective unconscious," an inherited group-mind capable of mythic associations. See Jung, *The Archetypes and the Collective Unconscious: Collected Works of C.G. Jung*, Vol. 9, Part 1 (Princeton, N.J.: Princeton University Press, 1981).

⁷ *Hokmah*, Hebrew for "wisdom," can be understood as a feminine dimension of God appearing most notably in the biblical book of Proverbs. *Sophia* is Greek for "wisdom" and is at times portrayed as a feminine figure, featured in both the New Testament and various apocryphal Christian texts.

⁸ See Apostle Boyd K. Packer, "'The Mantle Is Far, Far Greater than the Intellect,'" *BYU Studies* 21 (Summer 1981): 264–68.

⁹ See the following addresses, published in the *Ensign*, November 1993: President Gordon B. Hinckley, "My Testimony," 51, and "Bring Up a Child in the Way He Should Go," 54; Elder James E. Faust "Keeping Covenants and Honoring the Priesthood," 36; Elder Neal A. Maxwell, "From the Beginning," 18; Elder Richard G. Scott, "Acquiring Spiritual Knowledge," 86; Elder Boyd K. Packer, "For Time and All Eternity," 21; Elder Dallin H. Oaks "The Great Plan of Happiness," 72; Elder M. Russell Ballard, "Strength in Counsel," 76, and "Equality through Diversity," 89; Elder Russell M. Nelson "Constancy amid Change," 33, Elder Ronald E. Poelman, "Divine Forgiveness," 84; and Elder F. Enzio Busche, "Truth Is the Issue," 24.

¹⁰ In 2002, the Latter-day Saint Council on Mormon Studies (LDSCMS) formed to sponsor lectures, conferences, fellowships, and professorships, and to create the Howard W. Hunter Chair for Mormon Studies at Claremont Graduate University School of Religion. In 2003, Brigham Young University cosponsored a conference at Yale University Divinity School, "God, Humanity, and Revelation:

Perspectives from Mormon Philosophy and History." In 2004, the LDSCMS sponsored a conference on the academic study of Mormonism, "Positioning Mormonism in Religious Studies and American History," at Claremont Graduate University School of Religion. In 2005, BYU cosponsored "The Worlds of Joseph Smith" at the Library of Congress in Washington, D.C. Also in 2005, the LDS Church and the LDSCMS cosponsored "Joseph Smith and the Prophetic Tradition," the second conference on Mormon studies at Claremont Graduate University.

[11] Bruce C. Hafen, "Women, Feminism and the Blessings of the Priesthood," BYU Women's Conference, 1985, Women's Conference Collection, L. Tom Perry Special Collections, Harold B. Lee Library, Brigham Young University; see also Bruce C. Hafen, "Teach Ye Diligently and My Grace Shall Attend You," BYU, August 25, 1993, www.speeches.byu.edu (accessed January 12, 2010). Key phrases were: "Two very different forms of feminism . . . 'equity feminism' and the 'radical feminist critique'. . . Many forms of feminism . . . emphasize the unique dimensions of women's experiences and perspectives . . . female values as nurturing, cooperation, and personal relationships. These aspirations have great merit." See also Hafen, "Crossing Thresholds and Becoming Equal Partners," *Ensign*, August 2007, 24–29: "'For too long in the Church, the men have been the theologians while the women have been the Christians.' To be equal partners, each should be both a theologian *and* a Christian."

[12] Maxine Hanks, "Introduction" in *Women and Authority*, xxv.

[13] Joseph Smith, quoted in Minutes of the Female Relief Society of Nauvoo, microfilm of holograph, March 17, 1842, L. Tom Perry Special Collections, Harold B. Lee Library, Brigham Young University, Provo, Utah.

[14] Ibid., March 17, 1842.

[15] Snow, "To the Branches of the Relief Society."

[16] Minutes of the Female Relief Society of Nauvoo, March 17, 1842.

[17] Hanks, "Introduction," *Women and Authority*, xix.

[18] Joseph Smith, King Follett Discourse, April 7, 1844, *Times and Seasons* 5 (August 15, 1844): 612–17: "You never knew my heart; no man knows my history."

[19] Jan Shipps, "Prophecy, Canonization, and Institutional Authority," Council on Mormon Studies conference, "Joseph Smith and the Prophetic Tradition: A Comparative Inquiry," Claremont Graduate University, October 21, 2005. See also Shipps, "The Prophet Puzzle: Suggestions Leading toward a More Comprehensive Interpretation of Joseph Smith," in *The Prophet Puzzle: Interpretive Essays on*

Joseph Smith, edited by Brian Waterman (Salt Lake City: Signature Books, 1999), 25–47.

20. See Don Bradley's detailed rhetorical analysis of LDS scriptures.

21. Harold Bloom, *The American Religion: The Emergence of the Post-Christian Nation,* 2d ed. (New York: Chu Hartley, 2006), 96–111.

22. D. Michael Quinn, *Early Mormonism and the Magic World View*, 2d ed. rev. (Salt Lake City: Signature Books, 1998), 30–65.

23. "And now, behold, we have written this record . . . in the characters which are called among us the reformed Egyptian, being handed down and altered by us. . . . But the Lord knoweth the things which we have written, and also that none other people knoweth our language . . . therefore he hath prepared means for the interpretation thereof" (Morm. 9:32, 34). Nephi also refers to this mysterious language: "Yea, I make a record in the language of my father, which consists of the learning of the Jews and the language of the Egyptians" (1 Ne. 1:2).

24. Title page, Book of Mormon. The "Testimony of Three Witnesses" (Oliver Cowdery, David Whitmer, Martin Harris) reiterates, "We also know that they have been translated by the gift and power of God, for his voice hath declared it unto us." Front matter of Book of Mormon.

25. "The heavens were opened upon us and I beheld the celestial kingdom of God, and the glory thereof, whether in the body or out I cannot tell. I saw the transcendent beauty of the gate through which the heirs of that kingdom will enter . . . the blazing throne of God . . . [and] the beautiful streets of that kingdom which had the appearance of being paved with gold" (D&C 137:1–4).

26. Tolkien asserted that mythology contains spiritual truths and that myth-making discloses those truths. J. R. R. Tolkien, "Mythopoeia: Philomythus to Misomythus," 1931, in *Tree and Leaf* (San Francisco: HarperCollins, 1988). In this poem written for C. S. Lewis, "who said that myths were lies and therefore worthless, even though 'breathed through silver,'" Tolkien asserted that mythology contains spiritual truths, which myth-making discloses.

27. Joseph as prophet versus fraud has been argued in Brodie's *No Man Knows My History* and Dan Vogel's *Joseph Smith: The Making of a Prophet* (Salt Lake City: Signature Books, 2004).

28. Stratfordians see Shakespeare's work as authentic, while Oxfordians think the Earl of Oxford authored Shakespeare's works. Likewise, Smithians see the Book of Mormon as Joseph Smith's authentic work, while Spauldians believe it was au-

thored by Solomon Spaulding. In like fashion, the conservative view understands Smith as "translator" rather than author, while critics engage with Smith as "author."

[29] *The Gospel of Thomas*, 1–2, translated by Thomas O. Lambdin, in *The Nag Hammadi Library*, edited by James M. Robinson (San Francisco: HarperCollins, 1990).

[30] King, a professor of English and Shakespeare at Brigham Young University (1971–96), was also a published poet, critic, and essayist whose work focused on rhetorical devices and analysis.

[31] Ether is the last prophet in the Book of Mormon; his book appears just before the concluding editorial account of Moroni. However, Ether recounts the earliest events in all of the Book of Mormon describing events from 2200 to 2500 BCE.

[32] M. Russell Ballard, "The Doctrine of Inclusion," October 2001 General Conference address, *Ensign*, November 2001, http://www.lds.org/ldsorg/v/index.jsp?hideNav=1&locale=0&sourceId=e7f88c6a47e0c010VgnVCM1000004d82620a____&vgnextoid=2354fccf2b7db010VgnVCM1000004d82620aRCRD (accessed January 15, 2010).

[33] "Jesus said, 'If those who lead you say to you, "See, the kingdom is in the sky," then the birds of the sky will precede you. If they say to you, "It is in the sea," then the fish will precede you. Rather, the kingdom is inside of you, and it is outside of you." "It will not come by waiting for it. It will not be a matter of saying 'here it is' or 'there it is.' Rather, the kingdom of the father is spread out upon the earth, and men do not see it." "Gospel of Thomas," in *The Nag Hammadi Library*, 113, 126. Compare Luke 17:20–21: "And when he was demanded of the Pharisees, when the kingdom of God should come, he answered them and said, The kingdom of God cometh not with observation: Neither shall they say, Lo here! or, lo there! for, behold, the kingdom of God is within you."

[34] Mark 1:14–15: "Jesus came into Galilee, preaching the gospel of the kingdom of God, And saying, The time is fulfilled, and the kingdom of God is at hand: repent ye, and believe the gospel," and Matthew 4:17: "Jesus began to preach, and to say, Repent: for the kingdom of heaven is at hand."

[35] Scott Bartchy is a professor of Christian origins and the history of religion at UCLA (1981–present) and is founder/director of the Center for the Study of Religion there. This conversation took place in March 2004.

[36] See Cass R. Sunstein, *Why Societies Need Dissent* (Cambridge, Mass.: Harvard University Press, 2005). Dissenters perform a vital function in every society, at great personal expense.

[37] *Hymns of the Church of Jesus Christ of Latter-day Saints* (Salt Lake City: Church of Jesus Christ of Latter-day Saints, 1985), no. 2.

Chapter 4
Lavina Fielding Anderson

Feminist, author, editor, excommunicated September 23, 1993.

Lavina Fielding was born on April 13, 1944, in Shelley, Idaho, the oldest daughter in a farming family of six children, and grew up with a significant interest in Mormon history and practice. She also yearned to serve and embraced the opportunity to do so as an LDS missionary in France at age twenty-one. Upon her return, Lavina reenrolled at Brigham Young University where she completed her B.A. (1968) and M.A. (1970) in English before moving on to the University of Washington for a Ph.D. in American studies.

In 1973, finished with her coursework and working on her dissertation, Lavina was hired on the editorial staff of the *Ensign*, the Church's recently organized magazine for adults, and was immediately caught up in collaborating with the young and energetic staff who provided an intellectually stimulating atmosphere. The managing editor at the time, Jay M. Todd, hoped to compensate for the recent abolition of the *Relief Society Magazine* by addressing women's issues more directly than the *Ensign* ever had before. This afforded Lavina the opportunity to explore women's issues through an official Church channel but also exposed her to what she considers a crucial encounter with the Church's authoritarianism.

Lavina's experience with authoritarianism came about through the *Ensign*'s chain of command. The Correlation Committee was in charge of unifying and mainstreaming the teachings of the various Church publications and thereby held veto power over any articles published in the *Ensign*. Lavina found it irritating to finish an article only to have the Correlation Committee reject it, often *in toto*, for what she felt to be inadequate reasons or inaccurate understandings of the issues. To exacerbate matters, it was impossible to sit down with the Correlation Committee and resolve the problem. Their changes always just "came down."

In 1973, Lavina met Paul Anderson, a Californian with an architecture degree from Princeton who had served his mission in Japan. They began dating as Paul continued working on the new Museum of Church History and Art. In 1976, Lavina completed her Ph.D. program at the University of Washington, and a year later, on June 13, they married. Their only child, Christian, was born in 1980. In 1981, Todd fired Lavina from the *Ensign* over a confidentiality policy of which she was unaware. She started her own editing company, which still thrives alongside the variety of pro bono editing projects she oversees: editor for the *Journal of Mormon History* (1991–2008) and *Case Reports of the Mormon Alliance,* copy editor for *Dialogue: A Journal of Mormon Thought*, and member of the reading committee for Signature Books. Lavina has also edited *Lucy's Book: A Critical Edition of Lucy Mack Smith's Family Memoir*, which won the John Whitmer Historical Association Book of the Year Award and the Steven Christensen Award for Best Documentary from the Mormon History Association.

Lavina's intellectual interests introduced her to what she calls "cases of spiritual abuse" in which leaders have unjustly used their office to manipulate and/or coerce members. It was not long after Lavina began documenting and publishing these cases that she found herself in the midst of disciplinary proceedings, culminating on September 23, 1993. Over a decade after her excommunication, Lavina still considers herself a believing and orthodox Mormon and attends weekly church services.

I met Lavina on December 16, 2004, at her home in Salt Lake City, four days after the disfellowshipping of Grant Palmer. Palmer, a three-time director of LDS Institutes of Religion and seminary teacher, was disciplined for publishing *An Insider's View of Mormon Origins*, which posited the Book of Mormon as a nineteenth-century document. With another case of Church discipline in the air, Lavina warmly invited me into her home. Casually dressed and with a genuine smile, she offered me a chair and shared her often heart-wrenching past.

The Excommunication

Philip: On September 23, 1993, you sat with friends eating popcorn and watching *A Man for All Seasons* as a Church disciplinary court met just a few blocks away to decide upon your future in Mormonism. How did it ever come to this?

Lavina: Where to begin? A crucial moment was in 1991 when the First Presidency and Quorum of the Twelve issued a statement against freely holding symposia on women's issues and intellectual issues, and everything began to look so bleak. Previously, there had been years of some openness under Leonard Arrington,[1] and this was a clamp-down on that freedom. I didn't know exactly where it was going, but I didn't like it. I had the feeling that we were sliding into another Mormon dark age where we lose our memory of our past.

It had happened before where women were concerned. The Mormon women who came out of the Nauvoo generation were deeply spiritual and exercised significant spiritual gifts, such as speaking in tongues, pronouncing blessings of healing, and anointing women before childbirth. Women from this generation ran the Relief Society from its revival under Eliza R. Snow until Emmeline B. Wells was released in 1921. They set the tone for the women of the Church. They had a tightly woven sisterhood that provided levels of emotional support largely unknown in the male hierarchy. All this was lost from just after World War I into the late 1970s, so the history and spiritual heritage of these women had to be reconstructed from documents. There was no living memory passed down through the generations, from grandmother to granddaughter. The faithful women of the Church had censored their own memories and erased their own heritage, and I could see in a nightmarish way that the same thing might be happening again by restricting symposia, by censoring history and oppressing women's exploration into their own spirituality. So, I wondered what I could do and decided to keep records.

I read the scriptures more attentively. I attended the temple more diligently. I read every word in the Church magazines; but perhaps more importantly, I began taking notes in every meeting I went to. I documented what people said during sacrament meeting and the monthly fast and testimony meetings in my ward. This was particularly interesting because it is a working class, central-city ward with members whose memories go back to before World War I. In doing all this, I started to coincidentally run into cases of ecclesiastical abuse—not in my ward, but among my friends.

Then, in January of 1992, I had a telling dream. I saw a stick figure on a blackboard and something was erasing it. For me the meaning was clear: By being silent I was being erased just as the Nauvoo women had been erased. That's when I started thinking that just keeping records wasn't enough. I had to start sharing what I was finding out about ecclesiastical abuse. So, I agreed to present a paper at the Sunstone Symposium in Washington, D.C., in the spring of 1992 and also here in Salt Lake in the summer of 1992. These presentations resulted in an article in the spring 1993 issue of *Dialogue* that documented 133 cases of what I considered ecclesiastical abuse, an unhealthy trend of mutual suspicion between Mormon intellectuals—primarily historians—and Church leaders, and acts of reprisal from Church leaders at the general and local level.

You know what, though? After those symposia, people started calling and sending me letters about how their brother or their sister-in-law had been abused by the Church, and so I started collecting those too. Now, of course, there's a long, healthy, and active anti-Mormon tradition. Some people become sort of professional anti-Mormons and even make an entire career out of being mad at the Church. That wasn't who I was or wanted to be; and to ensure that I wasn't overreacting about all this, I began paying more attention to my own spiritual life. I continued to read the Book of Mormon every year as recommended by President Benson, read Church magazines cover-to-cover, attend my meetings, listen to every session of general conference, pray more than ever, and have family prayer and scripture study. These activities were already normal, but now I really paid attention to them. All this confirmed that I was doing the right thing. It's hard to describe, but I felt an inner steadiness and clarity.

Philip: But you must have known that publishing 133 instances of ecclesiastical abuse in that spring 1993 issue of *Dialogue* would get you in trouble with Church leaders.

Lavina: I knew there was a possibility, but, as you know, September of 1993 was a turning point. It's clear *now* that something like that would get you into trouble, but it wasn't clear then, and that particular article wasn't anything I came up with on my own except for the conclusion where I gave some suggestions on how the Church could act better. I only used documents that were in the public record or individuals whom I had personally interviewed, and putting them together was not an act of creation, but one of organization. Though, in Mormon theology that's the same thing![2]

It was not until my stake president, Marlin Miller, called me into his office in the spring of 1993 that I realized a confrontation was coming. At that meeting, he made it very clear that I could not remain a member of the Church in good standing without repudiating my article, but he didn't know what a footnote was. He didn't understand that it was not me saying such-and-such—it was Elder McConkie at BYU.[3] Anybody could look this stuff up, and I kept thinking that if he could just understand that, then it would be okay, but President Miller grew up on a farm in central Utah and works for Utah's department of transportation. He'd never quoted anything in stake conference indicating that he has read anything but the scriptures. So, obviously, someone had put my article before him. He would not have run into *Dialogue* in a million years.

After the meeting with President Miller, I left for my summer cabin as I always do. This gave me time to think things over. While I was gone, President Miller sent me a letter saying that I had to give back my temple recommend. After thinking it over for a while, I decided not to give it back. That would be conceding that I had done something that made me unworthy to enter the temple. Instead, I told him that I would not use my recommend until we had resolved our differences. He responded by calling all the temples in the area and telling them not to accept my recommend if it showed up.

I was really hurt. I had never been treated like a liar before in all my life. While I was thinking and praying about it, I got a very clear answer—instructions but without an explanation. The answer was that I would be excommunicated in September, I was not supposed to go to the court, and it would be "some time" before I would be reinstated. I continued to pray about it for the rest of the summer—I didn't want to believe it—but I never got a different feeling or any other different information.

I should mention that, right after the first meeting with President Miller in the spring of 1993, I had that same feeling of steady clarity when I realized that he'd made it really easy. He told me I had to stop talking to people who were having problems with their Church leaders. If he'd taken the approach of talking about conflicting loyalties, how sometimes you have to sacrifice one good to get a greater good, then that could have tied me up in knots for months. But he was telling me to stop helping people in pain. Well, that wasn't a hard decision to make.

Two scriptures came to mind with great force. The first one was James 4:17: "Therefore to him that knoweth to do good, and doeth it not, to him it is sin." The second one was the scripture in Mosiah 18:9 where part of the baptismal covenant is to be "willing to mourn with those that mourn; yea, and comfort those that stand in need of comfort." I actually felt thankful that President Miller had so clearly presented me with an ultimatum that meant I had to be loyal to the Church by being cruel to people. I decided to be loyal to God.

Philip: President Miller never told you to stop listening to fellow Church members in pain. He just didn't want you to put it in print.

Lavina: You're right, but I think to him it was the same thing. No, wait. He did say that I had to repudiate the article and stop listening to people who were having problems with the Church. If he had said what you said, it would have taken me much longer to decide what to do, but he didn't, and that was a blessing.

Philip: How did it feel not to attend your disciplinary council?

Lavina: That piece in the instructions about not going to the disciplinary council really baffled me, because I had things to tell those guys. I had speeches! I would even wake up in the middle of the night with good points to make. It helped me to realize that two issues were involved. Though I acknowledged that the Church had authority over me and could decide whether I was allowed to be a member or not, it couldn't stop me from dealing with spiritual abuse. By not going to the council, I could keep those two issues separate.

Later, I realized how hard it would have been for me to continue going to church if I had attended the council, because some of those high councilors were in our ward or would be visiting speakers. I would have had to see them and remember that they had thought I was unworthy to be a member of the Church. I'm not very strong in some ways. The Spirit knew that and protected me. It would have been too hard to look at President Miller and not remember what he had done in that high council room. As it is, I wasn't there, and so I don't have to remember.

Philip: You say that the Holy Spirit told you in the summer of 1993 that you would be excommunicated that September, which gave you a few months to prepare. Were you truly prepared when the excommunication was finally handed down? How did that feel?

Lavina: I remember going through the day after getting the information that I'd been excommunicated and feeling literally heavy hearted. It was hard to breathe. There was a weight on my chest. But though I felt sad, I didn't spend the day crying. I wasn't angry or depressed. I was just carrying a heavy burden, and people were so supportive. Letters and casseroles just poured in. People I didn't even know brought food. At one point, the island in our kitchen had eleven flower arrangements sitting on it, and when people said they were praying for me, Paul, and Christian, I could feel it. It was like there were angels in the house. In some ways, though, I knew it wasn't all about me. By this time Lynne, Paul, and Maxine had all already been excommunicated.[4] People knew what was going on and responded to me because I was the one they knew.

It's interesting because excommunication is a terrible, ultimate punishment. It should have shattered my life, but it didn't. I don't want to sound presumptuous, but that was in part because I don't believe that what my stake president did was recognized nor validated by the heavens, even though I recognize that the priesthood keys can bind on earth and simultaneously bind in heaven. This is the Church of Jesus Christ, and the excommunication was a minor administrative matter that Jesus will deal with when the time comes. I don't have to worry about it. My only job is to make sure that when these parallel paths merge once again that I haven't done anything that would frustrate that rejoining. I have faith in that.

Philip: Are you sealed to your husband and your son?

Lavina: Yes, and one of the things that is supposed to happen in excommunication is that those eternal sealings and my baptismal covenants are wiped away. I don't feel any of that has, in fact, occurred. I realize the Church's official position is that I'm delusional, but that's how I feel.

Church Hierarchy and Authority

Philip: You were apparently excommunicated for speaking out on ecclesiastical abuse, which you defined as instances in which a Church leader exercises "unrighteous dominion" (D&C 121:39). You said he does this by imposing "his personal opinions as Church doctrine or policy, or resorts to such power plays as threats and intimidation to insure that his personal views prevail in a conflict of opinions."[5] Yet, isn't this part of the role of LDS Church leaders—to rebuke and admonish Church members?[6]

Lavina: One of the distinctions that my definition doesn't make and probably should is that frequently the leader perceives himself as representing the official position of the Church. He doesn't present his position as a suggestion or as his best thinking or as his reading of what the scriptures mean. Instead, he fronts it as an official position that he personally accepts and is therefore responsible for enforcing.

It is true that leaders enforce compliance, not only with Mormon orthodox beliefs, but also Mormon orthodox views on lifestyle, which have grown increasingly more detailed in the past twenty years. There are new rules not based upon doctrine but founded upon the cultural orthodox list, such as having no body piercings unless you're female and then only one set and then only in your ears. This means that diligent Church leaders who are looking for ways to exercise their authority now have dozens and dozens and dozens of ways of telling people they're wrong and also have quite a lot of power to enforce those views. That's a problem. People think that Church leaders stand between them and God, which allows the leader to be intrusive in a way that's automatically abusive. A leader should point to God, not to himself or a rulebook or . . . tattoos. Yes, indeed, rebuking and admonishing are part of a leader's job, but so are nurturing, uplifting, and inspiring.

Philip: Should Church leaders be able to impose doctrine and policies upon Church members?

Lavina: I think the Church has the right to make rules and enforce them, and members need to know what those rules are and to decide if they can live by them. However, I don't think those rules should be such that they require a member to violate his or her own conscience. An example is how the Church no longer discloses financial information, though it did at one time. That's an ethical problem. Members of the Church have a right to know where their tithing is going if they want to, and the Church should have a better reason for not disclosing that information than "I'm bigger than you" or "because I say so." That's ecclesiastical abuse.

Philip: Do you think that current leaders are ordained by God?

Lavina: I think they are chosen by God, and I think they are ordained in the system that God established. I acknowledge their authority and consider them to be in their positions because God wants them there. I sustain them as prophets, seers, and revelators, or at least I would if I weren't forbidden to do so by the terms of the excommunication.

Philip: So when leaders decide not to give a reason why they no longer disclose the Church's financial information, for example, how can you say that's ecclesiastical abuse and not the will of God if you acknowledge they are divinely ordained leaders?

Lavina: Because I think members have a right to ask and leaders have a responsibility to tell. I disagree strongly with the fact that leaders can dispose of a discussion without accountability. It's not that I think they are untrustworthy or irresponsible with the funds. I don't question their honesty or their competence, but I do have a problem with the idea that members cannot be trusted with that information.

Philip: But why isn't it just that God said so, period?

Lavina: God never deprives anyone of free agency by the mere act of ordination. The leaders, of course, remain human even after ordination, and there's a long tradition in the Church that the leaders make mistakes. Yet the parameters of who can be questioned and how have changed drastically over the years. This new idea that leaders are the only ones allowed to ask questions and members are required to give answers is a power differential that works clearly to the benefit of the leaders, but not to the benefit of the members.

Philip: In your essay, "The September Six," you argue that individual members need to be empowered. To do this, you recommend that they must feel a sense of duty to God rather than to an institution, i.e., the Church.[7] Can one differentiate between the two in Mormonism? Can one separate one's duty to God from one's duty to the Church?

Lavina: Yes, if the leaders are, in fact, manifesting the will of God in what they do. Mormon theology allows for the possibility that they do not, and Mormon history documents many occasions when they do not. Mormonism allows for exploration, communication, and negotiation—and much more of that should be happening. I feel more strongly about that, even more than I did before.

Philip: But Mormon prophets throughout the last 175 years have claimed that God would not allow them to lead the Church astray. Though human and imperfect, they can be trusted.

Lavina: Wilford Woodruff said that under specific historical circumstances, which I'm sure you're aware of.[8] It's a self-serving statement because he was denying that he could have made a mistake by announcing the Manifesto which withdrew official support for new polygamous messages. Traditionally, in Mormonism, when the prophet says something problematic or troubling—or doctrinally significant or instructional—each member is supposed to pray and get a confirmation that it is, in fact, true, but that position has not been explicated recently. The assumption has always been, of course, that the member who prays will get nothing but a confirmation, but in the past fifteen years, there has been a significant shift that emphasizes only that the prophet will not lead the Church astray. That's a subtle and disconcerting shift because it disempowers members. It means that the person with the best and biggest title always wins the argument regardless of its merit.

It's to the advantage of the Church hierarchy to teach members that they, the leaders, are always inspired. However, I think that position conflicts with other points of Mormon theology, history—and reality. Church leaders do make mistakes, and members are presented with a cruel dilemma, because there's no loophole that allows for this when they do. It puts members and leaders in a terrible bind, and I wish they'd stop doing it.

Philip: You've referred to yourself in the past as an orthodox Mormon. How orthodox is it to question Church leaders?

Lavina: I think it is the absolute mainstream tradition of Mormonism. Nobody became a Mormon in the first generation unless they questioned everything. They had to in order to accept Mormonism. Similarly, my own spiritual life is based upon a profound spiritual knowledge that God invites, respects, and answers questions, so it seems ludicrous that you can have this functioning religion leading people to Godhood while excluding questioning. That's so contradictory.

Philip: And yet you still attend Church every week.

Lavina: Yes.

Reflection

Philip: How would you characterize your belief in the LDS Church just before you were excommunicated?

Lavina: It's not a whole lot different than it is now. I have a very strong, comforting belief in the reality of God, the love of Jesus Christ, and I have deep, deep feelings about Joseph Smith—probably made up equally of love, admiration, and deep suspicion. I love the Book of Mormon, which is a book of scripture that really speaks to me. I have kept on reading it every year as I did before, and I always find new treasures in it. I love the community of the Church ward system. I love the people in the wards, the hymns, the language, and the temple ceremony. I am Mormon from my bones out. I have given up even trying to see the world as if I were not a Mormon. I *am* Mormon, and I love that.

Today, I feel exactly the same as I did before my excommunication with one notable difference: I no longer trust the Church. In any instance of ecclesiastical abuse such as I have experienced, trust is the first thing that goes, and it's hard to get back. That's painful, but I think it's universally true.

Philip: You have never stopped attending church. What has your experience been, doing so during the eleven years since your excommunication?

Lavina: My ward has been wonderful. Nobody has given me so much as a raised eyebrow. They've never hinted that I or my family are not welcome there, and for my part I try not to make it difficult by asking questions or making comments. There are certain restrictions laid down when one is excommunicated, and I try to observe those restrictions, and I acknowledge and respect the Church's authority to impose them.

We've lived in this ward since 1977 and have been through three bishops—all loving men. I love our ward. This is a compassionate ward with wonderful people in it. Though not theologically sophisticated, they all care about one another, and I think that being able to live by the Golden Rule is more important than being able to construct an argument.

Our son Christian grew up in this ward and has since served a mission, gone to Stanford, and been married in the temple. My husband Paul has received continuous callings in the Church, whereas I, of course, cannot receive any. I have, however, been the permanent substitute organist for Relief Society for the past six years. They can't call me and set me apart for that position, but the *General Handbook* does allow for non-members to play the piano and lead the singing. That's been an excellent way for me to still make a contribution.

Philip: Because you can't fully participate in Church, there must have been some awkward moments in the past eleven years.

Lavina: Once when a friend from out of state was visiting, she was sitting on the outside of the row next to me in church. When they passed the sacrament, she automatically passed me the tray forgetting that, as an excommunicant, I couldn't take the sacrament. I looked at her, shook my head, and handed the tray back. She just started to cry, but managed to do it without making a sound. I put my arms around her and said, "It's all right." She was shaking and whispered with great energy: "It's *not* all right." It wasn't that she felt embarrassed for putting me in a difficult place. She was hurt for me. That was an awkward moment for both of us, but I'll always love her for it.

Philip: Has the excommunication negatively affected your marriage?

Lavina: Well, Paul and I met when he was working in the Museum of Church History and Art. He eventually moved on to work for BYU as head of exhibit design and special projects at that museum. He has always been devoted to and active in Mormonism. In fact, all of our brothers and sisters on both sides are active in the Church, were married in the temple, and have served missions. Paul served a mission in Japan, and I served in France.

Throughout the whole ordeal with the Church, we discussed every aspect and possibility. We were both very concerned about the possible impact on Christian and concerned that Paul might be fired because of my activities. The situation falls under the patriarchal principle that "if you can't control your woman, then we don't want you around." However, that hasn't been a condition of his employment at all. Nobody has even said anything to him, which I think is pretty admirable.

During the two years that I was moving in this direction, Paul was playing devil's advocate. He was very good about that dialogue and is the fairest person I know. He will bend over backwards to see another person's point of view, whereas I am much more inclined to impose my point of view on the situation. Never once did he try to tell me not to do something. He always wanted to discuss all the information available, talk about it, and see it from every angle, then work with the consequences together. I absolutely cannot say enough good about him. When the letter was delivered saying that I had been excommunicated, though, he changed on a dime. He was 100 percent supportive. There was no more questioning and, not even once, any "I told you so's."

Up until that point I had worked really hard to prepare myself not to be angry if I were to be excommunicated. Paul had more difficulty with the angry part. It took him two or three years. He only got over it when he was able to actually pray for the Church leaders who had excommunicated me.

Philip: How do you view the September Six? Was their excommunication unique in the history of how the Church has disciplined its members?

Lavina: My first reaction to that question is that we weren't unique, because there was the case of the Godbeites in 1867.[9] Those excommunications were similar because they were politically charged and took a theological form. It was a power play where the force of good ideas could not win out against sheer power.

The other parallel occurred in the 1920s when the Church was moving in a progressive direction. It sought to distance itself from its nineteenth-century past and boost the Church Educational System. They wouldn't even say the word "polygamy" in public. Then John A. Widtsoe, who was a young apostle, slammed the brakes on liberalism. He said that we needed to once again stress what is unique about Mormonism, and everything went back to Book of Mormon, Joseph Smith, First Vision, prophetic authority, stuff like that.

All these things assert the primacy of the prophetic office and the authority of God's priesthood leaders to control the members in ways that I have to say call us back to some essential core of Mormonism, but do so at a tremendous cost. We lose the other vital part of Mormonism, which is free agency, eternal progression, growth, and improvement. So, the pendulum keeps swinging back and forth between these two cores of Mormonism: the prophetic part of Joseph Smith and the presidential part of Joseph Smith.

What the excommunications of September 1993 and their follow-ups right up until last Sunday[10] do is protect the organizational strand of Mormonism. I think those were unnecessary course corrections, but of course nobody was asking my opinion. I feel that my role is to document and clarify what happened. Time will ultimately tell us the cost of slamming the window down on so many fingers.

Philip: Do you ever worry that you've damaged the faith of others? After all, if a Mormon ceases to believe in the very same Church leaders that you rebuked, then losing faith in Mormonism altogether could well follow.

Lavina: You packed quite a lot into that question! I would first respond by saying that Mormonism is constructed theologically such that it allows for any individual Church leader to have a lack of faith or to do something wrong, even with legitimate apostolic authority.[11] But while Mormon *theology* allows for that, Mormon *practice* does not. The practice of Mormonism, the culture, is moving in a monolithic and totalitarian direction that is at odds with basic Mormon theology. I have confidence this will correct itself, but it usually does so over quite a few dead bodies.

Having problems with authority usually signifies problems in one's relationship to God. It's been my experience that a significant number of people who have authority problems are the same people who don't have a spiritual life where they have felt the love of God or the cherishing of the Savior. They don't have confidence that there is somebody there when they pray. The scriptures don't speak to them. Yes, they have problems with the Church and how it's working or not working, but from my perspective, actually, the least of their worries is the Church. They need to be looking at who they are in relationship to God and only after that will love and confidence fall into place.

Philip: Do you think your problems with authority point to a problem in your relationship to God?

Lavina: I don't think my problems with authority have anything to do with a problem in my relationship to God. I wouldn't have done any of those things if I hadn't felt so loved by God. I wouldn't have had the strength. I wouldn't have had the clarity. I wouldn't have the peace I still feel. It's so wrong for the Church to treat people in a way that they can't experience the love of God.

Philip: Did you deserve to be excommunicated?

Lavina: No, certainly not. Absolutely not.

Philip: What are Church leaders supposed to do when a member speaks out against them?

Lavina: Nothing I did broke Church rules. My behavior was orthodox; my belief was orthodox; I was leading a Mormon lifestyle. What I wanted was to discuss some things that I thought were problematic. I thought this discussion would make the Church better, and, therefore, it should have been welcome. There should be places in Sunday School and Relief Society to talk about questions and ways of being Mormon that are all acceptable. We should embrace diversity rather than fear it and punish it. I was not rebelling against the Church or attacking it. These were acts of love, which were part of witnessing in the house of faith.

Philip: The nature of excommunication is such that you can be readmitted into full fellowship. Why haven't you done that yet?

Lavina: The stake president has never told me what I needed to repent for. In the excommunication letter that everyone gets there's supposed to be a list of things to do to get back into the Church. That list wasn't in my letter. When I realized this, I sent the stake president a letter asking to know the conditions of my return. He sent a puzzling answer, saying I couldn't judge the General Authorities or think they were wrong. This topic had never even come up before, and I certainly didn't understand that members had to believe General Authorities couldn't commit errors. I asked him for clarification. He never responded.

We've changed stake presidents since then, and the new one certainly knows where to find me, but I have a feeling neither the stake presidency nor the bishop know what to say. But I also feel that there's another timetable at work, so I don't feel any sense of urgency.

Philip: But don't you want to be a full member of the LDS Church?

Lavina: Yes. It was not particularly fun sitting in the temple lobby while my son was getting married inside, though he did something really nice. In the sealing room, the two fathers are usually the witnesses and they sit on either side of the officiator at one end of the altar. In the chairs facing the altar are the two chairs for the mothers. Christian asked that my chair stay empty, so there was room for me there.

Philip: Why haven't you just gone to the new stake president and asked to be readmitted?

Lavina: I often ask myself that very question, but I don't feel a prompting in that direction, so I don't think I should do it. Now, God isn't exactly holding me back against my will. I feel at peace with the future, and I don't think it's going to be up to me to change things.

Philip: You once wrote that you felt "lucky" to have had the opportunity to take a stand for your beliefs.[12] Do you still feel that way?

Lavina: Yes. We live in a world of inevitable compromise with many gray areas of integrity and ethics. So, I think it's an honor and privilege when something is clear enough that someone can say, "This is an issue of integrity and conscience." When someone can take a stand, then I think he or she should, because there are many people who can't. I was blessed to be in a position where I could take that stand for truth, honesty, love, kindness, and loyalty to the principles of the gospel.

Philip: You once wrote that the main issue of all this is a "struggle for the soul of Mormonism."[13] How is that soul faring today?

Lavina: I have faith in the eventual outcome. I believe that the truth is mighty and will prevail, but I think that the path Mormonism is taking now is haunted by the fear used by Church leaders to keep the members corralled. Mormon women are especially fearful. They are scared of doing anything wrong or having their children suffer because of the choices they make. Mormon culture is becoming more controlling and constricting right now, as a completely Mormon lifestyle is being created—self-indulgent things like Mormon toys and Mormon interior decorating. All this busy-religion channels energy away from the vitality of Mormonism and the freedom that it brings. People must be free to do good and trusted to do so in their own way. The level of micromanaging in the Church is stifling and unhealthy. The vitality of Mormonism will eventually break out of its shell, but I'd guess not for another ten or fifteen years—swings like this usually last about a generation—and those are going to be tough years.

There are many aspects of Mormonism that don't liberate because they are part of the Church culture and not the gospel.

Members of the Church suffer enormous amounts of pain because of the culture of the Church. Talk to any family who has a gay son or daughter. The Church only presents one model of righteousness, and the continual message to members is "You don't quite fit" or "You aren't working hard enough." There is so much guilt, fear, and inadequacy that result from the culture and have nothing to do with the gospel.

Philip: What would Joseph Smith say if he saw Mormonism today?

Lavina: That's a great question. I think there are parts of twenty-first century Mormonism that Joseph Smith would rejoice over. I think he would rejoice over the unity and love in wards, the ready access to temples all over the world, the willingness of missionaries to share the gospel, and the sheer size of the Church. I think he would be disconcerted at the wealth of the Church, because he lived in such poverty all of his life. He would be less than pleased with the amount of time spent in Church meetings on rules of the Church rather than doctrine and testimony. When I read Joseph Smith's talks, it's obvious that he focused so clearly on Jesus, the reality of the atonement, the empowerment of knowing truth—those don't receive as much emphasis anymore.

Philip: Do you have any regrets about the way you acted toward the Church?

Lavina: That's a question I ask myself two or three times a week, and certainly every Sunday. But the answer is no. It was such an enormous blessing, and even eleven years afterwards I still can't see an alternative to the way I acted that would entail any fewer regrets than I have now. I feel totally at peace.

Notes

1. Leonard J. Arrington served as the official Church historian from 1972 to 1982.

2. Mormon theology considers the creation of the world to have been an act whereby God organized existing matter rather than creating it from nothing (*ex nihilo*). Joseph Fielding Smith, comp. and ed., *Teachings of the Prophet Joseph Smith* (1938; rpt., Salt Lake City: Deseret, 1976), 350–52.

3. Bruce R. McConkie (1915–85), a theological conservative, served in the First Council of the Seventy (1946–72), then as an apostle from 1972 until his death in 1985.

4. See chapters 1, 2, and 3. Maxine Hanks, though interviewed for this volume, did not complete the revisions as she desired by press time.

5. Lavina Fielding Anderson, "The September Six," in *Religion, Feminism, and Freedom of Conscience*, edited by George D. Smith (Salt Lake City: Signature Books, 1994), 4.

6. Joseph Smith outlined rebuking and admonishing as essential functions for those with authority. *Teachings of the Prophet Joseph Smith*, 112–13.

7. Anderson, "The September Six," 4.

8. Text accompanying Official Declaration—1, p. 292, in the 1979 edition of the single-volume ("triple combination") Book of Mormon, Doctrine and Covenants, and Pearl of Great Price.

9. William Godbe, a British convert, had been a good friend of Brigham Young before distancing himself from Brigham Young's position, first economically, then politically and doctrinally. The Godbeites formed their own spiritual community and published a great deal of anti-Mormon literature including the *Mormon Tribune* (predecessor of the *Salt Lake Tribune*) and *Utah Magazine*. See Ronald W. Walker, *Wayward Saints: The Godbeites and Brigham Young* (Urbana: University of Illinois Press, 1998).

10. Grant H. Palmer was disfellowshipped December 12, 2004.

11. Apostolic authority, in Mormonism, is considered to have been transferred from Jesus to his apostles, lost with their deaths, but eventually bestowed by Peter, James, and John, as heavenly messengers, on Joseph Smith as part of the restoration of the gospel.

12. Anderson, "The September Six," 6.

13. Ibid.

Chapter 5
D. Michael Quinn

Historian, placed on probation in June 1993, disfellowshipped in July 1993, excommunicated September 26, 1993.

Dennis Michael Quinn was born March 26, 1944, in Pasadena, California, to a sixth-generation Mormon mother and a Roman Catholic father, who had changed his surname, "Pena," to "Quinn" after the family had emigrated from Mexico. Michael grew up with an inquiring mind and decided to study at Brigham Young University after high school. Following his freshman year, in the fall of 1963, Michael served a two-year mission to England (where the interview below picks up). He subsequently returned to BYU to pursue an English major and a philosophy minor in 1968. During this time, he also proposed to Janice Darley on their third date; and the couple married in June 1967. After Michael graduated in 1968, he entered the U.S. Army and moved with Janice to Munich, Germany, where he served as a plain-clothes counter-intelligence agent for nearly two years.

Upon completing his military service in March 1971, Michael, Janice, two-year-old daughter Mary, and seven-month-old daughter Lisa (sons Adam and Moshe were born later) moved back to Salt Lake City where Michael entered graduate school in history. He had been accepted for a doctoral program at Duke University specializing in twentieth-century English literature; but reflecting on his undergraduate tendency to skip class and procrastinate on term papers to make time for his extracurricular interest in Mormon history, Michael decided to make this long-time hobby the principal focus of his graduate study.

After graduating in August 1973, he began studying at Yale where he completed his Ph.D. degree in history in May 1976. The following August, he obtained an assistant professorship in history at Brigham Young University and went on to a sparkling career there, resigning in 1988 as a full professor and director of the graduate program in history.

From 1988 to 1998, Michael produced his best research yet. He published a number of groundbreaking articles and books, including *The Mormon Hierarchy: Origins of Power* (Salt Lake City: Signature Books in association with Smith Research Associates, 1994), *The Mormon Hierarchy: Extensions of Power* (Salt Lake City: Signature Books in association with Smith Research Associates, 1997), and his prize-winning *Same-Sex Dynamics among Nineteenth-Century Americans: A Mormon Example* (Urbana: University of Illinois Press, 1996). Michael had seized the freedom allotted him after leaving BYU to pursue research without the oversight of Church-employed Mormon superiors. Though his manuscripts were never directly censored by Church officials or fellow academic staff while at BYU, Michael had begun to feel extreme pressure to self-censor and, perhaps more significantly, to continue suppressing his homosexuality.

Also enabling his status as an independent historian were a series of fellowships from the Huntington Library, Indiana University, the National Endowment for the Humanities, American Academy of Arts and Sciences, and an intervallic position as technical advisor for A&E, the History Channel, PBS, and the Canadian Broadcasting Corporation. With this support, Michael published four books between 1994 and 1998 alone. He has since served as an affiliated scholar at the University of Southern California in 2000–2002, and as a senior fellow at Yale in 2002–03. After leaving Yale, he returned to independent scholar status, where he remains today.

I interviewed Michael following his presentation at the August 2003 Sunstone Symposium and warmed instantly to him. Dressed casually and with a relaxed demeanor to match, he is a true gentleman and scholar.

The Mission

Philip: You were asked to excommunicate people as a twenty-year-old on your mission in England, and eventually, in 1993, you found yourself on the other side of the disciplinary action. How did you feel about excommunications while on your mission?

Michael: It nearly drove me out of the Church. As missionaries, we were told to baptize teenagers who would then convert their parents and family. That was the plan. Previous missionaries had gone to England and played baseball or basketball with working-class kids, and then they told the kids that they had to be initiated into the sports team in order to continue. To be initiated, they were supposed to go through this thing called "baptism," and many were baptized at YMCAs. These kids were being baptized by the thousands, thinking they were being initiated into a sports club.

Then, Mark E. Petersen[1] stopped these proselytizing abuses. He told missionaries to take a survey of all the inactive members and decide either to fellowship them into the Church or excommunicate them. That was really difficult because there was, of course, a huge amount of inactivity. In Crawley, England, for example, there were about eight hundred to a thousand members at the time, but only sixty of them were active—meaning coming to Sunday meetings. Included in that total membership were about three or four hundred boys under the age of sixteen, some of whom had been baptized as early as six. The parents usually didn't know their kids were being baptized, but the missionaries went ahead with their baptism anyway. When the parents did know, they gave consent, thinking that their kid was joining a sports club.

When Petersen's order came down to excommunicate, I had been called as branch president. At the time, there was an active membership locally of only six people, but there were 150–200 people on the rolls. So, doing my duty, I began excommunicating them one after another. I excommunicated fourteen teenage boys and had fifty more on my list when I was released from being branch president. That was horribly depressing, because I had only baptized four by that time. I was in the negative! I nearly lost my faith in the Church right then and there, because it was easier to think that Church membership didn't matter than to think of what I was doing spiritually to these kids. Some of them were happy to be excommunicated, because they didn't want to be known as Mormons. Most, though, were broken. Here were these wealthy, well-spoken, American missionaries who were paying attention to them, but then dropped them like a rock after they were baptized. The kids naturally felt bitter, exploited.

Though these "baseball baptisms" disappointed me, I wasn't disaffected. After my mission, I even served as a part-time temple worker. I continued to believe in the Church and sustained the hierarchy as God's anointed. Things began to change when I started working at BYU.

Censorship at BYU

Philip: You worked at BYU for twelve years. Did you ever feel that your academic inquiry was hindered by your superiors or Church leaders while there, and did that contribute to your resignation in 1988?

Michael: Oh yeah. In 1976 I had offers from two universities, which was rather uncommon in that job market. When I came to talk with BYU I told the dean, Martin Hickman, that I didn't think BYU would want me there. I said, "My dissertation at Yale was on controversial stuff, and I'm going to continue this work." I had anticipated that my research could create some problems down the road. He responded by saying, "Oh no. Let us protect you from those men up in Salt Lake." So I accepted BYU's very generous offer with the assurance that it was an open forum, that academic freedom was alive, well, and growing. I still had misgivings but set them aside for the time being.

I found that BYU expects a certain amount of self-censorship with controversial issues. And I think every historian must use a certain amount of self-censorship, especially when writing for a readership with a wide variety of backgrounds and different knowledge about the past. When writing on controversial issues, the sensitive historian may decide to paraphrase rather than quote a sensational statement. I'm sure, for example, that authors of the Kennedy biographies, who had the cooperation of the Kennedy family, engaged in a great deal of self-censorship. It is a reality, and certainly was a reality at BYU.

I always operated with a certain degree of self-censorship, because I wanted to present material in the best way I could. If I thought material would be difficult for Church members to understand or assimilate into their faith, then I tried to somehow provide a context that would encourage them or even provide alternative explanations. This type of self-censorship operated even in my very early publications.

I first felt external censorship at BYU in 1981, when I gave the talk, "On Being a Mormon Historian."[2] Academic leaders, including my dean, said that, though they did not want to order me around, "Giving the talk was a bad idea and you definitely shouldn't publish it." They made it very clear that there was a desired and an undesired course of action to take, but worked hard so as not to appear to limit my academic freedom. That's how BYU operates and has for many years. Direct orders are given in an indirect way so the person giving them can deny laying down an ultimatum. I was never given a direct ultimatum at BYU, though I knew of professors in other departments who were given direct ultimatums that if they published or spoke out again, then they would be fired. I was never directly threatened like that.

The second time I felt censorship at BYU was in 1984 after a conference held by the Mormon History Association at the BYU campus in Provo, and it really surprised me. I had given a talk about General Authority involvement in corporate leadership. It was based entirely on public records—records of corporations, officers, directors, county courthouses, and the *Standard and Poor's Directory of Corporations*. The research extended all the way from New York to Texas to Hawaii for the years 1832–1932, and I concluded the talk by giving a name-by-name list of current LDS General Authorities who were officers or directors of companies. My dean called me a few days later and said, "Mike, I want you to know that I'm not making this call voluntarily. I've been asked by a higher authority to make this call in order to tell you not to publish that paper as an article."

Philip: Did he mention the name of the higher authority?

Michael: No, and I didn't ask, but I later heard that it came from Church headquarters in Salt Lake City. I told Dean Hickman, "All my research came from public records. It didn't come from the bowels of some archive or vault. It's public!" He said, "I know, but Church leaders still don't want *you* to publish it." I said, "I'll agree not to publish it as an article, but you know I'm preparing a book on the Mormon hierarchy and this will show up as a chapter." Hickman replied, "Well, I wasn't asked to tell you anything about books. I was just told to tell you not to publish it as an article, and if I can go back and tell them that you've agreed to that, then we're both happy. I look forward to your book." That's how we left it. I never did publish it as an article.

In the spring of 1985, however, I published a long article of almost one hundred pages on what happened after Church leadership formally abandoned polygamy in September of 1890.[3] In that article I explored how the First Presidency secretly allowed and authorized new plural marriages for the next fourteen years. That alone made me a problem in the eyes of Church leaders, and as a result of that publication, the hierarchy started putting pressure on me directly.

The Chase

Philip: Leading up to your excommunication in 1993, you underwent three councils in four months. Can you explain the events leading up to your first council and why, if you were marked as a troublemaker back in 1984–85 as you say, it took leaders eight years to formally take action against you?

Michael: The entire time I was on faculty at BYU, I lived in Salt Lake City and commuted to Provo. I knew the stake president in Salt Lake, which made me feel safer because a member, theoretically, can only be punished by his local Church authorities—the bishopric or stake presidency. I had served as a high councilor with this particular stake president for nearly three years. I had even served as a bishop's counselor for over a year and a half before getting in trouble with that paper in 1985. Then I was a stake Sunday School counselor.

When the article came out in 1985, the area president—things get crazy with all of these echelons of leadership—contacted my stake president and asked to meet with him. At that meeting, the area president, James M. Paramore, said that three apostles had instructed him to tell my stake president to take away my temple recommend for publishing this article. They were also supposed to take any other "appropriate action" against me as they saw fit. This instruction clearly suggested taking action against my membership.

When something like this happens, the stake president typically follows orders, and that's what Paramore expected. My stake president, however, disagreed with it all and engaged in a two-and-a-half hour debate with Paramore over the appropriateness of what had been asked. The stake president and his two counselors had read my article and told Paramore that they found nothing objectionable in it that would warrant punishment.

Philip: Had Paramore read the article?

Michael: No. The stake presidency asked him, and he said, "No, I don't read anti-Mormon trash." After the two-and-a-half hour debate, the stake president agreed to take away my recommend but also said that he would explain to me exactly why he was doing it—at the demand of Church headquarters. Paramore said, "Oh, no. You can't do that. You have to tell him this was your own independent decision. You cannot in any way suggest that this came by the instruction of Church headquarters or me." Then the stake president told Elder Paramore, "I'm not going to lie to Brother Quinn, so you decide. Do I tell him anything, or do I not take any action whatever? If I'm going to take action, which I don't think is justified, then I'm going to tell him why." Paramore hadn't expected this. He had expected to walk in as the messenger of three apostles and have a quick five-minute meeting. Boy, was my stake president gutsy!

Paramore finally concluded, "I've been told to ask you to take away his temple recommend. If that's the only way you're going to take it, then I absolve myself of responsibility. The rest is on your head." My stake president said, "Fine," and the reason I know all this is because he told me. When my stake president called me in to take away my temple recommend, he said that he was not going to hold a disciplinary court, but had to do something. So, he took away my temple recommend. He also warned me that I might be fired from BYU in a roundabout way, since faculty members are supposed to be temple worthy. He said, "If you are asked by anyone at BYU if you have a temple recommend, then tell them you do. Don't volunteer that it's in my desk drawer, and when it expires I will renew it."

See, the temple recommend has to be renewed every year by the appropriate authorities, so the stake president was protecting me. He said, "If they try to push you about whether or not you have a valid temple recommend, then you can refer them to me and I'll handle it from there." That's very important background. I was being protected by my stake president who was determined not to let BYU fire me for not having a temple recommend. Second, he was not going to disfellowship or excommunicate me, which would have almost automatically terminated my employment at BYU.

Despite being protected, I knew I was dead meat. If I ever moved out of his jurisdiction, then I would get a new stake president who didn't know me and who would be given similar instructions. That stake president would likely follow directions to the letter. Also, my stake president could be released at any time, because these are temporary positions lasting anywhere from seven to ten years, and he had already been in that position for about three years. It was only a matter of time before they found someone willing to excommunicate me. That was hard to accept.

I finally just decided to resign from BYU in order to protect myself and moved to southern California to work at the Huntington Library. Moving there made it difficult for the Church to excommunicate me because they need to know where someone lives to take any action. They have to be able to transfer all Church records into the local ward and go from there. They began trying to locate me right after I left Utah, and I knew it was only for one reason.

Philip: However, if disciplinary action begins in one stake, then it can follow you anywhere you go.

Michael: Yes, but disciplinary action never began while I was in Utah.

Philip: When they took away your temple recommend, it didn't count as disciplinary action?

Michael: No, and they can't "try anyone in absentia" according to Church regulations. They had to locate me to discipline me, and they were really determined to do both. After only a few months in California, Church headquarters learned that I was in the Los Angeles area, but they didn't know exactly where—so they still couldn't transfer my membership records into the local ward and take any action against me. Then, one evening, two men appeared on my attorney's doorstep in Salt Lake City, dressed in black shoes, black suits, white shirts, and black ties. They identified themselves as being from Church Security and said, "We know that Michael Quinn is your client, and we want his address." My attorney said, "You can't have it. That's privileged information. I can't reveal that to anyone unless he gives me authorization to do so, and he specifically told me not reveal it to anyone." Then one of the men said to my attorney, "You are a former bishop and nephew of an apostle of the Lord, and you hold a temple recommend. You have an obligation to give us this information, an obligation that is higher than any secular, earthly obligation." My attorney just said, "It has been nice talking with you, gentlemen. Good night." He then quietly closed the door in their faces.

So, then the Church tried with my mother. She received a call from a lady who said that I had left Utah with a serious outstanding debt, and they needed my telephone number and preferably an address to rectify the situation. The woman also said that if this wasn't straightened out, it would damage my credit rating. Well, I had told my mother not to give my phone number out to *anybody*, so she told the lady, "No." After trying repeatedly, the woman finally gave my mother a toll-free 800 number to call. The number turned out to be for the Church Membership Department in Salt Lake. The woman who said she was a business representative was an LDS headquarters representative!

I later moved to New Orleans and lived in the French Quarter, and had all my letters going to a mail-receiving place a few blocks away from my actual residence address, just like in L.A. As you can see, Philip, I was very confident in the Church's ability to track me.

After a year and a half in New Orleans, I got a letter from the Midwest office of American Express offering me a free gold card without requiring the normal annual fee. I sent out the application two weeks later, and then got a call from a woman who said she represented American Express. They had approved my application but needed my residential address. I said, "How do you know that the address I gave you isn't my residence address? That is the address for all my financial transactions and credit ratings." After a long pause she said, "Well, you can give either your residential address or this mail receiving address." I just said, "That's what I did." She was really flustered. "Okay, that should be good enough. Good-bye."

Two weeks later, I got a letter from the Salt Lake City office of American Express, saying, "We have approved your application for a gold card, but we need to have your residence address." It all became very clear to me then that this was not really a concern of American Express. Some executive at American Express was in cahoots with the Church Membership Department and used American Express to track down members who did not want to be tracked. When I wrote back refusing to give my residence address, I never heard anything further. The Church was after me, and we both knew that they needed my exact residence in order to do anything. They couldn't just suspect that I lived a few blocks away from where I received my mail, which I did. They had to be sure.

After three wonderful years in the French Quarter, and toward the end of finishing my book on hierarchy,[4] I decided to move back to Salt Lake City in August 1992. I needed some resources there to finish this very complex book, and I was tired of hiding. By this time I had gone through lots of therapy and was thinking quite a bit about these issues with the Church. I was ready for a confrontation and decided to have all of my mail delivered to my residence once I moved back to Salt Lake. I knew it would not take the Church long to track me down, especially since I lived only three blocks away from the temple.

The Excommunication

One day, in February of 1993, I was utterly sick with a fever over 100 degrees when someone knocked at my door. When I opened the door, I found three men from the stake presidency who promptly asked to come in. I said no. I was sick. I was in a bathrobe, looked like hell, felt (and surely sounded like) death warmed over.

The stake president said, "Well, I'm here on a very important matter of business. We have evidence that you are in apostasy for recent publications and statements made to the media, and we'd like to talk with you about it."

"I'm sick," I said, "and as soon as I am well enough I am going to California on a prescheduled trip and won't return until May or June. This isn't a good time."

They left. I got another knock at the door two hours later—after I had fallen asleep. It was just the stake president this time. He said, "I have a letter to give you, and you must read it and meet with me before you go to California." Mind you, these were my first contacts with Church leaders in Salt Lake. In the Mormon system, normally there are home teachers who come by to welcome you into a new ward. I didn't have any of that. The first visit I had was these leaders accusing me of apostasy.

I read the letter, and it outlined all the evidence of my apostasy. First, they noted an article I had published in *Sunstone* in 1992 called "150 Years of Truth and Consequences in Mormon History" where I wrote about the pressure put upon people who had written about uncomfortable issues or doctrine in Mormonism from the nineteenth century onward. The second example of my apostasy was an article I had published in *Women and Authority* titled "Mormon Women Have Had the Priesthood Since 1843."[5] The third example was a statement I made to reporters for both the *New York Times* and the *Salt Lake Tribune* where I said that Mormon leaders today no longer accept the existence of a loyal opposition. Instead, the LDS leadership wants "cookie-cutter" members, which was the title of the article in the *Salt Lake Tribune.*

I wrote a letter back to my stake president saying that I had no interest in meeting with him and that I was going out of town. He was still determined and said he *had* to meet with me. He asked for a meeting when I returned, but I wasn't going to meet with him again. I just left for L.A.

Since the 1980s, I had told almost nobody about what was going on with pressures from the Church. People have assumed that every time I've been quoted in the newspaper it's because I ran to them asking to be quoted. In actual fact, the newspapers were tracking me down—*Newsweek, New York Times, Washington Post*—they all contacted me, with one exception. Before going to L.A. on this trip, I decided that I was not going to just fall over and play dead; I was not going to cooperate in my own intimidation. So I went to the *Salt Lake Tribune* and gave a reporter copies of my correspondence with this stake president. The *Tribune* published two articles about me in February 1993, which were followed by articles throughout the Western world in every Associated Press paper, including the *Los Angeles Times*. The articles presented both my position as running from the hounds of hell and that of the Church, and the story blew up in Utah, Los Angeles, and anywhere else carrying the AP story.

Once I got to California I decided to attend church in Los Angeles, hoping that I could go under any radar. After the meeting, somebody told me that the bishop wanted to talk with me. I thought: "Oh, shit." Here I was just trying to attend church, and the leaders can't help but get in the way. I sat waiting for the bishop for a while, and then he came up. I expected the ax to fall. He started off, though, by saying, "We've read all about you and we're very pleased to see you. I've read many of your writings. What are those people up in Utah thinking?" I hadn't expected this. Then he asked if I would speak at an upcoming meeting on women and the priesthood. I was shocked. This demonstrates the variance in local Church authorities. Here is another local LDS leader, just like my stake president in Salt Lake, who knew I was in trouble and still fully backed my research and participation in Church.

I decided to attend that ward for three months but eventually had to move back to Salt Lake to finish my research. Before leaving, though, I attended a Sunday fast and testimony meeting where everybody got up and bore their testimony that the gospel and the Church are true. I knew this would be my last opportunity to bear my testimony as a member of the Church, and so I got up and expressed gratitude for my years of Church membership. Anyone reading between the lines knew that this was my farewell. It was over. I knew they were going to excommunicate me when I returned to Salt Lake.

Sure enough, the stake president convened three Church courts (now called "disciplinary councils") to put me officially on probation in June, to disfellowship me in July, and to excommunicate me in September.

Apostasy

Philip: You were excommunicated for apostasy. At what point do you think someone is apostate? Surely there must be limits, so at what point do one's beliefs become unacceptable and deserving of formal Church discipline?

Michael: In the nineteenth century, it took very little to be excommunicated, but after being excommunicated one day you could be baptized the next. Forgiveness was paramount. For example, Joseph Smith excommunicated people for going to Gentile dances, but then let them right back in. Was that apostasy? They had disobeyed Joseph's rules, but he forgave them as quickly as he punished them. They weren't heretics, as apostates are considered now. It all just comes down to the fact that everyone likes to be obeyed, and nobody likes to be questioned.

Philip: More specifically then, you published your controversial article in Maxine's book that argued that women have had the priesthood since 1843. This directly opposed the official Church stance. Was that an act of an apostate and perhaps beyond the pale of accepted views?

Michael: My article didn't undermine current Church policy, because the perception that women already have the priesthood doesn't mean they are going to go out and perform ordinances. Revelations in the Doctrine and Covenants limit that function to someone who has been ordained to a specific office. To legitimately ordain an LDS woman to a priesthood office would require new revelation to the living prophet.

Philip: But the Church today denies that women ever even had the priesthood.

Michael: Yes, they have denied that. So the Church is in the position of dealing with a member who is teaching "false doctrine," even if that teaching comes from sound historical research and the sayings of past Church leaders. I think they should allow that vocal dissent; I really do. You can be a vocal dissenter and still be a loyal Mormon. Just like when a child says, "I hate you" to his or her parents—that is very hurtful and damaging to the relationship, but it doesn't break the bond between them. Those children are still the son or daughter of their parents. Loyal dissent is similar, though, unlike the child, the loyal dissenter doesn't say, "I hate you." The loyal dissenter is just saying, "You've made mistakes" or "I don't agree with what you're doing." That should not be punishable.

Philip: What if you chose to publish an article saying that Joseph Smith wasn't a prophet? Should the Church condone that type of "loyal dissent"?

Michael: That is not loyal dissent to the essentials of faith. It's like Paul Toscano saying that Jesus is just an idea.

Philip: That Jesus might just be a fictional character?

Michael: Yeah, that is very disturbing. That is not the position of the faithful, a Christian, nor even loyal opposition. That is a position of disbelief. That is the position of an unbeliever, but I still don't think it's excommunicable. I see Church as the temporal family of God on earth, and families are meant to stay together. God had a hard time even with his family, and one third of them were so messy that he kicked them out before the creation of the world, but I can't imagine that God felt any sense of triumph about that. He lost one-third of his children! I think that would be an eternal sadness. There is no triumph in that.

Everything ultimately depends upon how one fundamentally views the Church. I see the Church as a hospital, rather than a refuge for the perfect. It's a hospital for the spiritually injured, the damaged, and the weak. It's an asylum for those who are spiritually ill. None of those things would include excommunication.

Living as a Homosexual in Mormonism

Philip: Can you describe your experience of living as a homosexual in Mormonism?

Michael: I had a very early awareness of my homosexuality but didn't know what it meant. I *knew* I was attracted to guys when I was eleven and had evidence of it even earlier at age eight. I remember hearing "queer" and "homo" as derogatory terms, and so I went to the public library when I was twelve to look through the card catalog to find something to read on it. I finally found "homosexuality" in the index and read everything I could on the topic, but it was all negative. Even the novels I read that were written by homosexuals had a negative outcome. Everything was sad, and I just thought, "This can't be what God wants for me." So I decided when I was twelve to live a straight life and repress the things I wanted sexually. I would get married, have kids, and be the perfect Mormon.

I started dating girls when I was thirteen but couldn't avoid being attracted to guys despite never acting on it. I kept hoping against reality that the attraction would just go away. It didn't. Nevertheless, I married when I was twenty-three. My wife and I were both virgins, and I did respond to her sexually, which made me think things were going to be hunky-dory, and the other dominant attractions of my life would just fade away. That's not what happened, and by the time I realized they weren't fading away but were becoming persistently stronger, there was nothing I could do. So, I honorably tried to make the best of it. My wife and I tried to work through it, but every husband and wife need fulfillment.

My wife blamed herself for our marital problems with my homosexuality, even though I kept saying it wasn't her, which is a typical pattern. We went through hell. At a certain point in the 1970s I was praying daily just to die, because I couldn't see any resolution. Divorce surely wouldn't make her happy, and that's what I wanted for her. I thought that the only thing that could bring happiness was if I died and she would be a revered widow. Then I found out after many painful talks that she was also praying to die, because she thought that was my only hope for happiness.

Finally, we went to therapy, but neither her needs nor my needs were going to change, so we decided to divorce. Ever since, the pattern of my life has been to continually run away from my sexuality. Some people are made for relationships, but I'm not one of them. I guess I don't want to make anyone else unhappy, so it's easier not to try.

Philip: How about with interactions with the Church?

Michael: I avoided the issue entirely with the Church. I pulled away from older men when they would embrace me as a teenager, because it was hard to accept that kind of physical intimacy. I knew that it was not sexual to them, but it could be sexual to me. I remember being a missionary and you are encouraged to love your companion, which put me constantly on guard. My closest missionary companion once prayed that I would be able to break down the barriers between me and other people. I couldn't explain to him the irony.

I spent my life running away from my homosexuality but was continually thrown into difficult counseling situations with young men while in the Church. Returning from my mission, I entered a BYU ward that called me to work with fifty young men as if I were their bishop. The bishop, who was preoccupied with researching a book, told me to become acquainted with everyone and do the counseling he would do if he had the time. Here I was supposed to be their substitute-bishop for the most personal matters, and I was sexually attracted to these guys. I spent time in the dorms talking with them and falling in love with them. I constantly had to put up barriers.

Decades later a student of mine at BYU put it best. He had taken my summer seminar and three of my semester courses. After one of my classes was over, he came up and said, "You are the most perplexing person I have ever known. On one hand your friendship is so inviting, and yet on the other hand there is a cold barrier that you don't allow anyone to cross." I just said, "I guess that's who I am."

Reflection

Philip: How would you contrast your strong belief after your mission with your belief right before being excommunicated? Was there much of a difference?

Michael: I always had a great spiritual relationship with God and his Church. I knew there were problems in the Church and with Church history from the time I was seventeen. I decided then that I was going to investigate every anti-Mormon claim, find out the basis of it, and answer it. That way, if a member of the Church was troubled by the issue, then I could give them an answer that was both true and faith-promoting. That was what I wanted to do, but to do so I had to acknowledge a lot of problem areas that many Church defenders didn't want to acknowledge. And I knew that I would have to acknowledge them in advance, in order to help members anticipate anti-Mormon claims and defuse their attacks. This approach exposed me to many difficult things, but my belief was never really shaken. I was a conservative believer, and that never changed, even after my excommunication. I'm still a very conservative believer, though with a radical spirit.

Philip: May I ask if your faith ever wavered after your son, Adam, left the Church or in the wake of his suicide?

Michael: I miss him deeply, but my faith in God and Mormonism has not been damaged by the tragedy of my son's life or his decision to exit it. When Adam disappeared in February of 1996, he was twenty-one, and it wasn't anything too unusual because he had been on the road from the age of sixteen to nineteen. But, of course, his mother and I were basket cases. We weren't sure if he was on the street, hitchhiking somewhere, or what. He was gone for six weeks. Then later that spring, a hiker came across a body at the top of City Creek Canyon in Salt Lake City. It was Adam. He had hanged himself.

Adam had left Mormonism when he was young and became independently religious. Really, the bottom line about his suicide is that he had a mental issue that was never fully diagnosed. He had hyperactivity as a child but refused to take his Ritalin medication. He had always seen the world completely differently and had difficulty in school. As his father, I prided myself on treating all my children the same. Too late I realized that that was the wrong approach with him, because he didn't see it as equal treatment. He had expectations that he thought the whole world should conform to.

He dropped out of high school at sixteen, as soon as he legally could, and went on the road to find people he could relate to. During that three-year period he went through nearly every state in the Union. The problem was he just couldn't get along with anybody.

In August of 1992, he was recovering from bronchitis for a while. Sometime during that period, he decided to try and conform, to give society a try. He took the GED, enrolled in Salt Lake Community College, and made the dean's list! Things were going great with Adam until 1995 when he entered the workforce. He was fired from job after job, and his emotional life went downhill. So, when total rebellion hadn't worked, and conformity hadn't worked, he decided to check out. I don't begrudge his decision; I just miss him and regret that's the life he was faced with—high-functioning autism.

Philip: Were you ever angry at the Church after your excommunication? Are you now?

Michael: I'm angry at individuals. I was never angry at the stake president who excommunicated me, even though he lied. He was in a double-bind because, in addition to being stake president, he was also a senior administrator of CES [Church Educational System]. The Church was his livelihood, and the General Authorities were his employers as well as his spiritual leaders.

I did feel angry toward Boyd K. Packer as a malignant influence in the Church, but I cried when I read his biography. I had tears streaming down my face, because he was a scrawny little kid who was constantly picked on. He was beaten up at home by his brothers, and then he went to school and was beaten by classmates for years. I cried, because I feel sorry for every kid who is beaten up. These kids go in either one of two directions: They either became very compassionate or very abusive by acting out in response to the abuse they received. Packer became abusive.

He is a fighter who is used to fighting back, but physical violence isn't approved of in the Church. So, he eventually developed an approach of religiously aggressive behavior that was approvable, and he uses all kinds of proof-texts, like Jesus whipping the money changers, for the way he approaches people (Matt. 21:12, Mark 11:15, John 2:15). That is a destructive and a spiritually abusive approach. It diminishes people, which is not part of the gospel of Jesus Christ. Packer justifies it, but it's really just a tragic manifestation of his boyhood experiences.

Philip: After being excommunicated, did you ever take part in a different church or faith community?

Michael: Yeah, I've attended the Unitarian Church, the Metropolitan Community Church (the gay and lesbian fellowship), the Quakers, the Gnostic Church (with Maxine Hanks), Catholic high mass, and the Episcopalian Cathedral in Los Angeles. I haven't felt at home in any of them, and I don't want to go back to being an outcast in the LDS Church. I can't even partake of the sacrament as an excommunicant, which for me is the only reason to go to sacrament meeting. The spirituality and uplift you might get from the talks is only secondary to the spiritual connection you should always get by partaking of the sacrament.

I don't feel guilty for no longer attending Church, which surprises me. After attending Church meetings 100 percent for my entire life, ever since I was a toddler, it is amazing to stop and not miss it. I don't miss the Church because I always received a spiritual confirmation that what I was doing was the right thing. Frequently along the way I'd ask God, "Why!? Why is this happening? Why am I in a situation where I'm rebelling against your leaders? If I'm wrong, then tell me and I'll shut up." All of this was a very painful experience, but I had my spiritual confirmation that I was doing the right thing. Maybe Church leaders did as well.

Philip: This September will be the ten-year anniversary of your excommunication. How have your thoughts and feelings changed over that period, or are they largely the same?

Michael: No, they have developed in the last ten years. I now see the LDS Church as being very similar to medieval Christianity—very powerful, very corrupt, and with leaders and members who are devout but, in many ways, devoutly wrong. They might still be good people of faith and devotion, but I think the LDS Church is now in a state of apostasy without light at the end of the tunnel. It has been a longtime perception of mine that all is not well with the Church, but I wanted to give it my best nonetheless, and I did. That is no longer possible after my excommunication.

Philip: In your speech "On Being a Mormon Historian" delivered to BYU students in the fall of 1981 you stated, "Dedicated and believing Mormon historians are seeking to build the kingdom of God and to strengthen the Saints by 'speaking the truth in love,' as Paul counseled." Do you today wish to "build the kingdom of God" and "strengthen the Saints" despite being excommunicated?

Michael: Yes, in the best way I can within my abilities and limitations. I feel it is important to defend the faith with candidness and all the relevant evidence, even if it seems controversial or contrary to faith. To do otherwise would be a tacit admission of fear. I have never felt that fear from the day when I was seventeen and read an anti-Mormon pamphlet about changes in the published text of the Book of Mormon since 1830. With that philosophy, I have tried to put all evidence within context, allowing for faithful conclusions while acknowledging that others might logically draw different conclusions. Contrary to how I'm perceived by many Mormons, I do not go out of my way to trash LDS leaders or to emphasize their foibles and mistakes, but their fallibilities are often central to understanding various incidents in the development of LDS history.

Philip: Did you deserve your excommunication?

Michael: No, no. No, but people don't deserve many things done to them by other well-intentioned people. The excommunications of the September Six can be compared to excommunications in other faith traditions, especially the excommunications of Martin Luther, Joan of Arc, Galileo, and others by the Catholic Church. They were just plain folks who got into trouble because they didn't match the expectations the Church had of a righteous person.

Philip: Do you think the excommunications of the September Six were well-intended?

Michael: By the local leaders, yes. The evidence points, though, to Boyd Packer as the one who orchestrated all the excommunications. By his lights, he was well-intended. By his lights, he was not malicious.

Philip: What do you mean "by his lights"?

Michael: From his religious point of view, his view of personal inspiration. He doesn't understand why people don't like him. He has asked friends, "Why do people hate me?" It's tragic. He thinks he's doing God's service, but he's doing to thousands of people worse things than he's ever experienced. These people also feel like they're doing the service of God, but the difference is that Packer is acting out against oppression that he experienced as a boy. He doesn't see that. From his point of view, Jesus stands with a whip against the money changers, the Pharisees, the Sadducees, and every other enemy of God.

It's interesting that in Mormonism, and even in Catholicism, members of the faith who are disloyal are regarded with greater hostility than nonbelievers who may even be critical of the faith. The former are considered treacherous. It's ironic.

Philip: If you were a Mormon leader, how would you react to those members who chose to speak out against the doctrines and/or policies of the Church?

Michael: I've always worried and prayed about that. I remember making a telling entry in my diary once while working with Leonard J. Arrington, who was the official Church historian.[6]

Philip: You were his research assistant, correct?

Michael: Yes. One day, I drove into the underground parking garage of Church headquarters and showed my pass to the parking attendant. He was really rude to me and demanded that I get out of my car, walk to the booth, and show him my pass. I was fuming with anger and thought, "If I had the power, you'd be out of a job by five this afternoon." Then I thought, "My God, thank God I don't have the power to fire him or even know somebody who does. Thank God, I don't have that power!"

So, it's not easy for me to answer your question by saying that if I were in a position of leadership, then things would be different. I recognize that power corrupts and does so in subtle ways. I'm not convinced that I could be the type of leader that I want them to be. However, I must admit that I had aspired to be in that position. I used to be convinced that God was preparing me for leadership in Mormonism, but I also had serious misgivings about power. I've seen so much corruption in people I loved and admired who inadvertently did things that were hurtful, and I don't have any confidence that I could do things better.

What I'd like to see in the Church is a recognition that freedom—"free agency" in LDS terms—does not come from coercion, or threats of hellfire, or actual excommunication. Though I like obedience from someone under my jurisdiction, I have an obligation to encourage freedom and independent thought—even if it goes against what I want. I would hope that I would always recognize corruption as a danger if I came into power. Our leaders have forgotten that power corrupts.

Philip: But because you have never been a Church leader, you are able to speculate. Ideally, how should Church leaders deal with disruptive members?

Michael: Ideally the message should be one of inclusion and love, and it should be constantly repeated. For example, the Church should not teach parents to abandon or disavow their children if they smoke, drink, have sex, or are gay or lesbian. That message isn't being communicated, because the Church isn't an inclusive Church.

If I were president of the Church, then I would give a mandate to all leaders to go and teach this message and not hold disciplinary courts on *anyone*. To warrant excommunication, someone should have to do something awful, like sexual exploitation of children, rape, or murder, but even then excommunication allows them to return. A message of love should always be given publicly and privately. I mean, according to Mormonism, even Hitler is going to a degree of glory. And, according to Joseph Smith, he's going to be "happy" despite what many of us would like for him.

Same-sex unions in LDS temples? I'm not that much of a radical or unrealistic dreamer. Ordaining women to the priesthood offices? That's not my agenda, though I would like all women to realize that they already have the priesthood through their endowment in the temple.

My agenda, if I were to become a Church leader, would be to end all the claptrap that portrays God's love as conditional, which is the basis behind so many of the Church's policies. The Church doesn't need to sanction gay marriage, for example. If it would just stop the witch-hunt and show people unconditional love, then that would be enough.

Philip: Excommunication allows for you to return to full fellowship. Have you ever seriously considered that?

Michael: I was asked if I wanted to come back by the stake president who excommunicated me. He wrote letters asking me to repent and return to the Church, so it's not simply a theoretical option, but I told him that I would not acknowledge that I was wrong from the beginning and that my excommunication was legitimate. I couldn't do that! Even if they drove over and said, "Oh, Mike! We're so sorry! We were wrong. Actually, it wasn't even us. It was the bad people back then who were wrong. We accept you with open arms," I can't go back because I can't be openly gay in the Church. If the Church is still as unaccepting and repressive as it was, even if it were to give me some kind of exemption, I still couldn't go back. Even though returning would give me the opportunity to go in the temple again, take the sacrament, and fellowship with the faithful—I still couldn't go back.

Philip: Did your excommunication bar you from being with God in the afterlife?

Michael: No, it didn't affect my relationship with God at all. I've actually turned back to the relationship with God that I had as a teenager when I thought, "It's just you and me, God." My relationship is more one-on-one rather than through a community. Excommunication does not have eternal significance unless it is ratified by God, and I don't think mine was.

Philip: As you see Mormonism today, do you want it to grow and increase in influence?

Michael: Mormonism already has social and political power disproportionate to its numbers, and Mormons know how to use their power. The LDS Church has abused its power politically in a number of ways with unethical methods that seek to achieve what they see as righteous ends. That is only going to increase. LDS statistics show a huge increase in devotion among conservative Americans who are flocking to Church, which means the conservative political base is increasing. Also, because of its military-style organization, the LDS Church can marshal almost total participation of its active members toward particular political ends. Ever since the 1980s, whenever the Church has wanted to influence legislative or popular votes, it has succeeded in swaying the vote, even in U.S. states where Mormons are only 1% of the population.

Philip: Are you glad this is happening?

Michael: I'm not happy about the disproportionate political influence the LDS Church has been exerting nationally for thirty years, but I *am* happy about the Church's growth because I believe that Mormonism has a message that people should hear. I'm pleased that the Church is growing, as it continues to be a positive influence in the lives of millions; but there is an increasing process of Mormons manipulating the U.S. political process, and that's unnerving.

Philip: Do you miss the LDS Church?

Michael: There are things about being a member that I miss, like the temple ceremony, taking the sacrament, the opportunities to serve, and the general fellowship of the Saints who are wonderful people. However, because I have such a high profile, I've seen many of the negative aspects of Mormon culture. I've gotten hate stares at the grocery store and movie theaters. I have even received death threats. In fact, in October 1993, somebody called in a death threat to the house of a man who had a name similar to mine, thinking it was my house. A fifteen-year-old babysitter answered the phone, and it terrified her. As with many world religions, Mormonism has an ugly side.

Notes

1. Mark E. Petersen (1900–84) served as an apostle from 1944 until his death.

2. This address to the Student History Association in November 1981 was published as D. Michael Quinn, "On Being a Mormon Historian (and Its Aftermath)," in *Faithful History: Essays on Writing Mormon History*, edited by George D. Smith (Salt Lake City: Signature Books, 1992), 69–111.

3. D. Michael Quinn, "LDS Church Authority and New Plural Marriages, 1890–1904," *Dialogue: A Journal of Mormon Thought* 18 (Spring 1985): 9–105.

4. D. Michael Quinn, *The Mormon Hierarchy: Origins of Power* (Salt Lake City: Signature Books in association with Smith Research Associates, 1994). It was followed by a second volume three years later, *The Mormon Hierarchy: Extensions of Power* (Salt Lake City: Signature Books in association with Smith Research Associates, 1997).

5. D. Michael Quinn, "Mormon Women Have Had the Priesthood since 1843," in *Women and Authority: Re-emerging Mormon Feminism*, edited by Maxine Hanks (Salt Lake City: Signature Books, 1992), 365–409.

6. Leonard J. Arrington was the official Church historian from 1972 to 1982.

Chapter 6
Janice Merrill Allred

Feminist, author, current president of the Mormon Women's Forum, put on formal probation October 13, 1994, excommunicated May 9, 1995.

Janice Merrill was born on April 12, 1947, the second of eight children, in Mesa, Arizona. Her parents were deeply committed to the LDS Church, and her household was steeped in Mormon thought and culture. Though neither of her parents was particularly intellectual, Janice quickly developed an insatiable love of learning. Her mother strongly encouraged education in addition to exploring one's own creativity, and Janice did both—with great success. Her intellectual activity helped Janice rise to the top of her high school class, and for this she was named a Presidential Scholar and a National Merit Scholarship recipient, two awards that carried with them substantial funding for any school in the country. Janice decided to apply to the University of Chicago, was accepted, and was offered an additional scholarship, but her parents opposed this choice. They encouraged Janice to attend BYU instead, and she became persuaded.

In 1965, Janice entered BYU with a wide range of academic interests, and she found many of her classes and professors intellectually stimulating, particularly in the Honors Program. Although BYU did not have a major in philosophy at this time, she took all the philosophy classes that were offered, being drawn to the field's concern with truth, the nature of God and reality, ethical issues, and the problem of evil. As such, she studied both analytic and Continental philosophy, and existentialism and logical positivism were particularly influential in the development of her thinking.

In 1969, Janice graduated with an English major and philosophy and German minors. In September of that same year, she married a bright young chemist named David Allred who had just returned from a mission in Guatemala. In 1971, after David had graduated from BYU and the couple had their first child, Rebecca, they moved to Princeton, New Jersey, where David began doctoral work in chemistry and physics. Two sons, Nephi and Joel, were born during their subsequent five years in Princeton. As David studied, Janice focused on her children, her Church work, and her writing, which included a play based on the book of Job that explored the problem of evil. She also started subscribing to *Sunstone* and *Dialogue*, which drew her into the Mormon intellectual community and exposed her to ways in which philosophical questions could be explored in Mormon theology.

These interests continued as the family moved to Oak Ridge, Tennessee, and then Tucson, Arizona, following David's graduation from Princeton in 1976. Another son, Ammon, was born in Arizona. In 1978, Janice published the first of what would be many articles in *Sunstone* and was shocked in December of 1979 when she heard of Sonia Johnson's excommunication. Johnson created a stir when she ardently advocated the Equal Rights Amendment, which the Church strongly opposed, and Janice was appalled that the Church would punish one of its own for holding certain political views. Johnson's excommunication thereby focused Janice's attention squarely on problems of Church governance.

The Allreds lived in Michigan from 1980 to 1987 where Miriam, Enoch, and Jared were born. The family then moved to Provo, Utah—David had accepted a teaching position at BYU—and here, Paul and John, the last two of their nine children, were born. In Utah, Janice found a ready-made community of seeking Mormons and, for the first time, built a social life that consisted of inquiring intellectuals. It was in this milieu that Janice began participating in the Mormon Women's Forum, which her sister, Margaret Toscano, had helped found in 1988 with the purpose of providing an outlet for discussing women's issues in the context of Mormonism. Janice eventually served on the group's board, as its vice president, and has been, since 1994, its president.

In addition, Janice has presented papers on theological topics nearly every year since moving to Utah and participated in conference panels on a wide variety of topics. In 1992, Margaret and Paul Toscano invited Janice to be one of the founding trustees of the Mormon Alliance with them. The purpose of this organization is to identify and counter spiritual and ecclesiastical abuse in the Church; and since these issues were central to her own concerns, Janice accepted. Such attachments would ultimately prove fatal for her LDS membership.

In 1991, Church leaders issued a statement against unsanctioned symposia, and Mormon intellectuals started being called in by their local leaders. It is with reference to this tumultuous period in 1992 when Janice was pregnant with her ninth child that the following interview picks up.

The September Six

Philip: Did you anticipate the excommunications of the September Six in 1993?

Janice: There were indications before September that there might be courts held on these people. Paul Toscano, my brother-in-law, and his wife, my sister Margaret, had each been called in by their stake president several times. I also knew that Lavina had been questioned and would probably have a court. She was a close friend, as was Lynne Whitesides. Margaret, Lynne, and I worked in the Mormon Women's Forum together, and Lynne was the president at that time. I was also acquainted with Maxine Hanks. I had read many of Michael Quinn's writings on Mormon history. Although I didn't know him personally, I had friends who did, and so I knew something of his difficulties with the Church. There had been a lot of discussion in the Mormon intellectual community about tensions with the Church hierarchy for several years. Since I had contacts with all of the September Six, except Avraham Gileadi, I knew a lot of what was happening.

My family was actually in Mexico during September of 1993 because my husband, David, was on sabbatical from BYU, so it was difficult for us to keep up on the news. I knew that several courts were impending as we left Utah late in August. I did have one friend, though, who sent us newspaper clippings of everything that happened. That's how I found out about the excommunications. It was so difficult for me not to be there with all of my friends and go through it with them.

I was also aware that I could eventually be in trouble because of an article I had presented at the Sunstone Symposium in 1992 on God the Mother.[1] My stake president, Carl Bacon, had called me into his office shortly after I gave the paper. We had had several meetings and he had finally told me not to publish it. I had told him that I wasn't planning on publishing it at that time, but I might in the future and would inform him before I did so. In the summer of '93 one of the editors of *Dialogue* told me that they were planning a women's issue and asked me if I had something I could contribute. I had sent my article on God the Mother to *Dialogue* just before we went to Mexico. So, while the September Six were being called into court, I began wondering if the same thing was going to happen to me.

Philip: Can you describe your involvement with Sunstone and the Mormon Women's Forum leading up to your excommunication?

Janice: There were three different organizations I was involved in: Sunstone, the Mormon Women's Forum, and the Mormon Alliance. I was a frequent participator in the Sunstone Symposium and had published a number of articles in the magazine beginning in 1978. I gave my first paper at the annual symposium in 1980. After we moved to Utah in 1987, I gave a paper nearly every year.

I attended most of the functions of the Mormon Women's Forum, which was organized in 1988. My sister, Margaret Toscano, was one of the organizers, and Lynne Whitesides became president at the end of 1992. She then asked me to become vice-president, and that's how I became involved on the board. The forum is a feminist organization whose purpose is to provide a place for Mormon women to speak about gender issues and other topics important to them. Originally the idea was to include all Mormon women, whether or not they have feminist leanings, but the forum quickly became branded as radical, and that limited participation. Men are also welcome to participate in our activities, but only a few have. Our goal is to give everyone an opportunity to speak without censorship. We have sponsored presentations on God the Mother, women and the priesthood, the Proclamation on the Family, and other controversial issues.

The Mormon Alliance was formed by Paul and Margaret Toscano and Fred Voros in 1992. They asked me to join them, and I was one of the founding trustees. Lavina Fielding Anderson came in shortly after. The purpose of the Mormon Alliance is to identify, report, and alleviate spiritual abuse in the Church and work toward a better relationship between leadership and members, to work toward a church that is more egalitarian.

One of the first things we did was to try to begin a dialogue with Church leaders. We wrote a long letter to the First Presidency and Quorum of the Twelve expressing our concerns. In this letter we listed some spiritually abusive practices, cited a few cases, and then affirmed the correct principles that should govern the Church. We hoped for a response that ultimately never came. All we got was an acknowledgement from the First Presidency's secretary that our letter had been received. One of our ongoing projects is to publish case reports of spiritual and ecclesiastical abuse in the Church for the purpose of calling attention to the problem so that members can have better Church experiences.

Philip: Have you always been interested in such controversial issues?

Janice: Actually, my first publications were not at all controversial. The first article I published in 1978 was on forgiveness; and it was not until my paper in 1992, "Toward a Mormon Theology of God the Mother," that I started getting worried that my writing might be viewed as problematic. In fact, right around that time President Hinckley told members not to pray to Mother in Heaven. I don't recall exactly when.

Philip: Hinckley's "Daughters of God" Speech was given at the women's general meeting in the fall of 1991.[2]

Janice: Right. So I had an idea when I wrote my paper after Hinckley's speech that I could be in trouble. The thing was, I really disagreed with President Hinckley on what he had said about God the Mother, and it's a very important issue. The Mormon Church believes in God the Mother and has since the time of Joseph Smith.

After I gave that speech my stake president, Carl Bacon, called me and my husband in. He apologized for calling us in because he was worried that we might be offended. He told us that he had been asked by Salt Lake to investigate me because of the speech I had given on the Mother in Heaven. At first he was not sure what he should do, and he said he would have to check back with the area authorities. His approach was to do whatever he was told by those higher in authority. My strong belief in personal revelation was at odds with his approach. I believe that God speaks directly to people, which, to me, is a fundamental teaching of Christianity.

If we pray, then we will get answers to our prayers. That is the founding story of Mormonism. Joseph Smith, a young boy who had questions that neither the Bible nor his religious authorities could answer, went directly to God. One of my core beliefs is that every person has a direct connection with God. So, area authorities contacted President Bacon and asked him to investigate me, to check me out. Apparently, at that time, President Bacon didn't know that he wasn't supposed to tell me where the orders were coming from.

Philip: So you are convinced that your local leader didn't instigate your excommunication.

Janice: That's right. I believe it came from the General Authority level. There is a lot of evidence for this beginning with President Bacon's statements to me. Some people thought that President Hinckley might have been involved in my case, because he might have taken what I had said personally. My speech on God the Mother went directly against what he had said, and the other speech that figured in my excommunication started by quoting him and then arguing against his statement. I don't know if there was a direct order to excommunicate me, but I do have evidence of General Authority involvement. The Strengthening Church Members Committee was definitely involved in my case.

At first, though, President Bacon didn't know exactly what he was supposed to do. He just talked with me and tried to ascertain whether or not I was a loyal Church member. It turned out that his definition of a loyal Church member was quite different than my own!

Philip: What is your definition?

Janice: I considered myself a loyal Church member. I was active, believed in the foundational principles of the Church, kept the commandments that are required of Church members, such as the Word of Wisdom, had a temple recommend, and had had many Church callings, including teaching in Relief Society. I thought of myself as a good Mormon and most people in my ward would have agreed. I didn't agree with some of the teachings the Church was promulgating at that time, but I was a loyal Church member. I have always based my theology and doctrine on the scriptures.

President Bacon's definition of a loyal Church member was somebody who doesn't question Church authorities—someone who does what he's told—but that's not what Christianity is about. And I don't believe that's what Mormonism is about. I don't think that the gospel of Jesus Christ is authoritarian, nor should the Church be. Authoritarianism leads to many abuses, and I have written about that. In my meetings with Carl Bacon, I talked a lot about the question of freedom of speech in the Church, which was one of the major disagreements between me and the Church leaders. I didn't tell President Bacon the extent of my disagreements with the Church, nor did I give him all the information on my associations with the groups we have talked about. He, of course, knew that I had spoken at the Sunstone Symposium, but he didn't even know what Sunstone was. Ultimately, he instructed me not to publish my article on God the Mother. I told him that I didn't have any plans to publish it at that time but that I might want to in the future. I said I would let him know if I decided to.

Philip: You promised only to notify him?

Janice: Right, and I was careful about that because I knew he wouldn't give me permission. It was my prerogative to publish it or not, and I didn't want to make a promise that I couldn't keep nor wouldn't want to keep. He thought I had accepted his command not to publish without permission because that's what he expected, but that's not what I promised. He just thought, "Okay, she agreed, no problem here."

In 1993, there was a lot of apprehension in the intellectual community. This was right around the time David Knowlton and Cecilia Konchar Farr were having problems at BYU,[3] and it became apparent that the Church was cracking down on intellectuals, liberals, and feminists. That's when my family went to Mexico.

Philip: Was there any part of you that was glad to be out of Salt Lake and away from all the problems?

Janice: No, not at all. A lot was going on, and I wanted to be part of it. Close friends and family members were experiencing trauma, and I wanted to support them. I wanted to protest what was happening. Many people were sending letters to the Church saying not to discipline these people, there were petitions circulated, and there was a lot of media involvement, a lot of concern about what was happening and discussion of the issues. It was hard for me to be away. When we got back to the United States just before Christmas in 1993, I found a letter from *Dialogue* in the mail that had accumulated, which accepted "Toward a Mormon Theology of God the Mother" for publication in the women's issue. I decided to go ahead with publication even though I knew there might be repercussions. I didn't inform President Bacon right away, because I didn't want him to put pressure on me not to publish. Since my first meeting with him, my daughter Rebecca had been married in the temple, and my son Joel would soon be going on a mission.

Philip: And one of your sons was already on his mission right?

Janice: Yes. My oldest son, Nephi, was already on his mission. I didn't want the Church to take my membership or my temple recommend away before I went to the temple with Joel before he left for his mission. That was important to me and was my reason for deciding to wait until just before the article came out in *Dialogue* to tell President Bacon that I was publishing it. As it happened, he heard that the article was going to be published before I told him, and he called me into a meeting and asked me not to publish it. It was too late for me to withdraw it, and I would not have withdrawn it anyway as I wanted to publish it. So, in his eyes, I had become disobedient.

The Excommunication

I now knew that a disciplinary council was imminent, so I familiarized myself with the Church's *General Handbook of Instructions* (1989), which does not list disobedience to a Church leader as an excommunicable offense. Of course, if that weren't the case, then anyone who doesn't accept a Church calling could be called into a Church court because he or she would be refusing to follow a Church leader.

President Bacon thought I was disobedient because I was publishing the article. He thought I had lied. I hadn't, but even if I had, then it still would not have been an excommunicable offense. Even so, I anticipated a Church court after that.

This was in May of 1994. Also during this time, I was working on a paper to present at the Sunstone Symposium, which was in August. In the October 1993 general conference, President Hinckley, who was then a counselor in the First Presidency, had given a speech saying that God would never allow the prophet to lead the Church astray, which is a common belief among Mormons. I think this idea is unscriptural and very dangerous because it promotes authoritarianism. I believe that all questions and ideas are subject to evidence—spiritual, empirical, and rational—and every person is responsible for forming and examining his or her own beliefs. The belief that God will not allow the prophet to lead the Church astray means, for many Mormons, that whatever the prophet says in his capacity as Church president is true and cannot be questioned. Whatever counsel he gives must be obeyed, and to challenge him is, in the thinking of many Mormons, an excommunicable offense. So this belief that prophets can't be wrong means "obey or you're out." Many harmful repercussions come out of this interpretation.

When I read President Hinckley's speech while we were in Mexico in the fall of 1993, I decided to challenge this popular notion that the prophet cannot lead the Church astray in my next speech, which was the one I was working on in the summer of 1994. In this speech I attempted to show that this idea is unscriptural, illogical, and not in harmony with the gospel or the principle of free agency. The gospel teaches that every person has a direct connection to God through the Spirit and can receive inspiration and counsel directly from God and that we are each responsible for our own actions. We cannot and should not give our agency to another person, no matter how righteous that person might be. Indeed, a righteous person would not ask this of us but would encourage us to follow our own conscience.

In the summer of 1994, I started having regular meetings with Bishop Robert Hammond, who eventually scheduled a court on me. I was aware that there was the potential for publicity, and I decided to agree to talk to reporters. I felt this was important for bringing about a more open Church. I was also aware that the Church would be angered by my speaking to the media and publicizing the Church's punishing people for intellectual inquiry. The publicity, in and of itself, became an issue.

When Peggy Fletcher Stack[4] heard through the grapevine that there was an impending disciplinary court for me, she called to talk about it. I told her that I wanted to wait until after the disciplinary council had actually been scheduled before publicizing my case, and she agreed to wait to do an article. Just before the Sunstone Symposium I got a call from Associated Press reporter Vern Anderson who wanted to talk about my court and the talk I would be giving at Sunstone challenging the belief that the Lord will not permit the prophet to lead the Church astray. He was fascinated by my story because here was a seemingly good Church member and mother of nine who was challenging the authoritarianism of the Church. He thought this had great potential for an article and wanted to do a story on me. The article came out on the front page of the *Salt Lake Tribune* the day I gave my speech. I then did a television interview for Channel 4, which was very scary for me.

In the end I had two disciplinary courts, the first of which was on October 12–13, 1994. Many interesting things happened right before the court. President Hinckley gave a speech in Idaho in which he brought up my Sunstone speech. He said, "She can present her paper until doomsday, but God will see to it that the Church will not be led astray." This reference to my talk was very unusual, because General Authorities rarely refer specifically to people or texts they want to challenge. Usually they do it in a general way. It also showed that President Hinckley was aware of my paper and what I had said.

Then at October general conference, nine different speakers spoke on topics that touched on the authority and calling of the prophet, and the idea that the prophet would never lead the Church astray was mentioned several times. Many people felt that this was clearly in response to what I had said. In fact, Vern Anderson called me afterward and asked if I wanted to comment.

The court on October 12 started at 7:00 P.M. and lasted eight hours, ending at 3:00 A.M. on October 13. There was a vigil for me held outside the building, but most of the people and reporters left before the court ended. Only my family, a few close friends, and the reporter from Channel 4 were waiting when I finally left the bishop's office with the verdict. In the court, the bishop forbade me to publish my article challenging prophetic infallibility and threatened me with excommunication if I didn't promise not to publish it. I refused because I believe that a person should be free to follow truth and his or her conscience wherever they lead, and I felt that making such a promise would be agreeing to submit the authority of my conscience to Church leadership, which I felt was wrong. After my definite refusal of this ultimatum, I was sure that the bishop and his counselors would come to a quick decision to excommunicate me as he had threatened to do. I was surprised that they spent almost two hours deliberating and then did not excommunicate me, but put me on formal probation.

With formal probation, according to the *General Handbook of Instructions*, the bishop can pretty much do what he wants in terms of restrictions or requirements, but, of course, the expectation is that the limitations will be lighter than those imposed for either disfellowshipment or excommunication, which are for more serious offenses. But the restrictions my bishop imposed on me mirrored those of disfellowshipment. I couldn't take the sacrament, speak in Church, pray publicly, serve in a Church position, or hold a temple recommend. These restrictions, I felt, were within the rights of the bishop to impose, although I believed he was unjust in doing so. That is, I felt I was worthy to partake of the sacrament, pray in Church, serve in a Church calling, and attend the temple. But I do respect the authority and calling of the bishop, and so I agreed to follow these restrictions. Because I wanted to continue attending Church in my ward, that was necessary; I wanted to be respectful of legitimate authority. However, Bishop Hammond also imposed a condition which I felt was both unjust and beyond the scope of his authority. This was in regards to my speaking and writing. He wanted me to submit my speeches and essays to someone to be scrutinized for any false doctrine they might contain. According to his plan, I would then agree to either omit or correct the ideas which were considered contrary to Church doctrine. I wrote him a letter in which I objected to this condition on the grounds that it was an infringement of my right to believe, speak, and act according to my conscience. I told him I was willing to listen to his counsel, but it was my responsibility to make my own decisions.

The story of my Church discipline was picked up by the press, who loved the irony in the Church's disciplining a mother of nine for talking about the Mother in Heaven, and the story was published in newspapers all over the country. I did several radio and television interviews, including one with the BBC and one with some media people from Germany. My bishop got increasingly upset with me about these interviews. I, however, thought speaking to the media was well within my rights and important for promoting free speech within and about the Church.

Early in November I gave a speech at Counterpoint,[5] which was sponsored by the Mormon Women's Forum. In this speech I told the story of my experiences in being disciplined by the Church. I called it "My Controversy with the Church."[6] This speech also became a point of contention between me and my bishop. After reading an article about the speech in the local newspaper, he asked me for a copy of the speech and I refused to give it to him. He felt that it was his responsibility to determine if I had made any apostate statements publicly. There were two definitions of apostasy given in the *General Handbook of Instructions* that was in use during this time (1989). One stated that apostasy occurs when members teach as Church doctrine information which is not Church doctrine after being corrected by their leaders. I was always clear that I was presenting my own views. I tried to base them on the principles of the gospel and the scriptures, but I never claimed to be giving official Church doctrine.

My bishop accused me of damaging the faith of Church members by my writing.

The point I was trying to make in not giving him a copy of my Counterpoint speech was that alternative forums, such as the Mormon Women's Forum, are outside the Church's jurisdiction and do not damage the faith of the average Church member. Most Church members don't even know about these types of forums. Even if they did, they wouldn't come to these forums because they see them as dangerous because they are unauthorized and discouraged by the Church. People who participate in the alternate forums are already questioning Church teachings and practices. In fact, some people have told me that my writings have helped their faith because I addressed hard questions from the perspective of belief. Nobody has ever told me that what I wrote caused them to leave the Mormon Church. On the other hand, people have left the Church because of its treatment of people like me.

My second disciplinary court was in May of 1995. Given the position I had taken and my refusal to allow the bishop to supervise my speaking and writing, the court was inevitable, but it was bad timing for me. I have no idea why the bishop decided to convene a court at that time. My son was scheduled to have surgery on his jaw that morning, and I had had surgery on my foot a few weeks before and was still on crutches. Plus, they scheduled it for just before Mother's Day. Maybe I could be excommunicated in time for Mother's Day! At that court they went through everything I had done since the first court—talks, articles, interviews—everything. I was certain that the outcome would be excommunication—I felt that the court had been called for that purpose—and sure enough, they excommunicated me.

Philip: What exactly did they excommunicate you for?

Janice: Apostasy. Their reasoning was that I had been put on formal probation with conditions given for remaining a Church member and, according to the bishop, I had "flaunted" them. (He meant "flouted," of course.) On the contrary, I thought I had been respectful. I had agreed to the restrictions and followed them, and I had respectfully stated my objections to the condition I was unwilling to follow. And in refusing to submit my speeches and writing to a process of censorship, I was not disobeying any law of the Church. My speeches and writing were not apostate according to the definitions of apostasy given in the *General Handbook of Instructions*.

My excommunication was very hard for me. My family has been in the Church since the very beginning. Several of my ancestors knew Joseph Smith. I was raised in a home where the Church was central to our identity. As a young person with an inquiring mind, I had many questions, a love of philosophy and literature, and a commitment to follow truth wherever it led me. I didn't know if I would stay in the Mormon Church.

I have always believed in God and the reality of the spiritual world. Although I felt it was necessary for me to understand and give serious consideration to the arguments against the existence of God, I have always believed. As I studied the scriptures and attempted to understand the gospel, I came to an understanding of Christ and his mission that was deeply meaningful to me. I especially came to love the Book of Mormon and the New Testament and their teachings. I found many profound ideas in the teachings of Joseph Smith. It was harder for me to fit socially in the Church, but eventually I found a niche for myself.

My husband and I, at the beginning of our marriage, committed to being active in the Church. We always accepted callings and assignments, and we raised our children in the Church. Up until the beginning of my being disciplined by the Church, our involvement in the Church was mostly positive. I think that my children, until that time, had seen it as a loving and kind place. I freely expressed disagreements I had with some Church teachings and policies at home, and my children were raised to see open discussion and respectful disagreement as consistent with active membership in the Church. But when the Church disciplined me, it was no longer a loving and kind place that supported spiritual growth for me and some of my family. All my children know that I love God, that I love Jesus Christ, and that I try to live the gospel. I, of course, make mistakes, but they know I try to live the principles of the gospel. So it was very difficult for them to see that the Church could not accommodate my differences. It was especially hard for Joel, who was on his mission when I was excommunicated, and Nephi, who was just about to return when the discipline began. They said it was hard to invite people into a Church that was persecuting their mother.

The Church Hierarchy/Authority

Philip: Do you believe Church officials have God-given authority to guide the Church, doctrinally and logistically?

Janice: That's a really hard question to answer briefly. I believe that priesthood leaders have the responsibility to teach the gospel, to administer the ordinances, and to receive revelation to guide the Church. I believe that members have the responsibility to follow the principles of the gospel—to have faith in Christ, repent of their sins, keep the commandments of God, and seek to understand truth and be guided by the Spirit of God. Every person has a direct connection to God through the Spirit. Every person has the responsibility, the right, and the privilege to seek revelation from God for his or her personal life and also to understand the principles of the gospel and the mysteries of godliness. Members also have the right and responsibility to receive inspiration about any Church teaching or practice or policy—to know for themselves whether it comes from God.

Many people in the Church believe and teach that it is their responsibility to obey priesthood leaders without question. I believe this teaching is contrary to the gospel and harmful to the Church and the spiritual welfare of its members. I believe that Church officials have a responsibility to seek revelation and inspiration in their callings, but they do not always receive it. Whether they receive it or not depends on their own desire and commitment to receive and follow it. I believe that the Church organization should be consistent with the gospel, which teaches that every person has a direct connection with God and every person is ultimately responsible to God. It is consistent with the gospel to disobey leaders in order to obey God.

Members have the right and responsibility to know whether what they are being taught is true and whether what is being asked of them is consistent with gospel principles and in accordance with the will of God. Mormons have a wonderful scripture in the Doctrine and Covenants which says, "No power or influence can or ought to be maintained by virtue of the priesthood, only by persuasion, by long-suffering, by gentleness and meekness, and by love unfeigned; by kindness and pure knowledge" (D&C 121:41–42). This says that possessing a priesthood office does not authorize a person to exercise power or influence. The Spirit of God authorizes and ratifies only that which is done in love and truth. Therefore, it is wrong for the Church to demand that members accept whatever leaders teach or obey whatever they command. Members should take the teachings and guidance of leaders seriously, examine them, weigh the evidence for and against them, and pray for inspiration about them. And if they believe that leaders' instructions are not consistent with the gospel nor good for the Church, they have the privilege of rejecting them.

Philip: In your article "Toward a Mormon Theology of God the Mother," you wrote, "I must add that I am in no way whatsoever attempting an official reinterpretation of LDS doctrine. That prerogative rests solely with the leaders of the Church. I am interested in simply offering a new understanding and appreciation of the Mother based on my own reading and personal reflection."[7] From this one might presume that you believe Church leaders should listen more to members when establishing doctrine. Is that true?

Janice: That statement was not in the original article. It was added when the article was included in a collection of my essays. My editor suggested the addition. He felt that, because of the controversy surrounding my essay, I should make it clear that I wasn't attempting an official reinterpretation of Mormon doctrine, which, of course, I wasn't. How could I, since I wasn't and could never be in a position to do that?

My essay was offering a reinterpretation of the Godhead based on my reading and pondering of the scriptures. The phrase "that prerogative rests solely with the leaders of the Church" didn't exactly represent my views, but I let it stand in my review of the changes suggested by the editor as an acknowledgement of my understanding of the position of the Church and most Church members on this question.

Do I believe that Church leaders should listen more to members when establishing doctrine? Yes, but the question of what constitutes

Church doctrine is a complex one. I believe that Church leaders have the responsibility of teaching the gospel, but I think that establishing doctrine in an official way leads to many problems and is detrimental to the search for truth of individual members. Leaders should resist the temptation to establish doctrine. Church doctrine should not be established dogma, and members should not be obligated to believe it. It should be based on the teachings of the scriptures and accepted revelations and should arise out of the thinking and inspiration of leaders and members as they try to understand the gospel, the nature of God, and our responsibilities and obligations to God, our fellow human beings, and the world around us. Both leaders and members should seek revelation.

I don't believe that just anything can be Church doctrine. New Church doctrine should always be established on the basis of revelation, and members then have the responsibility to determine for themselves if that revelation is true or not. That's part of what it means to be an alive and aware person. Hopefully, before leaders offer new doctrine or policies, they have explored relevant issues, have sought and received revelation, and have come to a greater understanding that enables them to offer interpretations that are illuminating for us. But the process of reinterpreting scriptures and refining and expanding gospel understanding is continual. It is part of the life and development of a person committed to finding truth and serving God and others. This is *continuing* revelation. And when you study the scriptures with this perspective, you realize you are engaged in a continuing dialogue with the prophets.

I think this approach to doctrine would be a lot easier for Church members if Church leaders were more interested in theology, read widely, and were willing to get ideas from members and from theologians of other churches and religions. Joseph Smith certainly did that. Now, if a change in official doctrine needed to occur, it is, of course, Church leaders who would need to propose the change, but members have the privilege of accepting or rejecting the change, and they should have more of a say in the process of making changes.

Reflection

Philip: Do you think that, if you hadn't lived in Provo, Utah, in such close proximity to the Mormon epicenter, you still would have been excommunicated? If you had lived in England and given these same papers and talks, would they still have excommunicated you?

Janice: That's a good question. A number of people have expressed this idea to me: that if I had lived somewhere else, I would not have been excommunicated. My brothers and sisters who live in Arizona have said that if I had lived there this never would have happened. I don't know. I've heard of authoritarian practices and ecclesiastical abuse all over the Church, worldwide. There are some places where the membership is more liberal and people can write and express themselves in ways that might get you in trouble elsewhere. However, I think that this would have been a problem anywhere in the Church because Church headquarters sent copies of my speeches and articles to my local leaders, asking them to deal with me. The speeches and things I wrote that got me in trouble were not given on the local level. They weren't given in the official Church, but in alternate forums which are not set up by the Church. The Church has no responsibility for them. The papers that were the focus of the disciplinary process against me were both given at the Sunstone Symposium in Salt Lake City. My participation in my ward was never a problem. Given that the action taken against me was instigated by Church headquarters and probably influenced by it, it could have happened no matter where I had lived. Different local leaders might have acted differently, but I think that depends more on the character and beliefs of the leaders themselves than where they live.

Philip: Were you angry after your excommunication?

Janice: I've thought a lot about the meaning of anger. I've even written about it. There is always a judgment involved in anger. The belief is that someone intentionally harmed or wronged you or someone you care about. In that sense I was angry, because I believe that my excommunication wasn't right; it was unjust. I shouldn't have been excommunicated. It was wrong! So, in that sense, I was angry.

Feeling hurt is part of anger, and I suffered a lot of pain and grief during the process, and that hurt is not entirely healed. Another part of anger is a desire to right the wrong. I have tried to do that in ways that are consistent with Jesus's teachings about forgiveness and loving your enemies. Sometimes the desire for justice that is present in anger becomes a desire for retribution. Some theorists believe that a desire for revenge is a necessary part of anger, but I disagree. I think that what we call anger very often is this desire to hurt in return, but this is only the last step in a process and not a necessary step. The desire for justice can be pursued in other ways than retaliation and retribution.

I was not angry with President Bacon or Bishop Hammond in the sense of desiring retribution. I believe that retribution is wrong, and it's not in my character to desire revenge. I had no desire that any of the men who judged me be punished or suffer for the injustice they did me and the hurt they caused me and my family. Following Christ means forgiving those who sin against us, and forgiveness means not desiring retribution. So I actively sought to forgive those who judged and punished me. One way to do this is to try to understand them, which leads to compassion. I thought that Bishop Hammond was in a very difficult position and, given his background and understanding, he did the best he could.

Some people felt that, by speaking to the media about my excommunication and publishing my story, I was seeking retribution. I don't see it that way. My reason for making my story public was to expose the authoritarianism in the present Church structure and teachings and show how it is contrary to the gospel, how it leads to spiritual abuse, and how it impairs spiritual growth. I hoped that telling my story would raise awareness of the problems resulting from authoritarianism in the Church. Excommunication and the threat of excommunication are damaging. If the Church disciplines people for writing on controversial topics or saying things that challenge Church teachings or practices, then it's harmful to the Church as well as to those who are disciplined. I want the Church to be better, more egalitarian, more in harmony with the gospel of Jesus Christ. That requires allowing people to express their ideas and talk about problems and work together to find solutions.

Philip: If you were in Bishop Hammond's place, how would you have reacted toward this Janice Allred who wrote on controversial issues and spoke out against Church leaders?

Janice: I didn't speak out against Church leaders. My paper on God the Mother examined the theology of the Godhead and argued for a reinterpretation of it based on my reading of the scriptures. My work is mostly theological. In my paper challenging the idea that the Lord will not permit the prophet to lead the Church astray, I quoted President Hinckley making that claim. My reason for quoting him was not to oppose him but to quickly make the point that the idea I was challenging is widely held in the Church.

Arguing that an idea a person expresses is wrong is not speaking against that person. One of the definitions of apostasy in the *General Handbook of Instructions* is publicly opposing the Church or its leaders, and I was accused of this. I defended myself by pointing out that my motive in writing and speaking was to engage in open and honest discussion for the purpose of increasing understanding and helping to solve problems. One of the evils of authoritarianism is equating disagreement with disloyalty. This damages both the institution and the members of the institution because it impedes the process by which truth is understood and progress is made.

To answer your question about what I would have done if I had been in Bishop Hammond's place, I'll just make a couple of observations. First, I maintained then and I still believe that I did not deserve to be excommunicated. At one point, I told President Bacon and Bishop Hammond what I thought they should do. They had been asked by Church headquarters to investigate me. They should report that they had talked to me and learned that I believe in Christ, accept the scriptures as the word of God, love the Church, am committed to it, serve faithfully in my ward, and keep the commandments the Church requires of its members. They should drop the procedure against me and leave me free to write and speak according to my own judgment. President Bacon responded to this by saying that he couldn't remain stake president one week if he didn't do something about me, which points out the problem that Bishop Hammond, as the one who finally conducted the disciplinary councils against me, faced. I was not submissive to the system. Did he support a system that required submissiveness to authority? He was under pressure from the Church system to demand that I submit or be punished. He didn't see a problem with the system so he finally excommunicated me.

Your question invites me to view my situation from the perspective of a Church leader rather than a member. I think it's always helpful to try to view a conflict from as many perspectives as possible, and I tried to do that. I think I understand why Bishop Hammond acted as he did, and I bear him no ill-will for doing so. Nevertheless, I think it was wrong for him to excommunicate me. It was unjust; I didn't deserve it and the excommunication caused me and my family a lot of problems and pain. He could have acted otherwise. I hope that, if I had been in his position, I could have resisted the pressure to act in an authoritarian way.

Is my vision of an egalitarian, open church a feasible one? I think it is. I think that following gospel principles demands it. If I were in a position of leadership, would I view the problems differently? Perhaps I would, but I hope I would have the courage and integrity to try to solve them in non-authoritarian ways.

Philip: At what point does one deserve excommunication?

Janice: I don't believe that excommunication or the threat of excommunication should ever be used to control or punish people. It might be necessary in some extreme cases if someone presented a real danger to Church members. But that danger would need to be defined carefully, and a just and fair system of due process for judging and carrying out excommunications would need to be put in place. What is in place now does not meet even a minimal standard of due process.

In the area of doctrine, I think there should be a lot of freedom. The most effective means of dealing with false doctrine is to teach true doctrine. Truth stands for itself. Punishing people for their ideas doesn't help anyone learn the truth. And it often just makes those ideas more interesting.

Philip: Do you still believe in the basic tenets of Mormonism, that the Book of Mormon is true, that Joseph Smith was a prophet . . . ?

Janice: I still believe in what I consider to be the basic tenets of Mormonism. I do believe that Joseph Smith was a prophet. I don't subscribe to the beliefs that many Mormons hold about what it means to be a prophet. I think that Joseph Smith made many mistakes, especially in his dealings with people. I do believe that he received revelation and that the Book of Mormon is truly an ancient scriptural document. It contains important ideas about Jesus Christ and salvation. Jesus Christ is the foundation of my faith and belief system.

Some people have told me that I have a skewed view of what Mormonism is. For example, a lot of people would say that believing that the prophet will not lead the Church astray is a basic tenet of Mormonism. Perhaps it has become that. But if Jesus Christ and his gospel are the foundation of the Mormon Church, then its basic tenets should be in harmony with Christ and his gospel. I believe this idea about prophetic infallibility is not in harmony with the gospel, and so I have tried to persuade my fellow Mormons to renounce it.

Philip: And you would consider yourself Mormon?

Janice: Yes, I'm Mormon, but I would also say that I'm a Christian and a seeker of truth. I guess I'm a Christian in the Mormon tradition. My primary identification is as a follower of Christ, but I also look for truth in other religious traditions, in philosophy, literature, art, and science.

Philip: As you see Mormonism today, do you want it to increase in members and influence?

Janice: I disagree with many of the positions the Church has taken on political issues—its position against the ERA and its position against gay marriage, for example. I don't want to see its political influence increase, because I think it's taken the wrong side on many issues.

I think the Church can be a positive influence in people's lives, but it can also have negative effects. I believe in the importance of the ordinances, and I think the additional Mormon scriptures give many important truths about Christ and his mission, the nature of God, and the principles of the gospel. I would never presume to say whether a person should join or leave the Church—that's between him or her and God. The major problem in Mormonism is not the people or doctrine, but the institution. I am committed to Jesus

Christ and to teaching people His gospel of love and truth. Inasmuch as the Church teaches people about Christ and His gospel and gives people the opportunity to love and serve each other, I support it.

Philip: Do you have any regrets?

Janice: I don't regret anything I did in the context of my excommunication. As I look back, I know that I did the best I could.

Philip: What has stopped you from joining another faith community, one that might be more accepting of you and your past?

Janice: I've thought about that. One reason is that my husband still teaches at BYU, and we live in Provo. My husband and our youngest son, who is still in the Provo schools, attend our Mormon ward, and I go with them. I want to be with them. Part of what I desire in a faith community is a place where my family can build relationships with other people and take part in a caring environment. That, in many ways, is still available in our local ward. Also most of my extended family is still in the Church, and the Church is very important to them.

I don't think membership in the LDS Church or in any other presently organized church is necessary to salvation, although I believe participating in a church community is important in living the gospel. I believe that my faith in Christ and my willingness to repent of my sins and seek the spirit of truth make me a member of Christ's spiritual church. I think joining another faith community would take me away from my family, so it doesn't feel like a real option to me right now.

Philip: Can you describe what it's like, then, for you to attend church every week and not be able to take the sacrament or fully participate in Church meetings?

Janice: It's been very difficult, more so at first, because of the judgment that excommunication signifies. I felt that judgment and exclusion from many ward members. As I told you, my belief in Jesus Christ is the strongest belief I have. It's the foundation of all my beliefs and the basis from which I try to live my life. So, to be denied the sacrament, which is a symbol of a person's faith in Christ and his or her covenant to obey His commandments, is really difficult. One irony is that, from time to time, one of my sons has had the assignment to bring the bread for the sacrament. So, I give him the bread, he takes it to church, and that's the same bread that's served, but of which I'm not allowed to partake. Yes, it's hard, but I've accustomed myself to it. I have tried to avoid internalizing the judgment that excommunication represents.

It has been years since the excommunication took place and there have been changes in our ward boundaries and ward membership even though we've lived in the same house. Some people in the ward know nothing of my history. My Church experience is better now than it was just after the excommunication. At that time very few people talked to me. Many people looked away from me at church, and some Church friends distanced themselves from me. Now people are friendly with me at church and Church functions. Not having a Church job limits my ability to make friends in the ward, and being excommunicated makes me hesitant to pursue friendships. I don't know who knows about my history and I don't want to misrepresent myself as a good Church member when I've been excommunicated for apostasy. And I don't know to what degree knowledge of my excommunication inhibits people from associating with me, but my interaction with ward members is mostly limited to Church functions.

Philip: Has there been any support from other members outside your ward?

Janice: I don't really have contact with people in other wards. People in the Mormon intellectual community have been supportive and I have many friends that I made at retreats and in book groups that have been very supportive.

Notes

1. Janice Allred, "Toward a Mormon Theology of God the Mother," *Dialogue: A Journal of Mormon Thought* 27, no. 2 (Summer 1994): 15–39.

2. Gordon B. Hinckley, "Daughters of God," *Ensign*, November 1991, 97.

3. David Knowlton and Cecilia Konchar Farr were two BYU professors (sociology and English respectively), whose contracts were not renewed, allegedly because Church leaders considered them too liberal for the conservative campus.

4. Peggy Fletcher Stack has been a religion writer for the *Salt Lake Tribune* since 1991.

5. Counterpoint is an annual conference, sponsored by the Mormon Women's Forum, that began in April of 1993 as an alternative conference to the BYU women's conference. From 1994 to the present, it is held in the fall.

6. Janice Allred, "My Controversy with the Church," *Mormon Women's Forum: A Feminist Quarterly* 6, no. 1. A short account of Janice's second disciplinary council, "On Being Excommunicated," appeared in Vol. 6, no. 3, of the quarterly. The full account of her disciplinary experiences, including the relevant documents, was published as "White Bird Flying: My Struggle for a More Loving, Tolerant, and Egalitarian Church," *Case Reports of the Mormon Alliance, Vol. 2, 1996* (Salt Lake City: Mormon Alliance, 1997).

7. Janice Allred, "Toward a Mormon Theology of God the Mother," in her *God the Mother and Other Theological Essays* (Salt Lake City: Signature Books, 1997), 43.

Chapter 7
Margaret Merrill Toscano

Assistant Professor of Classics at the University of Utah, excommunicated November 30, 2000.

Margaret Ann Merrill was born February 12, 1949. Part of a family that reaches back through Mormon history six generations on both sides, the young Margaret grew up as one of eight children—four daughters and four sons—all of whom took part in animated discussions about religion with their parents. Their father, John Arthur Merrill, was a soft-spoken and hard-working man dedicated to his family and the Church, while their mother, Lenna Peterson Merrill, was a gentle and deeply spiritual woman.

In 1967, eighteen-year-old Margaret entered Brigham Young University as a freshman to study English and history. She excelled in academics despite being a first-generation college student and was a voracious student of classics and early nineteenth-century Mormonism. The latter was an interest shared with Paul Toscano whom Margaret befriended and eventually married in 1978. While initially just friends, both Paul and Margaret became strongly attracted to the other's christocentric faith and willingness to question, and they accordingly spurred on each other's intellectual inquiry, which would carry Margaret through her academic studies.

Margaret graduated from BYU with a B.A. in English and an M.A. in classics, and taught classical languages at BYU from 1975 to 1989. During this time, Margaret began to explore the relationship between feminism and Mormonism, and this research culminated in numerous conference presentations throughout the 1980s. One paper of note, titled "The Missing Rib," was received at the 1984 Sunstone Symposium with great interest as a cutting-edge theological work.

Margaret later went on to help found the Mormon Women's Forum in 1988 and hosted a controversial panel in 1989 for the forum entitled "Women and the Priesthood." In response, the LDS Church cancelled all of her classes at BYU, so Margaret focused even more on completing her Ph.D. at the University of Utah where she has taught classics and comparative literature since 1996. This was just one instance of Margaret's harsh confrontations with her Church leaders due to her involvement in feminist and women's issues, not to mention the excommunication of her husband Paul in 1993. Seven years later, she too was excommunicated.

On July 6, 2003, I interviewed Margaret at her home in the suburbs of Salt Lake City, just a day after she sat in on my interview with Paul, listening to her husband relate his tumultuous past in Mormonism. In the account to follow, she shares her perspective on the events surrounding the September Six, the excommunication of her husband in 1993 and of her sister in 1995, her own excommunication in November of 2000, and her life outside the LDS Church ever since. The interview is eloquent and provoking.

The September Six

Philip: You were excommunicated seven years after your husband and the rest of the September Six. Perhaps we could discuss those events first. Is it true that on July 11, 1993, Kerry M. Heinz called you into his office and demanded that you stop writing, speaking, and publishing about the church?

Margaret: Yes.

Philip: Was that in response to a particular paper you had presented?

Margaret: Yes, I had done a slideshow called, "Images of the Female Body, Human and Divine," which was an exploration of feminine identity and female deity through archetypes and icons. Originally, I gave it at the Counterpoint Conference,[1] and some people liked it, so I was asked to give it for a feminist club at BYU, called

Voice, on June 15, 1993. There were about forty students on hand at the presentation, mostly women.

At that meeting there was a reporter from the *Daily Universe*, the student newspaper, who wrote a front-page article headlined something like, "Mormon Feminist Talks about God the Mother." Of course, the reporter quoted the most controversial things from the paper, and this got back to Apostle Boyd Packer, according to Kerry.

When Kerry called me in, he said, "I got a phone call from my friend Melvin Hammond,[2] who said Elder Packer asked him, 'Can't Kerry control that woman!?'" Packer had been angry, he said, and Kerry was embarrassed because he felt like he had fallen down on his duty to keep me under control. Kerry wasn't a dictator; I liked Kerry, but he was caught in a situation and decided to call me in after he talked to Packer himself.

Kerry told me, "You really shouldn't be talking about these kinds of things. I would like you to promise me that you will never talk about this topic again." Then he started questioning me about my views on whether or not women should have the priesthood. It started as a theological argument, but after about half an hour, he withdrew from that approach. It seemed he couldn't answer all the issues and evidence I was bringing up, so he switched directions and wanted to make it a matter of obedience. I should agree not to talk about these issues because he asked me to as my priesthood leader, but I just couldn't agree to be silent and thereby perpetuate a kind of community I didn't believe in. I don't believe in a community where people can't say what they feel, because I think it is damaging to spiritual growth and the free flow of the Spirit.

I have never tried to tell anyone that they must believe what I gave as my own opinion. And I never claimed my own ideas were Church doctrine. I was teaching the adult Sunday School class at the time and never brought up controversial stuff like this there, because it wouldn't have been appropriate. In my Sunday School class, I tried to preach the gospel and explore the scriptures. It wasn't like I was denying basic Church teachings either, saying that the Book of Mormon isn't true, Joseph Smith isn't a prophet, or Christ isn't Lord. I believed those things, but I also think that the gospel of Christ and him crucified isn't preached like it should be; women are second-class citizens, and "all is not well in Zion." If I ever said anything critical at Church meetings, it was about our failure as members to follow Christ's teachings. Mormons think that the gospel is legalistic, that one must follow every single nitpicky commandment, but salvation does not depend on not smoking, drinking, or having multiple piercings. People think things like these too often in the LDS Church, and it's damaging. You are not morally worse than anyone else just because you have a tattoo. Yet, even though I felt this way, I still wasn't saying the Church was false.

So, while on a certain level I was trying to change the Church to be more open for women and to show more charity and believe more in grace, I was not trying to subvert Church authorities. I just think it's spiritually damaging when people can't speak from their hearts and say what they really believe. It's damaging to promote a kind of group-think. Can't we love each other as brothers and sisters without agreeing on everything? How does that hurt the Church?

In actuality, there is a climate of fear that does hurt the Church and the members. I've talked with many people who are afraid to say what they really feel. All of these things came out in my discussion with Kerry.

Philip: Later, on August 5, 1993, you and Paul met with President Heinz and Bishop Wilson Martin to discuss your paper, "Images of the Female Body, Human and Divine." What took place at that meeting?

Margaret: Well, between July 11 and August 5, they sent me a formal letter; it was unbelievably restrictive and said I couldn't speak, discuss, publish, or write anything about Church history or doctrine in any forum or they would hold a court on me, with probable excommunication. It was so all-inclusive it was shocking. I couldn't communicate about anything, according to their demands. One paragraph even said, "This is not meant for everybody. This is just a personal command for you, and we ask you to obey us on the basis of faith." That precipitated the meeting with Paul and me on August 5. Paul's very intuitive, and he knew that I wouldn't back down, so he tried to draw the fire away from me by insulting Kerry so he wouldn't come after me. Paul was doing the savior thing.

Philip: So, after the Sunstone Symposium in August of 1993, the Church held a court on Paul in September, instead of you, because he insulted Kerry at your August 5 meeting?

Margaret: Yes, I'm certain that was his main reason for going after Paul first. Certainly we found out later that Packer wanted Paul out of the Church too, so it would have happened eventually, but maybe not first. It's not like I obeyed them though; I didn't stop writing or speaking. I gave a talk at the Sunstone Symposium later on in August that same summer. I was part of a panel that Maxine Hanks put together, with Michael Quinn and Linda Newell, called "If Women Have Had the Priesthood since 1843, Why Aren't They Using It?" The panel was even broadcast on the radio, and my part was later published in *Dialogue*.

Philip: So you specifically disobeyed the Church's ultimatum?

Margaret: I told them in that August 5 meeting that I wasn't going to obey—not because I wanted to be rebellious but because I could not in good conscience be silent. Freedom of speech is too basic to my sense of personal identity, so it's not something I could give up even if I wanted to. It's just so basic to anyone's spiritual development and individual growth that I felt it was wrong for them to ask me to give it up. I felt I would be participating in abuse and colluding with a wrong model of community if I agreed. I actually explained all of this both on that radio broadcast and later at a talk I gave at Harvard because I felt it was important that the issue itself be addressed publicly.[3] We need to talk about these kinds of problems.

Philip: And they still did not call a council on you?

Margaret: No, and I was very surprised they didn't. Bishop Martin told me a couple of years later that he was supposed to call a bishop's court on me but wouldn't. The Church hasn't called him to a leadership position since, though. So, Paul's technique worked marvelously in 1993. Kerry was very upset with all the personal insults Paul gave him, which made Paul a more satisfying target for Kerry than I was.

Later, in December of 1993, when Kerry read us a letter denying Paul's appeal of his excommunication, Kerry turned to me as we were walking outside and said, "I really should do something about your situation, too. It's something I need to take care of but haven't gotten around to it yet." I think, though, that by the time he finished with Paul, with all the publicity and uproar, Kerry just didn't want to deal with me. I don't think he would have done any of it on his own anyway without directions from above.

Philip: How did it make you feel when Paul tried to save you from excommunication by directing your stake president's attention toward himself?

Margaret: A part of me was really upset at him because I didn't want to be rescued, although I knew he did it out of concern for me. Why run in and try to rescue me? Let me speak for myself. I did feel upset that he rescued me because what ended up happening was that my voice, my person really, got lost for quite some time. Because I wasn't one of the September Six, people forgot about me. I felt subordinated to Paul by both the Church and the intellectual community. Yet, even though I wasn't excommunicated until 2000, I had essentially been excommunicated with Paul in 1993. The effect was the same in many ways because I couldn't function in the Church anymore. I was labeled as a bad person. Right after Paul was ex'ed, we even had a few people telephone us anonymously, saying that we were of the devil. While you know rationally that these kinds of people are a little wacky, it still makes you wonder what mainstream members think of you. I eventually had to get to the point where I stopped worrying about whether other people thought I was an evil sinner or not. But it's hard when you've tried to live an ethical life and be a good Mormon. For seven years I was still officially a member of the Church, but I couldn't function in it. And at the same time, I didn't have the status or honor of being someone who had stood up to the Church for personal conscience and truth. After the September Six happened, nobody asked me to speak anymore, and all my feminist work seemed to be forgotten for several years. This left me in limbo for the next seven years, feeling uncertain how to define myself. Was I Mormon or not?

I remember that, during Paul's court, our daughter Sarah, who was nine at the time, sat outside the stake president's office for the whole nine hours. Two days later, we were going to McDonald's, and

I asked everyone what they wanted. Sarah said, "I want some iced tea." I looked at her and asked, "Sarah—iced tea?" She said, "I'm not Mormon." The nine-year-old had already decided that she would never go back to the Church. In fact, none of the children wanted anything to do with the Church after Paul was excommunicated. I continued to attend meetings for two months after they kicked Paul out to say publicly, "I'm still part of this community." But one day Sarah came up to me and said that she felt I was betraying the family by going to church. So, I stopped going and obviously chose the family over the Church.

That was when I had to face a lot of stuff I didn't want to face, including my own anger. Growing up, I was always taught not to be angry, but I think it's a natural response when you're hurt, and it doesn't do any good to pretend otherwise. Facing my anger made me reexamine everything, including my own beliefs and motives.

Philip: Did you actually agree with your daughter Sarah that by attending church you were betraying the children?

Margaret: On a certain level maybe, because it's very hard to have a united family when people have strong but different feelings toward something as important as religion. I did stop going to church because of how Sarah and the other girls felt, but a part of me also had to acknowledge that I didn't want to be connected to this religion anymore either, because it was very abusive and not acting according to basic Christian principles. But still a part of me also wanted to keep going to show the Church, that, even though I'd been treated badly, I could still be a faithful member. But then I stopped going, and the reality of not being part of this thing that had been my whole life began to sink in. The weight of the loss and the feelings of grief were so enormous. I guess I thought that because I was a believer that things would go on as they had in some way without going to church. But they didn't, and eventually I even took off my garments, which was very hard.

Philip: When did you do that?
Margaret: 1996.
Philip: So you wore your garments even after you stopped going to church?

Margaret: Oh yes, because I took those garments and the covenants they represented very seriously. They were something between me and God rather than me and the Church. They were part of who I was, and I thought that not even excommunication could stop me from wearing them. I can certainly respect someone who decides to take this stance, just as I can respect those like Lavina and my sister Janice who continue to go to church every week. They will be faithful "members" no matter what. Part of me wanted to do the same thing, but I didn't and went through agony over my decision. I felt torn spiritually about who I was and what I wanted or believed.

From 1994 to 2002, I almost completely withdrew from the Mormon intellectual community, too, and became an academic recluse. Part of this was because I was trying to finally finish my Ph.D. But I didn't want to do much with Mormon scholarship either. In many ways I had shut down emotionally and didn't want to open old wounds. Publicly I didn't want to play the part of the excommunicated martyr. I even made self-deprecating jokes about not wearing garments so I could wear more fashionable clothes, but the reality is [weeping] I really had wanted to be God's priestess. I had felt this call in the temple, which is one thing my garments symbolized to me. For me to take off the garments . . . it was . . . I just wanted. . . .

[At this point, we took a break.]

Philip: Did your faith in the Church diminish after your husband was excommunicated in 1993?

Margaret: My faith in the Church diminished a lot. I thought (and still do) that God works through the Mormon Church and its people, and I believe there is a lot in Mormon theology that is an important addition to the Christian message. I just couldn't handle the authoritarianism. In my twenties, I believed more in obedience to Church leaders and also that what they said in general conference was often revelation. Gradually that all disappeared, especially after Paul's excommunication. I'm still not an anti-Mormon in any way and, in fact, often defend Mormonism at the University of Utah where some of my colleagues think it's mostly bad.

Philip: How did the excommunication of your sister Janice in 1995 affect you?

Margaret: It was like one more nail in the cross. It was very upsetting to me. I went to her trial as a witness and for emotional support. When she came out and told us that she had been excommunicated, I said, "I hate them," and ran out the door. I was so upset that I couldn't even think about how this sounded.

Janice is two years older than I am, and growing up, I always admired and respected her so much for her dedication to truth seeking and her strong desire to do what is right. From the time she was a little girl, she always read difficult books to stretch herself. She always had so much self-discipline, too; she's a real stoic and concerned with ethical purity. She is a truly good person and mother, so it hurt me a lot to see what they did to her and how it hurt her. In outward terms, she fit the model of the perfect Mormon mother, having nine children and never working outside the home, and she always obeyed Church rules faithfully, even small things like refraining from cola drinks (unlike me!).

Philip: Janice, like you, has done a lot of work on women's issues. Did you feel that her excommunication was one more hit to the feminist voice?

Margaret: Definitely, which was very discouraging. When we first started the Mormon Women's Forum in 1988, there was a lot of interest from many different kinds of Mormons, even BYU people, who wanted to participate in everything. The Mormon Women's Forum sought to create a middle ground where everyone could voice their views, whether they were feminists and intellectuals or more mainstream members. We wanted a space where both active members and estranged Mormons could dialogue. However, this ideal never really worked. And the more people that have been excommunicated, the more there is the feeling that you either have to stay in and shut up, or you have to leave. The excommunications have polarized the community in a very damaging way.

A lot of women have told both Janice and me, "I left the Church because of what happened to you. I could see the handwriting on the wall, that there is no place for a thinking woman who expresses concerns." The fallout has definitely extended beyond our personal situation. It creates a damaging climate. I can't tell you how many women have expressed these sentiments to me—lots. And lots have told me they have left over gender issues too.

The Excommunication

Philip: Can you explain the immediate events leading up to your excommunication in 2000?

Margaret: Yes. In November 1999, Dale Blake, my stake president here in the Salt Lake South Cottonwood Stake, whom I had never met before, called me into his office. It was a bizarre experience because he was grilling me while pretending he wasn't and acting all friendly while setting up the background for the disciplinary court. He kept mispronouncing my name—"Sister Tos-CAN-oh" rather than the more Italian "Tos-CAWN-oh." That was so annoying. A year later, in November of 2000, right after Thanksgiving, I got a phone call from the secretary to the stake president who said, "The stake president wants to see you again." I went in, and he handed me the summons letter to the court, which said . . .

Philip: Wait. What instigated the letter?

Margaret: That was the weird thing—we never knew. I had been very low profile. I had published a couple of things and was still working with the Mormon Women's Forum, but the forum had nearly disappeared because of the polarization. Women who were still interested in feminist issues said, "I don't care about the Church anymore." And women who were in the Church said, "I'm scared to come to the Forum." The Forum almost died. We barely kept it alive. So I had done almost nothing and was concentrating on my university work. The summons was totally out of the blue. It was very strange.

Personally, I think that they wanted me excommunicated in 1993 and that it took them seven years for several reasons. Kerry was supposed to hold a court on me but was too psychologically damaged. Bishop Martin wouldn't do it either, so the Church couldn't find a willing leader for a while.

I think the Church was also somewhat scared. They don't like negative press, and I think they were very afraid I was going to call in the media like Tom Murphy did. If Tom Murphy hadn't gone public, he would have been excommunicated. They thought I was going to do the same thing by bringing in the press and a big vigil, which we did for some of the September Six. I could have done this, but didn't want to.

Philip: Why not?

Margaret: There were three reasons. I didn't want to make a big deal out of my trial, because I didn't know how I felt about it and how I would explain it to others, so I didn't want it in the news at that time. I also didn't want to draw attention to myself because I was too emotionally exhausted with trying to finish my doctoral dissertation. Also, because of my children. After Paul was excommunicated, we had all this publicity and almost nonstop phone calls for over a month. The BBC from London called, this thing and that thing. The children had to face classmates at school, most of whom were Mormon. That was hard on them. In fact, when I got the summons, they said, "Oh no. Are we going to have to go through that again?"

"No way. I'm not putting you through that again," I said.

So I told nobody, other than my immediate family, our close friends the Voroses, and Lavina, because I wanted her to record the whole thing. Also, after being unofficially excommunicated back in 1993, I thought, "Let's just get this over with quickly. Shoot me. I'm done. Let's end the agony."

Philip: Going into the council meeting, did you know that you were going to be excommunicated?

Margaret: I pretty much knew it was already decided. They had given me the summons letter four days before the court, totally out of the blue. The charge was apostasy. They stated it like this: "You are reported to have been in apostasy." Well, who reported me? Who said I was an apostate? What had I done that was apostate? I confronted my stake president, Dale Blake, when he gave me the letter. "Sister Toscano, we don't need to discuss that now. We'll talk about that at the council." I said, "Have you been given any directions by anyone, such as the Strengthening Church Members Committee?"[4] He said, "Oh, Sister Toscano, it makes me feel so sad that you don't trust the Church. We wouldn't do something like that. We're going to start at seven o'clock sharp on Thursday night. You can bring two witnesses, but they have to be members in good standing, you have to give their names to your bishop by tomorrow night, and you have to tell exactly what their testimony is going to be." This seemed so unfair since he wasn't telling me anything about the charges. But since I decided right away not to take witnesses, I didn't protest. It seemed to me like my fate was already sealed. I didn't want to tell anybody because I felt very private about it. I just wanted to go by myself, but I did want to go. For some reason, I wanted them to have to face me. I wanted to know how they were going to handle the whole thing too.

When I got there, the whole building was dark. A man let me in because the door was locked. I found out later that it was dark and locked because they were afraid the press and Paul were going to show up, along with a big crowd of supporters. All the lights were off so nobody could see, and it was locked so nobody could get in. They were shocked that I came by myself. I waited five or ten minutes before President Blake came into the hall where I was. I then was led into a room to sit in a lone chair in front of the twelve high councilors in chairs arranged in a semi-circle. The stake president sat to my right at a table with his two counselors and the stake clerk, who was taking notes the whole time. I brought in a yellow writing pad and a pen, hoping to try and defend myself and write down notes at the same time.

The stake president was like the prosecuting attorney, the judge, and everything else all in one. He directed the whole thing, telling the high council from the beginning that I was an apostate. First, they all rose from their chairs when I entered and wanted to shake my hand. It was crazy because I knew I was going to be executed, and yet they're introducing themselves like we're at a ward social? It felt like a Kafka novel.[5]

In the two meetings we had before, the stake president was always a happy-go-lucky guy. As soon as we get into the court, all of a sudden he's a hard-hitting prosecuting attorney. Throughout the trial he had a typed script in front of him. He also had in front of him everything I'd written and published; they even had transcripts of a couple of talks that had never been circulated and had to have been taped at the time of delivery. There was almost everything I had done since 1984, even newspaper articles about me. This was a thorough research job, so they obviously had been building a case against me for years. And President Blake couldn't have done it alone.

The stake president read the definition of apostasy and asked me what my response was. I said, "I'm not guilty," and made a brief statement why I wasn't. They then brought in a surprise witness: Kerry Heinz. They asked him a few questions where Blake mostly tried to show that I had been disobedient to Heinz by not obeying his instructions to stop speaking and publishing. After Heinz left, Blake continued to present his case against me by going through my writings and showing both how I had not obeyed the order to be silent and how my writings themselves were dangerous, focusing mostly on the issues of Heavenly Mother and women and priesthood. I was not allowed to respond much as he proceeded. Once when I tried to defend myself against his attacks, the stake president stopped me in mid-sentence saying, "You will only speak if I give you permission. We will not allow you to lecture us." He was very stern and, frankly, kind of intimidating.

At the end of his presentation, he finally let me speak. I knew it wasn't going to do any good to argue doctrine because he had shown that was not his main concern, so I talked about the importance of free agency for moral choice and how it is vital to a healthy spiritual community—basically the notion that we can disagree and still love each other. I also talked about the distinction I made between speaking in academic forums and in Sunday School. I gave an impassioned speech about freedom of speech, which obviously got to them as I saw later from the questions and responses from the high council.

First, seven of them asked me questions, such as whether I intended to publish any more. Then they did the dividing thing ...

Philip: The drawing of lots?

Margaret: Yeah. Then Blake said, "To save time, we're going to have two people defend you and two people argue on the Church's side." One of the guys that defended me, who was the sweetest man, said, "I can tell that she has a testimony of Christ and that she has a good spirit." The other man that was supposed to defend me damned me with faint praise because he said, "There's the spirit of the law and the letter of the law. I think her intentions were right, so she is innocent by the spirit, but she did something wrong by not obeying her priesthood leader. Therefore, she is guilty by the letter of the law." Basically, he gave the same argument that the two people against me gave.

The first man arguing for the Church said, "She is leading people astray, and we have to protect the purity of the Church. If we let her stay in the Church, then the purity of the Church is damaged." "What purity?" I thought, but I had no chance to respond. The second man repeated the fact that I had disobeyed my priesthood leaders, thus showing my apostasy.

I was then led out while they deliberated for half an hour. When I came back in, they said, "Well you're nice, and you're respectful, but you're also excommunicated." I thought, "If I am such a nice and delightful person, then why are you barring me from heaven!?" It just didn't make sense.

The main argument for my excommunication during the disciplinary council was that I had disobeyed Church leaders. However, the official letter later added to this by saying I had promoted pernicious doctrine and damaged the testimonies of Church members. Evidence for the second claim had never been given at the council.

The whole thing was three-and-a-half hours long, from 7:00 to 10:30 P.M. At the end they told me that I couldn't have any of the privileges of membership, pay tithing, speak in Church or even make comments, speak at a funeral, participate in the Church in any way, or even wear garments.

I get up to leave, and they all wanted to shake my hand again and talk to me. I was exhausted. This had been devastating. I just wanted to leave. It's like, "You just sent me to hell, and you want to shake my hand and tell me you actually enjoyed some of my writings!?" It was bizarre. Then the stake president walked me out to my car, and that's when he told me, "Oh, we were afraid your husband was going to come and be belligerent, because Kerry Heinz told us how protective he is of you. We also thought you might have a vigil." He spoke with relief, implying, "You made it so easy for us."

Philip: How did you feel the moment you walked out the door?

Margaret: My first feeling was relief. The mercy killing was over. I was emotionally drained and happy to be gone. I was no longer in limbo. When I got home, Paul and my four daughters were all waiting, as well as a couple of family friends. We ate pastries, and I told them what happened. They were constantly making jokes to cheer me up.

Since the trial was on a Thursday, I still had my 9:00 A.M. Latin class the next morning. I had promised myself I wasn't going to cry, but I couldn't stop crying when I got up the next morning, which was going to make it really hard to teach. So I did this girl's trick: When you have been crying but want to pretend that you haven't, then you slap your face, wash it with cold water, and put on lots of make-up. That allowed me to teach my class looking really strong. Nobody knew what had happened. As soon as the class was over, I started crying again and couldn't stop for three days. It was at the end of the semester, so I had stacks of papers to grade and finals to give. I was teaching three classes, still working on my dissertation, had Christmas to prepare for my family, and was just trying not to have an emotional breakdown.

The Status of Women in the Church

Philip: In the chapter "Women, Ordination, and Hierarchy" in your book *Strangers in Paradox*, co-authored with Paul, you state: "The scriptures contain nothing claiming priesthood is inherently and unalterably linked with maleness." However, Mormon prophets, who are perceived to be the divine mouthpieces of God, are unified in declaring that the priesthood is for males alone. How can you disagree? Couldn't there be a divine reason that the priesthood is only for males that you are not aware of?

Margaret: There could always be a divine reason that I'm not aware of, but for me the underlying question was this, "Why do you think it's dangerous for me to talk about this issue?" I always said that I could be wrong and that I was only giving my opinion. How could that be dangerous when I have no authority?

Besides, the Mormon prophets have not been unified on the idea that priesthood is only for men. Certainly, both Joseph Smith and

Brigham Young taught publicly that priesthood belongs to women as well. When I talked to current Church leaders, they were not willing to deal with the historical documents. They weren't willing to say, "Yes, I admit that Joseph Smith said that, but we have had another revelation and this is what holds now." They would say there was never a revelation, and I felt that such disingenuousness was disturbing. They were not being honest and were telling people not to bring certain topics up simply because they didn't want to deal with the issues.

It is true that finally in my excommunication letter the stake president told me, "No statement of Joseph Smith or the scriptures outweighs the current prophet." He never gave me a chance to respond to that idea. I feel that if there is a new revelation that contradicts Joseph Smith or the scriptures on something, there has to be an acknowledgement of the change and a stated reason for it. It has to fit in with the other pieces of our doctrine, or truth means nothing and we have no foundation for belief or action. As the Apostle Paul said, "An angel cannot bring a different gospel."[6]

Philip: Why would you want to be part of a church that you disagree with?

Margaret: There are a lot of things that I agree with, both in the doctrine and in the practice. Besides, this was my heritage, and I'm connected to the people and feel they do a lot of good. But I don't want to be part of it anymore. I don't want to go back. I couldn't go back to what it is now because of the authoritarianism, the anti-intellectualism and dishonesty about the Church's history, their treatment of gay people, their continued racism, and their subordination of women.

Do you know that Heavenly Mother has fewer rights in the Church than Mormon women? Some Mormon women think *they* have it bad—look at Heavenly Mother! She is locked in a closet. We're not even supposed to talk about her. What kind of a husband doesn't let the kids talk to their mom?

Philip: But Mormons would respond that they don't speak of Heavenly Mother out of respect.

Margaret: You think it's respectful to lock a woman up, not mention her name, and act as though she doesn't exist? Is that respectful?

Philip: The explanation is that, because Heavenly Father has been mistreated by human beings taking his name in vain, he does not want Heavenly Mother to receive the same treatment.

Margaret: I know, but this really upsets me. I've heard that explanation a thousand times, but it's patronizing and makes God look like a controlling patriarch. Do you think that God is so petty that he is enraged every time someone uses his name in something other than a reverent context—if we say, "Oh God, I hate you. I hate this world. I hate everything!"? Students get mad at me as a teacher. Sometimes because they get mad at the system and because I'm the one in charge, they take their anger out on me. I would hope I'm mature enough to handle that. And I think a loving Heavenly Mother could handle her children's pain and frustrations and swearing without feeling that her dignity was slighted.

Philip: Are the Ten Commandments wrong then when they say not to take the Lord's name in vain?[7]

Margaret: No, but what does it mean to take God's name in vain? I'll tell you what I think it means (and I hold the name of God sacred): To take God's name in vain is to tell somebody in the name of God that they should do something when it's not God speaking. To speak in God's name to justify going out to kill nations. That's taking God's name in vain. It's what people do in the name of God to justify their sins. That's taking God's name in vain.

Philip: Can you summarize why the LDS Church should open up the priesthood to women?

Margaret: Well, first I think I need to clarify that I didn't start out as a feminist who was trying to import "worldly" ideas into the Church. I didn't start with the idea that women should have the priesthood and then begin looking for evidence. My process was just the opposite. All the leaders thought I was trying to impose feminist notions on the Church, but my question started out as, "Does God want me to be subordinate to men? And if so, why would God want that of me?"

At first I accepted that God had decreed women weren't to have the priesthood, according to present Church teachings. It hurt me, but I felt I had to accept God's role for me because I wanted to do what was right. Then in trying to understand and learn more, I changed my views. Going through the temple was part of this process because the rituals there connect women with priesthood, and I felt personally endowed with priesthood there through the Spirit of God. And then I found statements by Joseph Smith, Brigham Young, and others saying that women had received the priesthood through the endowment in Nauvoo in 1843. Then I examined Christianity, with the help of other Christian feminists, and came to the conclusion that women should have the priesthood just because of the equality that the gospel calls for. St. Paul says, "In Christ Jesus there is neither male nor female."[8] I came to believe it was a just concept, one that was in accordance with the gospel.

I came to believe that priesthood is not simply the right to have leadership in the Church, but it deals with spirituality and the use of spiritual gifts. In *Strangers*, there is a chapter called the "Nature and Purpose of the Priesthood" where we argue that Joseph Smith's teachings on one level are similar to Martin Luther's notion of a priesthood of all believers. Joseph defines priesthood as connecting a person with the Spirit of God. In his view, when you receive the Holy Ghost, you receive a portion of God's Spirit, and the process of becoming more sanctified in the Spirit is a process of receiving more and more of God's Spirit, which is ultimately receiving the priesthood. When you look at it that way, it seems ridiculous that women would be excluded because it would exclude them from full sanctification.

So, to go back to your original question, I think the LDS Church should open up the priesthood to women for several reasons. First, I believe it is a revelation from God to the Church through Joseph Smith and that the fullness of the priesthood and gospel cannot function without women exercising their God-given priesthood. Second, it is unjust to withhold it from women because it violates the gospel principles of equality and reciprocity. Women cannot be full citizens in the kingdom of God without it. Having an organization where every decision is made by male priesthood leaders, which is true in the Church today, means that women's voices are not heard. The men just assume that they know what women want without actually letting them speak for themselves. Third, women have enormous spiritual gifts that they can contribute to the Church, which they need the priesthood to exercise. If all the leadership is men, then women's gifts are not used fully in the way they could be, which ultimately robs the Church. And finally, it comes down to women's self-esteem. They have no spiritual role models. They think, "I have motherhood, my husband has priesthood, so he is my spiritual leader." They don't even see themselves as the spiritual equals of men like President Hinckley or able to speak in God's name.

I know what mainstream members will answer to this argument. If all of this were true, we would hear it from the present prophet. But is this really so? What about the history of blacks and the priesthood in the Church? Joseph Smith never withheld the priesthood from blacks. There were several black men who held the Melchizedek Priesthood under Joseph Smith, men like Elijah Abel. Then Brigham Young, who was very prejudiced, decided to change the policy on priesthood. He didn't take it away from Elijah Abel, however, because Brigham wouldn't go against Joseph directly, but he would never let Elijah hold a priesthood office in the Church. Then racial statements by Brigham Young started coming from the pulpit, and all of a sudden everyone began to believe that it's God's will to withhold the priesthood from black men. When the revelation came in 1978 to reverse this policy, no one could admit the previous policy was a mistake. They just said, "We don't know why God withheld the priesthood from the Blacks." I can tell you why: because of the prejudice of the people. God *didn't* withhold it. Joseph Smith gave it! The Church didn't want to admit that it had made a mistake because that would mean that Brigham Young made a mistake, and that means current leaders could be wrong too. The Church doesn't want the members to have the ability to question it and make their own decisions on things. That is wrong! I'm not saying that I couldn't be wrong on the issue of women and priesthood. But I shouldn't have been punished for exploring this issue.

Reflection

Philip: Do you think your excommunication was justified?

Margaret: According to their definition of apostasy, I was an apostate because they defined it as anyone who disobeys a Church leader for any reason. They defined an apostate in my court by saying that it's someone who doesn't do something his or her stake president has asked, no matter what it is. Kerry Heinz told me not to speak, and I did. So, by their definition, I am an apostate; by their definition I am dangerous to the Church because they see public disagreement with Church policies as harmful to members' view of a sanitized, unified religion. I don't buy their definition at all. I think what they did was wrong, both to me personally and also to the larger Church community. It allows no room for disagreeing with a Church leader about even unsettled questions. When I disagreed, I was polite about it! I tried to show respect for authorities while disagreeing with them.

After being excommunicated, I tried to sever my ties with Mormonism by standing in front of the mirror and saying the word "fuck" without choking. I wanted to distance myself from that veneer of niceness that often characterizes Mormon culture—and certainly my disciplinary council. Politeness can be a way of cutting off discussion about very real problems that need to be worked on for healing. I've worked hard at not being nice because the problem with niceness is that it can cover up violence, like it did at my court. I tried to be very nice in that disciplinary council. Actually, I didn't try—I was trained that way from childhood; it wasn't hard.

People have said Paul deserved his excommunication because he was not nice. He was rude even to leaders. I don't think he deserved excommunication any more than I did. Neither one of us intended to harm the Church. We both cared about it very, very deeply. We wanted the best for the Church and tried to act in a way that could help it be more true to its Christian principles. What they did to me in the disciplinary council was violent. If they really believe that excommunication cuts a person off from heaven, they shouldn't inflict it on someone unless they think that person is pretty horrible. They told me I was nice. Don't tell me I'm nice if I'm so dangerous. Don't pretend to be nice to me when you're inflicting serious harm on me.

Philip: Did you ever try a different church after leaving the LDS Church?

Margaret: No. For me excommunication was like a divorce after a really bad marriage. You're not really anxious to jump into another one. I avoided entering into any new or close relationships or a spiritual community after that because I was pretty damaged from my sense of betrayal. I felt that things would eventually fall apart as people betray you and you betray them. It's been painful and frustrating. I was so wounded after leaving the LDS Church that I would go to some public meeting and get physically ill. I would have a physical reaction to the spiritual wounds and, of course, a spiritual reaction as well. Who knows if that will always be so, but that's how it has been. I have no desire to find another spiritual community.

Philip: From the mid-1980s on, you didn't hesitate to publicly address controversial issues in the Church, such as Heavenly Mother or the patriarchal status of the priesthood. Didn't you ever worry that such activities could result in excommunication, even before the events of 1993?

Margaret: When I gave my first paper, "The Missing Rib" [1984], I was just trying to pursue an issue that was really important to me personally. I never thought it would cause a stir. I was just naively pursuing what I thought was truth, and I was astonished when everybody was amazed at the paper. I had never thought of myself as an activist. Of course, on some level I always knew there was danger because you sense the taboos in the Church, and Paul and I had some run-ins with leaders. But I felt the issues I was talking about were important and that my writing clearly showed my belief in Mormonism. Besides, I was never controversial in Church meetings.

By the time we got to the Kerry Heinz conflict in 1993, I knew that I didn't want to lose my membership and that it was likely. So I was really tormented. There was a part of me that thought maybe I should be quiet because my membership means so much, but I just felt like I couldn't do that in good conscience. It would be betraying my deepest spiritual convictions. For me, silencing people really does promote something very, very bad. It's unhealthy for a community. I was torn, very torn. But there does come a time where you feel like the die has been cast and you're on death row, so there is no need to hold anything back because you're going to be killed anyway. That happened in 1993, but it had been a process. I also eventually got to the point where I realized I had to show opposition, because not to speak out against injustice is to support the injustice. I felt I had previously done that in racial matters and didn't want to do that again. I couldn't just be quiet.

Philip: In *Strangers*, you refer to Joseph Smith's statement that "by proving contraries, truth is made manifest." And then you expound upon that statement by saying, "In other words by examining various, even contrary views, new truths may be revealed."[9] Do you believe it's the duty of members rather than Church officials to make doctrinal assessments for the Church? Should everyone examine contrary views so they can reveal new truth to the Church at large?

Margaret: Yes, I do believe that everyone should examine truth, but I wouldn't say that it should be members rather than leaders. I just think members have an equal duty, which would be one of the areas where I disagree with current leaders. I don't see how examining contraries is going to hurt the Church, as long as people aren't trying to force their ideas on others. One of the flaws in the theory of having a living prophet who gets revelation as a solution to life's problems is that he can't be with all the members all the time to tell them what they should do or think. And if he did, then you would remain a child. God doesn't do that with us either. We are constantly dealing with conflicts and issues that the scriptures don't make clear. Struggling with such difficulties is a process one must go through to become a mature spiritual adult. Wisdom *is* proved in the contraries.

One of the damaging things in the Church is the model of priesthood hierarchy that keeps people in a childlike, immature state. That is very damaging because it lets people avoid responsibility for their own moral, spiritual lives. They think they should be told everything that they are allowed to do, like what to wear, or read, and what movies to watch. They are afraid to think for themselves about complex questions.

Philip: According to you, then, why should there even be Church leaders?

Margaret: To lead us to Christ. On one level, I've overstated my position. If you don't have somebody in charge of an organization, then things don't get done. There's always a point where somebody's got to say, "We're going to do this in this way." It's very hard to rule by consensus. So you need somebody to make decisions on a day-to-day level. You can't have a democratic vote about every little thing. And there need to be general policies and doctrines that define the Church. I'm not against that; I just think there should be room for dissent and minority opinions.

Power issues come up in every human situation. If they're not stated and clear, if there is not some kind of a structure, then it all goes underground. You must delineate how the power is running, because the power issues don't disappear. But we don't want to admit that power ever gets abused in a Church context.

Philip: Was Joseph Smith a prophet?

Margaret: I definitely think he was inspired, but I don't like the term "prophet" because it has come to mean an infallible leader in the Church today, someone who always talks to God and speaks for God in a simple linear fashion. I don't think anybody speaks for God like that. I think revelation is more complicated. And I think you can be a prophet and make a lot of mistakes. I believe in visionaries and in people who have inspiration and are touched by the divine, and then try to communicate the divine to other human beings. Joseph was certainly a prophet in that sense, really the most prophetic leader we've had. I've always liked him because he is flawed and complex—and luminous.

Philip: Do you consider yourself Mormon?

Margaret: I do. I think "Mormon" is more of a cultural thing, while "LDS" is about membership in the Church. I'm no longer LDS, but I'm still Mormon.

If I hadn't believed so much, it wouldn't have hurt so much to be kicked out. I think that when you have invested a lot of yourself into something, then being kicked out hurts more. I am not as certain of my beliefs as I used to be, so it's harder for me to define myself. I have been in an existential crisis, and there is a part of me that wants to reject everything because of the hurt. I do believe in the human soul though; I believe in God, or at least some kind of divine purpose. I believe that human beings are complex, that language, laughter, and relationships are all so complex and important. Life cannot be reduced to the merely physical, to molecules, but I do have more questions than I have answers.

Philip: How have your thoughts and feelings toward the Church and the events that occurred changed since your excommunication?

Margaret: I think I'm starting to heal a little bit. I was deeply wounded, more than I'll ever let anyone know. I was so deeply wounded spiritually and emotionally that I had to shut down. I think I'm getting healthier now, but it has been very slow.

Philip: Final question: do you miss the Church?

Margaret: Yes. Part of it, I really do miss. I still find myself defending Mormonism. It has a lot of good, and certainly it's no worse than most other religions. I very much dislike ignorant slander against the Church. I think there's a lot of good stuff you miss when you're not part of the organization. But, as I said before, I have no desire to go back. I don't feel that I could fit in anymore and certainly don't want to be in a place that rejects me so much and that I am so unhappy in. I'm not a masochist. And I don't want to support something that damages people because of its narrow-mindedness about so many important issues.

I felt that God called me to try to make a difference, but it didn't work. The Church is more closed now than it was in 1984 when I gave "The Missing Rib." There seemed to be more hope and equality for women and their voices then. Since then, there's been a backlash. I didn't make a difference, and that's painful, but I don't want to go back.

Notes

1. The Counterpoint Conference was organized in response to the actions of the BYU Women's Conference committee. The committee had rejected the proposal that Pulitzer Prize-winning author Laurel Thatcher Ulrich serve as keynote speaker for the upcoming conference due to many earlier, allegedly controversial publications. So a small group of women organized an alternative conference, the Counterpoint Conference, in April of 1993. From 1994 to the present, the conference has been held in the fall.

2. F. Melvin Hammond was sustained a member of the Second Quorum of the Seventy April 1, 1989, then was named to the First Quorum of the Seventy April 3, 1993, where he served until age seventy.

3. The talk, titled "Outsiders Within," was given in November 2003 to the Women's Studies in Religion Program at Harvard. The presentation can be viewed online at http://www.hds.harvard.edu/wsrp/scholarship/rfmc/video/speakervid5_3.htm.

4. According to Apostle Dallin H. Oaks, the Strengthening Church Members Committee is a "clipping service" that "pores over newspapers and other publications and identifies members accused of crimes, preaching false doctrine, criticizing leadership or other problems. That information is forwarded on to the person's bishop or stake president, who is charged with helping them overcome problems and stay active in the Church." Quoted in "News: Six Intellectuals Disciplined for Apostasy," *Sunstone* 92 (November 1993): 69. The First Presidency further clarified the nature and history of the Strengthening Church Members Committee when it stated, "This committee serves as a resource to priesthood leaders throughout the world who may desire assistance on a wide variety of topics. It is a General Authority committee, currently comprised of Elder James E. Faust and Elder Russell M. Nelson of the Quorum of the Twelve Apostles. They work through established priesthood channels, and neither impose nor direct Church disciplinary action." Quoted in "News: Church Defends Keeping Files on Members," *Sunstone* 88 (August 1992): 63. Many of those called in for investigatory interviews or discipline have claimed that this committee is responsible for compiling incriminating evidence against targeted members.

5. Franz Kafka (1883–1924) was a Jewish novelist from Austria famous for his anxiety-ridden portrayals of social situations.

6. "But though we, or an angel from heaven, preach any other gospel unto you than that which we have preached unto you, let him be accursed" (Gal. 1:8).

7. "Thou shalt not take the name of the Lord thy God in vain; for the Lord will not hold him guiltless that taketh his name in vain" (Ex. 20:7).

8. "There is neither Jew nor Greek, there is neither bond nor free, there is neither male nor female: for ye are all one in Christ Jesus" (Gal. 3:28).

9. Margaret and Paul Toscano, *Strangers in Paradox: Explorations in Mormon Theology* (Salt Lake City: Signature Books, 1990), 3.

Chapter 8
Thomas W. Murphy

Professor and chair of anthropology at Edmonds Community College, nearly excommunicated in December 2002, proceedings halted indefinitely on February 23, 2003.

Thomas W. Murphy was born on August 14, 1967, in Los Angeles, California into a strong Mormon household. His mother, Cheryl Harmon, a product of Mormon pioneer heritage, had been born and raised in the Church, while his father, Roy Murphy, had converted in part to marry her. Within a couple of years, the family returned to southern Idaho, where both his parents had originated. Then, when Tom was seven, his parents divorced, leading to his moving back to Burley, Idaho, in 1968.

It was in Burley that Tom, between the ages of seven and ten,[1] attended the family's LDS ward, though more out of habit than personal volition. Accordingly, he was baptized at the age of eight but considers doing so largely because it was expected of him. It was not until being inspired by his bishop, who told him that he would one day be a Church leader, that Tom began to seriously consider his place in Mormonism. In Pocatello, Idaho, his family's next move, Tom's reflections resulted in a focused effort to obey every rule and commandment. He would also serve in a variety of leadership roles before the age of eighteen, including deacons' quorum president, senior patrol leader in the Boy Scouts, teachers' quorum president, and seminary class president. Tom strove to be the model Mormon teenager.

Despite such intense Church involvement, Tom's adolescence was not free of doubts. He was deeply affected by his experience in debate as a junior in high school, which required him to argue all sides of an issue. This approach demolished what he calls his "black and white view of the world." Simplicity gave way to complexity and blind faith to intellectual rigor. Tom was then introduced by a friend to Ed Decker's scathing anti-Mormon work *The God Makers*. Claims that Joseph Smith slept with teenagers, that Mormons took orders from Satan, and that the temple ceremony demanded blood-oath covenants motivated Tom to look beyond the surface level of this faith to which he had committed himself. Then occurred one of the many defining moments for Tom's relationship to Mormonism.

In seminary class, the teacher, a member of Tom's local ward and a good friend of his mother's, lost his temper and kicked one of Tom's fellow students. Tom shared his concerns with his mother and refused to return to seminary until the issue was addressed. His mother defended the teacher against Tom's accusations and punished him for obstinacy. As a result, Tom quit attending church.

In his senior year of high school, after his family had moved to St. Anthony, Idaho, Tom met a vibrant freshman from the Church-owned Ricks College (now BYU-Idaho) named Kerrie Sumner, daughter of a career Church Educational System employee. The two dated, quickly fell in love, and married on September 5, 1985, not long after Tom graduated from South Fremont High School. While they were dating, Tom had a second major confrontation with the Church that began to undermine his belief that leaders were guided by the Holy Spirit.

One night, Tom and Kerrie were working together at McDonald's when a vicious winter storm hit. Tom and his brother, Greg, struggled to drive Kerrie home through heavily falling snow. By the time they reached her apartment, return was impossible—and, despite Ricks College regulations, Kerrie invited them to stay the night. Her roommates duly told the local bishop that Tom and his brother had stayed over and added the unsubstantiated claim that Kerrie was a drug dealer. When Kerrie went to the bishop to explain, he told her that, through divine inspiration, he knew that she was having an inappropriate relationship and was in fact a drug dealer. The bishop was plainly mistaken. Kerrie and Tom had a chaste relationship, and Kerrie had not—and still never has—touched, let alone used or sold, an illegal drug.

This misguided claim of divine inspiration watered the nascent seeds of anti-authoritarian sentiment for Tom and Kerrie alike, though they did return to church within a year of their marriage in hopes of rekindling their faith, and their only child, Jessyca, was born soon thereafter. The couple's renewed attachment to Mormonism, however, was sharply strained when they were sealed in the temple in April of 1988, where the following interview picks up.

I interviewed Tom in his office at Edmonds Community College on September 11, 2003. Books crammed the shelves on every wall and stood in piles on the floor. Tom's inviting nature made the informal atmosphere that much more pleasant. In black jeans, a green Seattle Mariners shirt, and spiked hair, Tom cordially offered me a seat. He then leaned back in his office chair and related his story.

Seeds of Doubt and the September Six

Tom: Kerrie and I went through the temple to be sealed in 1988. Beforehand, I suppressed any doubts that I had about the faith and actually got quite enthusiastic about the Church, but the temple was a traumatic experience. First, I realized that Ed Decker hadn't made it all up. Some of the things he said were actually pretty accurate.

Philip: Well, he had been a temple worker before leaving the Church.

Tom: Yeah, and his being right was a shock for me. Mormons do follow instructions from Satan! We do swear to slit our throats if we reveal the temple rite—bizarre. Kerrie and I also had a horrible experience in the temple with regard to our daughter, Jessyca, which brought up a lot of issues for me. Jessyca was young then, not quite two years old, and was still nursing. All morning she had been in the nursery while we were going through the endowment ceremony. As we were going into the sealing room we saw the altar and all these people dressed up in white to watch, and we were dressed in white. Everybody looked unusual, and it shocked Jessyca who had just come out of the nursery. So she started crying. Kerrie tried to console her short of nursing by taking her out in the hall and bringing her back in, but she would immediately start crying upon reentering the sealing room. So the temple worker told me to hold her down on the altar so they could perform the sealing . . . and . . . and I did it. The guilt for doing that is still with me to this day.

Afterwards, the temple worker said that the Church doesn't usually force children to do something, but this was just too important. For me, though, that brought up a lot of issues, because my stepfather had been physically abusive, and I felt that holding Jessyca down was abusive. I wasn't beating her or doing something that would be considered child abuse by the letter of the law, but it felt like abuse, ethically.

My way of dealing with the child abuse I had experienced was to agree with Kerrie not to physically punish our child, and I never did. I never spanked Jessyca; I never physically punished her. I was afraid that if I started down that track of physical punishment, then I wouldn't be able to control myself. So, I set a high bar that was lowered when I held Jessyca down on the altar to perform the ceremony. I was using physical force in a way that I was uncomfortable with. That was very emotionally traumatic for me, and it became a turning point. It didn't have an immediate effect. We still kept on going to church, but it all began to build up.

At the time we were sealed, Kerrie and I were managing a popcorn store in Davenport, Iowa, and one of the regular customers was a Christian guy whom we got into lots of discussions with. He kept telling me things like there is no archeological evidence to support the Book of Mormon, and I didn't believe him. So, he brought in a couple of books for me to read, like Walter Martin's *Kingdom of the Cults* . . .

Philip: Ah, a classic . . .

Tom: Yeah, and also Thelma Geer's *Mormonism, Mama & Me*. I read them along with that book on the Salamander letter.[3] The salamander book impacted me more than the *Kingdom of the Cults* book, because it was written by Mormons who were balanced in their approach to the subject. Martin and Geer obviously had an agenda, and I was skeptical of many of their claims.

All these books began to raise questions for me, and I decided to embrace the typical Mormon response—prayer. I remember as a kid praying to get a testimony of the gospel, and nothing really happened. So, now as an adult, I started praying harder than ever to get this confirmation. I was a believer, but I didn't know for a surety that it was true.

I prayed and prayed . . . nothing. And you know how, in Mormonism, there is a scripture in Doctrine and Covenants that says if you get a stupor of thought then something is not true, whereas if you get a burning in your bosom then something is true.[4] I wanted that burning in the bosom, but what I got didn't feel like a burning in the bosom *or* a stupor of thought. It didn't feel like anything.

One evening, I decided to be more patient because I found myself rushing through my prayers. After a while, though, I ran out of things to say and just sat there to see if anything would happen. Then, as I was kneeling, a thought started creeping into my mind: What if the Church isn't true? What if it really is *not* true? So I asked if the Church wasn't true, and for the first time, I felt something! My spine tingled, and my hair stood up, which stunned me, because it was totally unexpected. That was the crucial climax: the experience in the temple, the books, and the conversations with this Christian friend had all built up the pressure to that moment. The response still didn't make sense though. How could I follow scripture, do the prayer, and get the opposite response? It didn't make sense and still doesn't. I still wonder.

Anyway, the prayer freed me up to explore the issues in Mormonism in a way that I never could have before. I started reading everything I could find on Mormonism voraciously and eventually quit going to church early in 1989. I entered the University of Iowa that fall. That's when I read Fawn Brodie for a research paper in a history course.[5] After reading Brodie, I was pretty certain, not just emotionally but intellectually, that the Church wasn't true.

Philip: Did you complement Brodie's work with any of the Mormon responses?[6]

Tom: Not initially, but eventually I did. I wouldn't be exposed to much of the scholarly literature until after returning from the Gulf

War. I was activated in November of 1990 and went over to the Gulf very clearly not a believer. In fact, I took the statement "there are no atheists in a foxhole" as a personal challenge. I wanted to be that atheist. I'm not sure if I would describe myself as an atheist today, but I surely did at that time.

I believe that gods are, at the very least, powerful social forces. It isn't that I don't believe in God or gods, but I believe in them as something different than other people do. I agree with one thing Carol Delaney recently said while speaking at Edmonds Community College, "Calling yourself an atheist is a cop-out, because it allows you to walk away from the hard questions."[7] I agree, but have always hesitated to publish it . . . so here I am telling you [laughing]!

After returning from the Gulf War, we were having financial difficulties, so we went to the Church for financial help. I was very impressed and still am with the Church's social programs. It is one of the great things about Mormonism. But the way the Mormon welfare program works is that you don't simply get a handout; you always have to do something in return. What the bishop asked my family to do in return was very, very clever: We had to set up chairs for church every week, which meant that we had to go! [laughing] So, we went to church on a regular basis, and that's when we started talking very seriously about difficult issues with a member of the bishopric, whom I'd rather not name because he's still there.

I told him that my anthropology classes had raised lots of questions about the truthfulness of the Book of Mormon. He responded by saying, "Oh, I believe the Book of Mormon is a nineteenth-century document." I was stunned. Here is a member of the bishopric who doesn't believe a key element of what I thought was necessary to be considered a Mormon! He didn't think that Joseph Smith actually translated the Book of Mormon from ancient plates! This leader is in fact the one who introduced us to much of the alternative Mormon literature like *Sunstone* and *Dialogue*, and we began going to the Sunstone Symposiums in 1992.

After Kerrie and I had finished repaying the loan to the Church, we had a conversation in our car to decide whether or not we wanted to continue going. We asked Jessyca about her thoughts. She told us that she was really uncomfortable at church for a couple of reasons. First, her Primary teacher had told her that women aren't supposed to work outside the home. Jessyca knew that her mom was going to school and had worked outside the home, and couldn't see what was wrong with that. We said that the Church does teach that, but we don't believe it. The other thing she mentioned was that in Primary they said that dark skin was a curse from God, that the Lamanites were cursed, and one of her best friends was from Venezuela and had darker skin. We told her that we didn't believe that either and that she shouldn't feel like she had to. She replied, "If you don't believe this stuff, then why do you go to church?" We couldn't answer that question to her satisfaction or our own, so we quit going.

This is about the same time as the September Six, which was a crucial episode for me. At the same time that the liberal Mormons at Sunstone were reaching out to us, they were being pushed out of the Church. If the September Six hadn't happened and my daughter hadn't asked that question, then we still might be going to church, because there were so many aspects that we liked. I know I enjoyed the social atmosphere, the people, the opportunities to serve, and the teaching (I taught Sunday School). We even had people in our Iowa City Ward who were very open and tolerant of alternative points of view, including this member of the bishopric, and I was impressed. But when the September Six were kicked out, I suddenly felt very unwelcome and pessimistic about the ability of those people in the Church whom I admired to make the changes I thought the Church so desperately needed. We haven't been active since they were kicked out, except while living and conducting research with Mormon communities in Guatemala and Mexico.[8]

Philip: Why did you attend Church at that point?

Tom: As part of my research. Cultural anthropologists employ participant observation as our primary methodology, so participation was a vital component of my investigation.

The Research

Philip: The Church commenced disciplinary proceedings against you because of your controversial DNA research. Can you describe the two geographic schemas, the hemispheric and limited geography models, both of which your research claims to refute?

Tom: The traditional Mormon view is that the Book of Mormon accounts for all or nearly all of the genetic ancestry of the Native American Indians. That is called the hemispheric model, and that's what's still taught and remains in the Introduction to the Book of Mormon—that the Lamanites are the principal ancestors to the American Indians.[9]

In the twentieth century, a number of scholars have proposed a limited geography model, which states that the Book of Mormon assigns Middle Eastern ancestry only to a smaller regional group of Indians. The main reason they argue for this is because the archeological evidence shows that there were people here long before what's mentioned in the Book of Mormon, and also that they came from somewhere other than the Middle East, most likely Asia. So, in order to accommodate the archeological evidence and some internal contradictions in the Book of Mormon about things like population growth, Mormon scholars have narrowed the Book of Mormon's claim down to a small area of Central America.

The genetic evidence clearly refutes the idea that people from the Middle East of any background were principal ancestors of the American Indians, as a whole or in a particular region of Central America. There are *no* Middle Eastern genetic markers found in any region of the Americas. This genetic evidence refutes both the hemispheric and regional models. I published these findings first online on mormonscripturestudies.com in August of 2001 and then in *American Apocrypha* in May of 2002.[10]

Philip: You briefly alluded to an assertion you have made elsewhere, namely that there is no archeological or numismatic evidence that attests to the population growth purported in the Book of Mormon. Yet, isn't the archeological evidence rather scant in this regard, illuminating only isolated periods of American history? Isn't there at least a small possibility that archeologists don't have the complete picture and the Book of Mormon is true?

Tom: I doubt the Book of Mormon is true. Archaeology, of course, presents only a partial picture. Science is never proven and you always have to keep other possibilities open.

Philip: Kevin Barney claims that you and your colleague Simon Southerton, grew up with a narrow and fundamentalist view of the Book of Mormon.[11] Is that true?

Tom: I would agree, but so did just about everybody else. That's what all of us were taught as children. The Church doesn't teach Kevin Barney's view of the Book of Mormon. Missionaries don't teach it, the Introduction to the Book of Mormon doesn't teach it, and prophets don't teach it in conference. He's right that I grew up with a narrow, black-and-white view of the Book of Mormon, but that doesn't mean I still have that point of view. I don't. I've weighed the arguments from FARMS and found them flawed and wanting.

Philip: But Barney claims that your "narrow" view growing up has resulted in a scientifically naive assumption that Lehi and his family were the sole ancestors of *all* the American Indians and so accepting of the hemispheric model. That doesn't allow for the limited geography model.

Tom: First of all, I don't agree with him that I'm making a theological argument. He says that we rejected the Book of Mormon on the basis of theology and that's a ridiculous argument. I reject the Book of Mormon on scientific grounds. If he would actually read my paper "Lamanites, Genesis, Genealogy, and Genetics,"[12] then he would see that limited geography is not supported by the genetics either. There is no genetic evidence at all to support the limited geography model. So it has the same problems that the hemispheric geography does. There is no more support for the one or the other.

The Church's official position—what I would call official because it's in the Introduction to the Book of Mormon—is what leads me to what Barney calls a scientifically naive conclusion. I don't like that term. I would say that the Book of Mormon is incompatible with the findings, not that it's scientifically naive.

Philip: The Mormon Church didn't allow black men to hold the priesthood until 1978. Yet, wouldn't many anthropologists argue that race doesn't even exist as we normally think of it?

Tom: Race is a social construct that we invent. Its origins are social, not biological. We make reference to observable differences in our biology and then put people into categories on the basis of things like skin color. There is no biological evidence to support the racist claim you see in Mormonism that dark skin is a curse from God for wickedness and there never has been. There are clearly real biological differences between people, but those differences do not fit neatly into our socially constructed racial categories. You could easily walk by someone and see them as white when they see themselves as Native American.[13]

If you look at genetic diversity at the continental level—in Africa or Europe, for example—you find that about 94 percent of the genetic differences that exist in the larger human population can be found within small population groups. Only a small amount of diversity exists. In fact, humans differ from one another by a maximum of only .1 percent. You could go all the way down to the village level and still find that 85 percent of the genetic differences found among all of humanity will be found in any given village. That means that when a white person sees someone with dark skin, he or she may have more in common that with that person biologically than another white person. That's a serious issue that both the Mormon Church and the United States need to wrestle with. In fact, the racism in the Book of Mormon and Mormon history is a more problematic issue for me than the DNA research that has garnered so much attention in the press.

The Near-Excommunication

Philip: In November of 2002, you were called in by Matthew Latimer, the stake president of the Lynnwood Washington Stake, for publishing your opinion that DNA studies provide no evidence of Middle Eastern Israelite lineage for the American Indians. What took place at that meeting?

Tom: When President Latimer asked me to come in, I anticipated he would discipline me for something I had written. At this time, I wasn't even attending church on a regular basis. So I talked with several people beforehand about what to expect, including Lavina Fielding Anderson and Brent Metcalfe.[14] I also read through the *Church Handbook* in order to be familiar with the disciplinary procedures.

I didn't want to go alone to the meeting, so I brought Kerrie with me. After a little chit-chat, Latimer said that someone had given him a copy of the article I had written for *American Apocrypha*, and he was concerned that it contradicted the Church's position. I responded, a little facetiously, that I didn't know the Church had a position on genetics. I acknowledged that I thought the evidence says that the Book of Mormon is a nineteenth-century document and said, "If you've got a problem, then you should argue with the evidence." He said he was not a geneticist. In fact, he was a lawyer.

Then he started asking about my view of the Church more generally, and I shared with him my concerns about the racism in scripture, the various sexist teachings of Church leaders, the mistreatment and place of women in the Church, like not allowing them to have the priesthood, the Church's political action against and mistreatment of homosexuals, patriarchal authority—these were all issues we talked about. He tried to be nice about the whole thing and was really passive-aggressive. There was no yelling whatsoever. We were able to respectfully disagree with each other.

Latimer said he didn't think it was good for a member of the Church to be saying the things I was saying, because it was giving people the wrong impression. The way to deal with that, he said, was to initiate a disciplinary council that would consider removing me from the Church. Then he told me to think it over and said, "This is not a threat, but would you maybe just consider rethinking your conclusions?" It certainly seemed like a threat. If I would change my conclusions, then I could maintain good standing in the Church. I responded, "I'm not going to change my mind or my position."

Philip: Was it ever an option to alter your findings or change your conclusions to accommodate the Church?

Tom: Not for me personally, and I made that very clear. I said "If you're going to discipline me, then I think it would be best to get it over with." So, we agreed upon the date of December 8. Before the date came I spoke with my colleagues here at Edmonds Community

College, because I knew I didn't want to go quietly and wanted to make sure that publicity would not negatively impact my job.

Philip: Were they supportive?

Tom: Yes, very supportive. I came home after that meeting with President Latimer and wrote a letter to them, members of the Mormon intellectual community and family members. Later, when Lavina asked me if I was comfortable going public and I told her yes, she forwarded this letter to Ron Priddis, and it eventually made its way through to Patty Henetz with the Salt Lake Bureau of the Associated Press. She called me the day after Thanksgiving, and I told her my story, and by that afternoon it was on the AP wire.

I did a search on my computer the next day and was shocked—my story was one of the top forwarded stories! I thought there would be a couple of small articles on it, and then the story would just blow over. The search was the first hint that this would be a major story. Beginning that next Monday I got constant phone calls from the press, and by the end of the next week, the story was in the *Chronicle of Higher Education*, *Wall Street Journal*, *L.A. Times*, and *National Post*.

I think the *L.A. Times* article had the biggest impact. The angle they wanted was to make me into the "Galileo of Mormonism." The reporters seemed to have that in mind when they talked to me. One reporter asked me what I thought about being called the "Mormon Galileo," and I said I thought it was a bit presumptuous. He quoted Maxine Hanks saying that I was the "Mormon Galileo."[15]

The stake president then suspended disciplinary actions, because he was so upset by the press reports. I said that I didn't think I was saying anything that wasn't true, and he responded, "Yeah, I know I can't blame you for the way the press reported this, but the implication is that this is an inquisition."

Philip: Did you think going public would help you stay in the Church?

Tom: Stephen Clark [from the Salamander Society] told me he thought if I went public they would change their mind, and I didn't believe him. I didn't think it would make a difference one way or the other. It certainly didn't make a difference for the September Six, so

I was blindsided by the retraction. I think it was the *L.A. Times* article that did it.

Latimer gave two reasons for not proceeding. One was that Church disciplinary action is supposed to help bring people to repentance and back into the fold, and he didn't think disciplinary action in my case would achieve that goal. The other was that disciplinary action is supposed to protect the Church, and he didn't think it was protecting the Church. In my case, it was actually counterproductive.

Philip: What were the stated reasons for the disciplinary council according to your summons letter?

Tom: It said they were going to consider disciplinary action against me that could include disfellowshipment or excommunication for apostasy. I was glad to see they only listed apostasy, because I know other people were charged with conduct unbecoming a member.

After they stopped disciplinary proceedings, President Latimer asked that we have a continuing dialogue. I haven't taken him up on that offer. I don't see much point in it. I've got other things to do. I don't have the time.

Apostasy and Doctrine

Philip: At this time you were not attending church?
Tom: Right.
Philip: Your faith was shaken, to say the least?
Tom: Right.
Philip: Was apostasy then a legitimate charge?
Tom: There are different ways to answer that question. If you look at it from my perspective, then what am I apostate from? I'm not going to church and interfering with what they're doing. I'm just publishing my research. If this was just another Christian denomination, then I wouldn't even be considered a member of the Church.

The way Mormonism counts its members is misguided. In Mormonism, anyone who has been baptized in the Church is a member no matter how they live or whether they attend Church or not. So, from their perspective I'm still a member of the Church, even though I'm not a participating, active member, and from their perspective that makes me apostate.

Another way to answer that question is in terms of boundary making. Every human institution has to create some sort of boundaries including the Church, but it doesn't need to use excommunication as a means of doing that. Why couldn't everybody be Mormon? You could create boundaries in different ways. You could create boundaries to raise the faith.

The larger Christian world is a membership by belief, but believing in Mormon theology is different than actually being a member of the Mormon Church. So, if they would set boundaries around belief like the larger Christian world, then I'd already be out. What's the point? It's the prerogative of the institution to set its own boundaries, and I respect that, and if they want to draw me outside of the boundaries, then the difference is really for them. For me, the question as to whether or not I'm on the official Church records is not important. Discipline would hurt, but it wouldn't change who I am.

I guess I just think it's foolish to feel justified in drawing the boundary in a way that would exclude me. Why not just accept my inactivity as evidence? Yes, I'm apostate, but I don't accept that way of maintaining boundaries.

Philip: Well, according to the boundaries they have set, you are still on the rolls.

Tom: I think they should rethink that. It looks good to have eleven million members right? But now it's a potential embarrassment. The people are saying, "I'm not a Mormon," and the Church is saying, "You are." The Church is defining people as Latter-day Saints who don't self-identify that way, which raises credibility questions. Most people don't write in to the Church when they stop attending and say, "Take me off the rolls." In fact, when a friend of mine left the Church, I told her specifically, "If you want to be taken off the list, then you need to write and tell them." She did, but never received a reply so we still don't know if it worked.

There's a lot of irony in my situation. When I was seventeen and a senior in high school I went to the bishop's office asking to be excommunicated. I asked him to take me off the rolls. He said, "No, you haven't thought that through." He refused my request! He could have saved the Church a lot of turmoil [laughing].

Philip: To clarify, you recognize that the Church defines apostasy differently than you do. Further, you acknowledge that their definition means that whether you believe or not has little bearing on whether you are excommunicated. It is how you act about your work and toward the Church that matters most. So, were they wrong for charging you with apostasy?

Tom: I'm not trying to waffle around the answer, but it's not a simple answer of right or wrong. I think it was foolish. What harm was I really doing? Most of the people paying attention to my research prior to that time were already questioning the Church. It's not like I was going out on the street preaching what I believed to be right. I was publishing for the academic community, many of whom were already harsh to the faith. The people reading what I wrote were already questioning and challenging.

Philip: Yes, but you must have been aware that your research would eventually make its way into the hands of the average Mormon whose faith could be shaken by your conclusions. Did that ever bother you?

Tom: No! I hoped for that. My Mormon-ness, my sense of being part of the culture and religious tradition, is bound with the ability to think critically at the same time. I was very inspired by Brigham H. Roberts,[16] and I hoped to inspire other Mormons to think critically. This is an important time in the development of the Church, even though the membership numbers are exaggerated, and there is a chance to make a huge impact.

Philip: Should the LDS Church take an official stance that says the Book of Mormon is an ancient document translated by Joseph Smith without any qualification?

Tom: I do not envy the Church's position, because I don't see any real answer to that. I suppose the simplest answer is that they should be tolerant of scholarly attempts of all stripes to weigh that question. There wouldn't be any reason for Joel Kramer to produce that video[17] if Mormons were already producing it, if Mormons were looking honestly at their own history. Some Mormons, like me, are obviously already doing that, and if the Church would be half as honest as its scholarly component, then it would have nothing to fear from so-called anti-Mormons. The Church could gradually evolve and move away from claims that no longer stand up to scholarly scrutiny just as the Community of Christ has done.[18] However, I know enough about the history of religious institutions to know that there would be repercussions to that approach.

Philip: Do you mean that if the Church took an official stance at all, then there would be severe division?

Tom: Yeah. It's a no-win situation no matter what the Church does. For example, if it takes a real hard line on creationism with respect to evolution, then that would be a competitive advantage because stricter churches, more dogmatic churches, grow faster than those that are more tolerant. Conservative Protestantism is doing much better in the marketplace then liberal Protestantism. However, when you take too dogmatic of a position, as do young-earth creationists who insist that the earth is not more than 6,000 years old, your credibility really suffers. The LDS Church has that problem with its hard-line approach, because it is so easy to disprove. It sets you up to lose the best and brightest of your children as they grow up and learn. The hard line may recruit people temporarily, but it won't keep them. So, it's a trade-off.

The LDS Church would have more difficulty recruiting if it said that Joseph Smith was just another guy. If Joseph Smith became like the Methodist John Wesley, a founder of the Church who was inspired but human, then Mormonism would lose some of its market appeal. People would think it's just another Christian faith, but that's a legitimate path to take. That's Grant Palmer's approach.[19] He argues that the Church should acknowledge that Joseph Smith was just a man and should instead emphasize the highest Christian message: loving one another and having compassion. That would make the LDS Church just another Christian church, but one which I would like to see. If they continue to take a hard-line approach, then they're going to continue to lose credibility.

They could just come out and say, "We were wrong." Apologize. I think some of them even know they're wrong.

Reflection

Philip: In your meeting with President Latimer on February 23, 2003, you agreed to address controversial issues through academic channels, rather than in or through the Church. Didn't you ever feel that you were leading a double life as an intellectual on one side and a Mormon on the other?

Tom: No, which is the reason why I never felt comfortable in church. I couldn't fully express myself. Ever since that prayer that I told you about, I felt out of place, even though I went back to church. The only exception was when we were fellowshipped by people at Sunstone and *Dialogue* where I felt, even though I had some differences of opinion, that they always respected my right to believe what I wanted to. I didn't feel out of place at Sunstone symposia, Mormon History Association meetings, or while reading *Dialogue*.

Philip: I remember attending your lecture at the AAR regional meeting in Moscow.[20] In those types of situations you are speaking to a largely non-Mormon audience, and I can recall points in the lecture when audience members laughed when you talked about Mormon theology. You laughed right along with them. Do you consider yourself a good representative of Mormonism in those arenas—in academia—when you're laughing right along with the audience?

Tom: I think for obvious reasons I'm an attractive image of what it means to be Mormon—critically thinking, reflective, a Mormon who is not afraid to laugh at Mormonism. It's important to laugh at your own tradition and recognize its peculiarities, and the response I get from other academics has actually been quite positive. Most have been enthusiastic and supportive of my research, though not always in anthropology, where there is more of a prejudice. Anthropologists are very dismissive of religion and Mormonism in particular.

Philip: How does that prejudice manifest?

Tom: It's difficult to get grants to do research on Mormonism. It's as if they're implicitly saying, "How can you be Mormon?"

Philip: Many people often wonder how one can be an intelligent academic *and* a Mormon? How do you respond to that?

Tom: My response is that I didn't choose to be Mormon, just like I didn't choose my parents. I study hard, and people call me intelligent, and I'm fortunate to be intelligent, but I was born Mormon.

Today, I'm a cultural Mormon, and when I say "Mormon" I use it differently than "Latter-day Saint." "Mormon" would apply to meta-Mormon culture, and within meta-Mormon culture, I would include not only the Church but the Sunstone and *Dialogue* crowd. I would even include what some people call anti-Mormons. Within the meta-Mormon culture I would include Ed Decker and Jerald and Sandra Tanner,[21] who are involved in Mormon culture. That would also include fundamentalist Mormons and the Community of Christ. Within that larger context, I'm part of the community.

Whether I'm listed as a member of the Church or not I'll always be a product of the culture, and I don't try to run away or hide from that. Here I am. I didn't choose to be born Mormon, but because I was born into a particular tradition, I try to improve it. And just as in science or other human endeavors, the most provocative work is done by marginal or outsider-type people. That's true of Mormonism. The movers-and-shakers of the LDS Church are often marginal.

Philip: But for those Mormons who do fully ascribe to Mormon theology and attend Church, how would being an intellectual and a Mormon reconcile in their eyes?

Tom: I don't know. It must be hard. There are some things that cannot be scientifically tested—for instance, no evidence could prove if God really visited Joseph Smith. With the Book of Mormon, there is hard evidence that it does not recount an accurate history of ancient America, making it a different sort of thing. Many Mormons don't really believe that the Book of Mormon is an ancient document.

There is overwhelming evidence that the Book of Mormon is not true, so people who get a spiritual affirmation to its truthfulness are not getting historically reliable answers. Maybe there is a different kind of truth—spiritual or emotional truth—I would accept that. Yet when I prayed, I got a different answer than most Mormons. I believe they do experience something, but I don't know what it is. Maybe some of them make it up, but quite a few genuinely experience something; and whether that's psychological, spiritual, or divine, I don't know.

Philip: Was Joseph Smith a prophet?

Tom: In the social sense, I'd say yes. He filled a special role. Now, I doubt that he communicated with the divine, but I wouldn't rule it out. You *can't* rule it out. But that doesn't mean that the Book of Mormon is historically accurate. Mormon prophets don't deliver historical truths.

Philip: Do you think the Church could feasibly say that Joseph Smith was not a prophet who spoke with God, but only what you call a "social prophet"? Wouldn't that oppose many of its fundamental claims?

Tom: Yeah, and that's a problem, but they could deal with that by saying he was a product of his time. They could just change what they mean by "prophet." They could say we're all prophets, and that argument could be made using traditional Mormon theology. Using traditional sources, they could lower the status of a prophet. There are ways to do it—and who knows, they just might. It'll be interesting to see what happens in the future, but I don't envy their position.

Philip: You were aware of the September Six in 1993. Did you ever think that your research could lead you to the same result?

Tom: Oh yeah, that was a very real possibility. I thought they were encouraging models for how to deal with it, and I couldn't let the way the Church treated them stop me. If anything, it inspired me. Just like me, they believed they were doing the right thing.

Philip: Would your life as a "meta-Mormon" have changed if you had been excommunicated?

Tom: If you had asked me that in October of 2002, then I would have told you that excommunication would make no difference whatsoever. I wouldn't say that today. It hurt a lot more than I ever thought it would. I really felt rejected. I felt unjustly punished. Despite the fact that Lavina told me to expect a lot of different emotions, I was appalled at the emotions I went through. Excommunication is a more powerful weapon than I ever realized. Emotionally, professionally, it's a powerful weapon! The people who have responded to my research, like FAIR and FARMS, have to be very careful about what they say, or else.[22] Some of them have already been called in by the Church to be interviewed.

Since this ordeal my life has changed in ways that I hadn't anticipated. For one thing, everybody knows who I am, which wasn't the case before. Another thing is that I don't have any closure with the Church, which might have been resolved if I would have been excommunicated. I don't wish for excommunication, but I feel in limbo, even though the stake president has said nothing will happen. One day there will be a new stake president and a new prophet, and who knows what will happen then?

You can think of the situation like a child who was abused by a stick. I was partially beaten, but the stick hasn't gone away. It will stay there, permanently. It would be easier to move on if I had been excommunicated. It would be easier to walk away from it all. I might do that anyway.

Kerrie would not even consider going back. I actually would (you know, if the Church would change [laughing]). All they have to do is ordain women to the priesthood, acknowledge that the Book of Mormon could be a nineteenth-century document, toss the patriarchal BS of the hierarchy, stop the homophobic political action and action against women—basically become like a liberal Protestant denomination, and I would start going.

Philip: Regarding the ordination of women to the priesthood, how would you respond to Mormons who say that the priesthood is given solely to men because Christ ordained it as such?

Tom: Who says Christ gave it to men? You may be a better biblical scholar than me, but I don't know of anywhere in the Bible where that's supported. Who did he appear to after he died? He appeared to women first.

Philip: But that does not mean he gave women the priesthood.

Tom: Evidence drives the way I think, and I don't see any evidence that Jesus would have opposed giving the priesthood to women. In fact, one could make the argument that he was quite open to women. One could say that Paul opposed it, I suppose, but it would be hard to pin that on Jesus.

Philip: But there is no evidence of Christ laying hands upon a woman for the purpose of endowing the priesthood.

Tom: But of course that's assuming that the laying on of hands is the same thing as giving the priesthood.

Philip: Sure.

Tom: I see those as two totally separate things. I see one as an institutional practice that emerged in the nineteenth century in a totally different cultural context than that of Jesus in the ancient Near East. I don't think Jesus thought of priesthood in the same way that any modern institution does.

Philip: How would you presume he saw it?

Tom: I don't know. I'm not a good enough biblical scholar to know. I'm not even sure Jesus intended to set up a church. We don't really have any evidence that Jesus intended to establish a church. We don't really have any direct evidence for Jesus. All we have are oral traditions that were passed on, and most of them were not recorded until two or three generations after he was dead. We don't have anything directly from him, and so we don't really know what Jesus thought. So, I'm a bit skeptical.

Philip: You are skeptical about much of Mormon faith. Why haven't you just asked to be taken off the official Church rolls yourself?

Tom: I told you that I did when I was seventeen.

Philip: Yes, but . . .

Tom: I actually came very close to resigning my membership rather than face the disciplinary council, because I don't like conflict. Given what happened to the September Six, I seriously thought about resigning, but a conversation with Kerrie kept me from doing that. She encouraged me to take a stand. She said, "Don't make it easy for them." I still think about resigning, but this whole issue with genetics and the Book of Mormon is not really about me. The Church needs to wrestle with that issue on its own, and getting rid of me won't make that any easier to deal with.

Another reason I stay in the Church is because, though it may sound strange, I hang on to the hope that I'm actually making a positive contribution to the Church. I think of Sterling McMurrin,[23] who was a confessed nonbeliever but maintained his status in the Church. He made a difference. I admire people like that and hope for that. I want to provide for people what Fawn Brodie and Brigham H. Roberts provided for me, which is being within the Church and still wrestling with questions. That was tremendously valuable for me—maybe not as a Mormon per se, but as a human being. I hope to be able to do that for other Mormons.

Philip: Do you think that your ability to make a difference would change if you resigned your membership?

Tom: [long pause] That's a good question. I don't know for sure, but I suspect it would be lessened. Not entirely, because I would still choose to write about Mormonism despite being excommunicated, and that would hopefully make a difference. That's a really hard hypothetical question to answer.

I have had influence thus far inside the Church. In fact, FAIR and FARMS will now basically acknowledge openly that there is no genetic evidence to support the Book of Mormon. That's an impact. They weren't saying that before. Now, I imagine that most Mormons frankly don't give a hoot about me or DNA for that matter. All this doesn't matter much to most Mormons, but I can say from other responses that it has impacted an awful lot of people.

I have a log in my computer of all the emails I received from people who are making some sort of response to what I'm doing. I have 831 emails in there, and that's just email. I have a file full of letters over there from dozens, if not hundreds, of people who have contacted me. That doesn't even count the telephone calls. It's making a difference. It's making a difference for probably close to a thousand people who have reached out to get in touch with me.

Philip: Can you generalize the sentiment of the responses?

Tom: It has been overwhelmingly supportive and encouraging, especially early on. As time has passed I more frequently get people who want to argue with me, but positive responses still account for more than 95 percent of the total.

I'll read you an example [pulling a letter from his drawer]:

> Mr. Murphy, Thanks so much for your brave stand for objective truth in the face of official LDS Church opposition. I've read about

your situation in the paper and have since been very inspired by your story. I'm a member of the LDS Church as well, but have been non-practicing for about five years. I wish you the very best. You're definitely not alone in your stand.

That's very characteristic of the response.

Philip: After all this, do you want the Mormon Church to prosper as it stands currently?

Tom: You know what? I find the Book of Mormon's portrayal of the American Indians ethically repugnant and its perpetuation of the idea that a dark skin is a curse from God for wickedness abhorrent. I object to the Church growing at the expense of native people. My doctoral dissertation, for example, examines the origins and perpetuation of Book of Mormon portrayals of Lamanites. It invites Mormon scholars to take seriously Native American views of the Book of Mormon, both those coming from within and outside Mormonism.[24] To garner my support in the future, the Church must find a way to grow while moving away from its fundamentally racist portrayals of Lamanites in the Book of Mormon.

* * *

By February of 2008, Tom had decided to abandon Mormon studies. He donated much of his large collection of books in Mormon studies to the Seattle non-profit Eco Encore, and the remainder to Angelo Baca, a Navajo filmmaker at the University of Washington, who is using documentary films to explore Lamanite identity.

Notes

1. Tom used his stepfather's last name, Bean, at church, at school, and in public, between ages ten and eighteen.

2. Ed Decker, the founder of Saints Alive, in Issaquah, Washington, converted to Mormonism when he was twenty and stayed in the Church for over twenty years. He held the Melchizedek Priesthood, worked in the temple, and held many leadership positions. In 1975, Decker left Mormonism to become one of its most vehement critics. In 1982, he later released an infamous exposé film, *The God Makers*, followed by a book of the same name in 1984, and a later film sequel, *Temple of the God Makers*.

3. Linda Sillitoe and Allen Dale Roberts, *Salamander: The Story of the Mormon Forgery Murders: With a New Afterward* (Salt Lake City: Signature Books, 1988).

4. "But, behold, I say unto you, that you must study it out in your mind; then you must ask me if it be right, and if it is right I will cause that your bosom shall burn within you; therefore, you shall feel that it is right. But if it be not right you shall have no such feelings, but you shall have a stupor of thought that shall cause you to forget the thing which is wrong; therefore, you cannot write that which is sacred save it be given you from me" (D&C 9:8–9).

5. Fawn Brodie, *No Man Knows My History: The Life of Joseph Smith, the Mormon Prophet* (New York: A. A. Knopf, 1945).

6. See Newell G. Bringhurst, ed., *Reconsidering No Man Knows My History: Fawn M. Brodie and Joseph Smith in Retrospect* (Logan: Utah State University, 1996); or Hugh Nibley, *No, Ma'am, That's Not History* (Salt Lake City: Bookcraft, 1946).

7. This is a paraphrase of a statement made by Delaney, an anthropologist at Stanford University, in her lecture at Edmonds Community College, "The Social Legacy of Abraham," on October 23, 2002.

8. See Thomas W. Murphy, "Reinventing Mormonism: Guatemala as a Harbinger of the Future?" *Dialogue: A Journal of Mormon Thought* 29, no. 1 (Spring 1996): 177–92; "Guatemalan Hot/Cold Medicine and Mormon Words of Wisdom: Intercultural Negotiation of Meaning," *Journal for the Scientific Study of Religion* 36, no. 2 (1997): 297–308; "'Stronger Than Ever': Remnants of the Third Convention," *Journal of Latter Day Saint History* 10 (1998): 1, 8–11; "From Racist

Stereotype to Ethnic Identity: Instrumental Uses of Mormon Racial Doctrine," *Ethnohistory* 46 (Summer 1999): 451–80; "Other Mormon Histories: Lamanite Subjectivity in Mexico," *Journal of Mormon History* 26 (Fall 2000): 179–214.

9. In October 2006, Doubleday, which published a trade edition of the Book of Mormon, changed that phrase, which had been part of the introduction since the 1979 edition, from "principal ancestors" to "among the ancestors" of the American Indians. Carrie A. Moore, "Debate Renewed with Change in Book of Mormon Introduction," *Deseret Morning News*, November 8, 2007, http://www.deseretnews.com/article/1,5143,695226008,00.html (accessed July 31, 2008).

10. Thomas W. Murphy, "Lamanites, Genesis, Genealogy, and Genetics" in *American Apocrypha: Essays on the Book of Mormon*, edited by Dan Vogel and Brent Lee Metcalfe (Salt Lake City: Signature Books, 2002), 47–77.

11. In his response to Murphy and Southerton's, "Genetic Research a 'Galileo Event' for Mormons," *Anthropology News* 44, no. 2 (February 2003), Barney writes, "Murphy and Southerton appear to be nice guys. They are sincere, and they believe in what they are doing. Both seem to have had a similar experience. They apparently grew up with narrow, fundamentalist assumptions about the Book of Mormon, believing in and presumably knowing only of the hemispheric model. When they learned that the hemispheric model was scientifically untenable, each experienced unfulfilled (unrealistic) expectations and an ensuing crisis of faith, upon which each lost his belief in the antiquity and historicity of the Book of Mormon, and the Church with it. Now they desire to enlighten others under the banner of science." Kevin L. Barney, "A Brief Review of Murphy and Southerton's 'Galileo Event,'" FAIR, http://www.fairlds.org/apol/bom/bom08.html (accessed September 8, 2003).

12. Murphy, "Lamanites, Genesis, Genealogy, and Genetics," 47–77.

13. Thomas W. Murphy, "Sin, Skin, and Seed: Mistakes of Men in the Book of Mormon," *John Whitmer Historical Association Journal* 25 (2005): 36–51.

14. Brent Lee Metcalfe, raised a Mormon, currently describes himself as an agnostic. He edited *New Approaches to the Book of Mormon: Explorations in Critical Methodology* (Salt Lake City: Signature Books, 1993), and is co-editor of www.mormonscripturestudies.com. He was excommunicated in 1994.

15. Thomas W. Murphy, "Inventing Galileo," *Sunstone*, Issue 131 (March 2004): 58–61.

16. Brigham H. Roberts (1857–1933) served in the First Council of Seventy for forty-five years and wrote copiously on LDS Church history and doctrine.

17. Living Hope Ministries, the media segment of Living Hope Christian Fellowship, produced a video, *DNA vs. the Book of Mormon*. Living Hope, pastored by Joel Kramer, is an evangelical, non-denominational congregation based in Brigham City, Utah.

18. The Community of Christ, previously known as the Reorganized Church of Jesus Christ of Latter Day Saints, after a preliminary organizational period by Mormons who refused to follow Brigham Young (1852–60), formalized its existence in 1860 under the leadership of Joseph Smith III. It renamed itself the Community of Christ in April 2001. World headquarters are in Independence, Missouri, and worldwide membership currently numbers over 250,000.

19. Grant H. Palmer, *An Insider's View of Mormon Origins* (Salt Lake City: Signature Books, 2002).

20. American Academy of Religion, Pacific Northwest Regional meeting, University of Idaho, Moscow, Idaho, April 26, 2003.

21. Jerald and Sandra Tanner grew up in Mormon homes with strong ties to prominent figures in the early Mormonism. Sandra Tanner is the great-great-granddaughter of Brigham Young. The couple renounced Mormonism and spent much of their life criticizing the faith. They have published more than forty books on Mormonism and at the time of this interview were operating the Utah Lighthouse Ministry, originally known as Modern Microfilm Company. Jerald Tanner died in 2007.

22. FAIR stands for the Foundation for Apologetic Information and Research. It is a non-profit organization established in 1997 by Mormons who emphasize the internet as a medium of defending Mormonism. FARMS stands for the Foundation for Ancient Research and Mormon Studies, which, similarly to FAIR, defends Mormonism against its critics, but especially with regard to scriptural studies. FARMS was established in 1979 and acquired by Brigham Young University in 1997.

23. Sterling McMurrin (1914–96) was often known for his willingness to question Church doctrine and practice. Among other positions, he served as the E. E. Ericksen Distinguished Professor at the University of Utah and as U.S. Commissioner of Education in the John F. Kennedy administration. He also wrote influential works on Mormon philosophy, including *The Philosophical Foundations of Mormon Theology* (1959), *The Theological Foundations of the Mormon Religion* (1965), *Religion, Reason, and Truth* (1982), and *Toward Understanding the New Testament* (1990).

24. Thomas W. Murphy, "Imagining Lamanites: Native Americans and the Book of Mormon" (Ph.D. diss., University of Washington, 2003).

Chapter 9
Donald B. Jessee

Former employee, Church of Jesus Christ of Latter-day Saints, Public Affairs Department.

This interview transcript has been reviewed, edited, and approved by Mr. Jessee, who has asked to include the following disclaimer: *"The statements that follow are my own opinions. I am not speaking for the Church of Jesus Christ of Latter-day Saints on any issues, including the issues below. Only the Church president speaks for the Church."*

Donald B. Jessee has long been devoted, both personally and occupationally, to the LDS Church. After graduating from BYU, he was hired to work for the Church, commencing what was, at the time of this interview, a forty-five-year career in its service. Mr. Jessee began his career as a Church Educational System seminary instructor and principal. Among other employment opportunities, he has worked for the Aaronic Priesthood Department and the Family and Church History Department, where he served as the manager of Missionary Training. Subsequently, Mr. Jessee entered the Church's Public Affairs Department. At the time of this interview, one of his duties was to respond to "man-on-the-street" questions that came to Church headquarters via phones and emails.

In all this, Mr. Jessee never let a demanding workload undermine his commitment to his family or his local community. He and his wife have ten children, and Mr. Jessee has served in a variety of

Church callings over the years, including bishop, stake president, regional representative, mission president, and, at present (2010), stake patriarch.

On the afternoon of August 25, 2004, Mr. Jessee and I sat down together on the second floor of the Joseph Smith Memorial Building in downtown Salt Lake City, Utah. A congenial man, dressed sharply in a blue suit and red tie, he relaxed in the chair across from me and exemplified the ease with which he defends the LDS Church against those who would be critics.

Mormon Identity

Philip: Perhaps we can begin by exploring Mormon identity. How does the Mormon Church define a "Mormon"?

Donald: First of all, let me correct a misconception. Even though we are commonly called the Mormon Church, it is not the Mormon Church; it is the Church of Jesus Christ of Latter-day Saints. We are called Mormons because we have the Book of Mormon. The world seems to feed off that, but that is not the name of the Church.

To become a member, or to define a Latter-day Saint, one must have faith in the Lord Jesus Christ, believe that He is the Savior of the world, and believe that He took upon Himself the punishment for the sins of all who follow him. He gave his life on the cross and was resurrected as a celestial being, assuring that all mankind would be resurrected. Thus, through the atonement of Jesus Christ, He was who He said He was. Prospective members should repent of their sins and be baptized by immersion for the remission of their sins, which we believe is in the similitude of Christ's death, burial, and resurrection.

Following baptism, hands are laid on their heads by one having priesthood authority, for the gift of the Holy Ghost. They then are presented to a congregation to be accepted as a member into a ward or branch of the Church. This is not a popular vote, but a formal recognition by other members of the congregation and a welcome to a new member. At that time, a record of membership is made, and their names are placed on the official records of the Church. That constitutes a convert becoming a member in the Church of Jesus Christ of Latter-day Saints.

Philip: How does the Church justify including some people as members when they do not self-identify as such? For example, some adults have not attended church since they were kids, but are still considered members in good standing.

Donald: What do you mean "self-identify"?

Philip: They do not consider themselves members of the Church of Jesus Christ of Latter-day Saints.

Donald: You mean those who are inactive and no longer come to our meetings?

Philip: Yes.

Donald: If a membership record exists for a person who no longer attends church or others who may choose not to identify with the Church, we look upon them as members of the Church and do all that we can to bring them into fellowship. Unless they ask that their membership be removed from Church records, local leaders strive to bring them back into activity. The most basic program to identify and help these members is what we call "home teaching." If we know where these people live and can identify them as being in a particular ward or branch, then the home teachers should visit them regularly to help them rekindle their testimonies and encourage them to come back to Church activity.

Philip: So what you're describing is maintaining one's membership by virtue of a past baptism rather than a continued belief. What would happen if the Church determined its membership strictly by belief, where one must continue to believe in the Church and its doctrines to be considered a member? Would the membership numbers change?[1]

Donald: We don't have such a program.

Philip: Right, but if there were a change . . .

Donald: You can't get in any other way except through baptism and the process I described, and you cannot get out unless you officially request your name be removed from the records of the Church. While a belief system is essential, it is not the only determining factor. If you frequently read the scriptures, do all of the things that the prophets of God say to do but are never baptized, even if you were to attend church on a regular basis, you're not a member of the Church.

Jesus and the apostles in the New Testament taught that there is only one way. Unless you come in the right way, your name will not be placed on the official records of the Church. So we're different from other religions; some only ask that you confess that Jesus is the Christ and then you are accepted as a member of the congregation and are then counted on its records. Other religions accept membership if a person makes consistent financial contributions. The Church of Jesus Christ of Latter-day Saints requires a process of belief and ordinances.

The Status of Women in Mormonism

Philip: How does the Church respond to the all-too-frequent claim that the LDS Church is sexist because it encourages women to stay at home rather then pursue a career, and it also withholds the priesthood from them?

Donald: If we're sexist, then God is sexist, because that's His plan. When God created women, He gave them the power to bear children, He established the family, and we are His children. He is our Father in Heaven. Women in the Church may choose for themselves whether they pursue a career. All women are encouraged to get as much education as they can. The prophets encourage even the young women to get as much education as they can and plan on furthering their education past high school. Married women are encouraged to have sufficient education that they can provide for their physical needs, if necessary. All women are encouraged to develop their talents and have a broad knowledge of things both on earth and in heaven. Single women are encouraged to be engaged in their education and a career until they are married; then it becomes a matter of priorities.

The influence mothers have is profound. It is difficult to work outside the home or pursue a career and influence their children and not give them to others to raise. The Church encourages mothers to be at the crossroads of the home when their children are there. Heavenly Father gave the priesthood to His sons. There is no indication in the scriptures that He ever gave the priesthood to women. There is no evidence in the Bible that He ordained women to the priesthood. Were it His intent, He would have revealed it to the ancient prophets, and it would have been practiced in the ancient Church. In fact, back in the days of Israel, He gave the priesthood to only one of the twelve tribes of Israel—the tribe of the Levites—and even then only the older sons could hold the Aaronic Priesthood, which qualified them to work in the temple while the others couldn't. There is no mention of women holding the priesthood. Joseph Smith was given clear instruction and revelation concerning who should hold the priesthood.

Philip: As far as comparing the responsibilities of priesthood with motherhood, as you just did, Maxine Hanks has remarked, "It's fallacious to equate them. Motherhood is a biological process that requires reproductive organs while priesthood isn't. If motherhood is priesthood, that excludes many women, and it requires pregnancy. Meanwhile, Mormon women do have priesthood in several ways—priesthood roles, duties, and divine power." (See chap. 3.) How would you respond?

Donald: I have no comment on her statement. What she tried to say by her statement is her business. Family is about the priesthood, and a woman shares in the blessings of the priesthood just like every other member of the family. Males who are ordained to the priesthood magnify their calling by bringing to bear the power of the priesthood in the lives of others. Women are entitled to the blessings that come from the priesthood—the freedom to pray and to receive revelation, and blessings associated with Church ordinances, including temple blessings. They can hold leadership and teaching positions in the Church and have all the rights and powers that Heavenly Father has reserved for them. All these and other things are interconnected with the priesthood and its power. A mother in the home relies on the Spirit of the Lord for daily direction. The angels of heaven are given watch over her and sustain her in time of need. These things come through the powers of heaven, which are priesthood directed.

Excommunication and Intellectual Freedom

Philip: Can you describe what warrants excommunication?

Donald: Yes. A member may be disciplined for conduct contrary to the laws and order of the Church, such as taking a person's life or violating the laws of chastity. We don't expect that members will be perfect, but if they violate the laws of the land and are convicted, or violate their temple and other sacred covenants, if they teach as Church doctrine philosophies or principles that go contrary to the teachings of the Church, are involved in an abortion, murder, or immoral sexual acts—these and other actions could be reasons for church discipline.

Philip: Lynne Whitesides, who was a member of what the media have called the "September Six," six Mormon intellectuals all disciplined in September of 1993, has claimed, "I don't think anybody deserves to be excommunicated or disfellowshipped. I don't think anyone *deserves* that. If this was a Church of love, then there would be another way to entreat people to come back into the fold. . . . When your Church excommunicates you, then where do you go for mercy? I'll tell you where a lot of people go—they just throw it all out. God's gone. All of it's gone. We need to find a way to love people. Neither murder, nor rape, nor child abuse deserves excommunication." (See chap. 1.) Can you explain how the Church can view excommunication as an act of love?

Donald: Well, if the Church tolerates these sins, then there's no basis for the integrity of the Church. Jesus taught that God gives no allowance for sin, but still loves the sinner. Those who violate the commandments, the tenets of the Church, by choice, give up their membership in the Church. To suppose or state that to discipline a Church member indicates that they are not loved is a false assumption. Members who break Church rules are disciplined because God loves them, and Church leaders are vitally concerned for their eternal welfare. If they were not loved, they wouldn't be disciplined, for discipline is a divine act of love. It is an eternal principle. True happiness comes as a result of divine discipline.

Philip: In some disciplinary cases, such as Thomas Murphy's, it has appeared that the LDS Church discontinued disciplinary action because of the negative press it would incur. Is this true, and if so, could one then infer that the Church is more worried about its public image rather than about properly dealing with its members?

Donald: Regarding these councils, Church leaders or members do not comment on disciplinary actions because to do so violates an individual's privacy; therefore, any attempt to find out about the proceedings will result in "no comment." It should be noted that, if information is made public, it is a result of a choice the individual made to do so, for the Church is committed to safeguard a person's privacy. As far as being coerced because of the media, there is no truth or substance to that statement. The Church is not governed by situational ethics, and it is not in the business of pleasing the world or catering to the media or compromising its standards because of pressures brought upon it by worldly influences. I am talking here about the Church of Jesus Christ. One purpose of the Church is to lead people to Christ in hopes that they will embrace his teachings and ordinances, which will perfect them over time. Perfecting the Saints and helping them come unto Christ is a major Church objective, and much effort is given in an attempt to achieve it.

Philip: Vern L. Bullough has written, "Use of excommunication to control dissent is like an alcoholic taking the first drink."[2] Could using excommunication as the Church does be a slippery slope, a tool difficult to stop using once employed?

Donald: Absolutely not. Discipline is part of the kingdom of God from the beginning. The Church did not invent or create discipline; it is an eternal principle. The God of Heaven gave us the commandments and counsel and the consequences if they are violated. If God did not instigate discipline when giving the Ten Commandments, why then did he say "thou shalt not"? Asking people to repent of their sins and disciplining them were the task of the prophets of ancient Israel. Throughout the Old and New Testament, the message to follow God's commandments was the heart of Jesus's message. It was a frequent issue in ancient Israel—a matter of the people not keeping the commandments or worshipping idols and not the true God, so He disciplined them. Those were the rules; those were the guidelines, and today the Church does not compromise them for any reason. If there is compromise, it has to come from God Himself, not from the Church. The Church is sensitive to what the media are saying; however, those are the guidelines God set down and what His plan is all about. The Church accepts the principle of discipline, and it is a part of its teachings and practice. Joseph Smith through latter-day revelation taught the principle of discipline and its role in the Church.

The Church teaches that following discipline, leaders and members show forth an increase of love toward those who were disciplined and do all they can to bring them back to full fellowship. Members who go through disciplinary councils and return to activity in the Church oftentimes express their gratitude for this redeeming process. Many comment on the sincere interest and the love that members and leaders show in their behalf. More important, because of the discipline, they feel that God has forgiven them of their trespass and sin. This is the most significant aspect of Church discipline.

There are some who decide they don't want to come back and will use whatever excuses they want to show that they shouldn't have been disciplined and even profess they were never loved. Well, they're entitled to their opinion, but in reality, they have, for various reasons, refused the hand of love and fellowship, which is a significant part of Church discipline. The God of Heaven will look at that at the Judgment. No humans are in a position to judge how justly they've been treated. All that can be said is that, when discipline is applied according to the evidence and the promptings of the Spirit, a basic Church principle or ordinance has been violated, which in turn has violated the commandments of God and the integrity of the Church.

Philip: Allen Dale Roberts has claimed that the Church conducts surveillance on liberal or "unorthodox" Mormons and has even employed spies to enter BYU classrooms.[3] Are you aware of any such activity?

Donald: I cannot speak to that, as I have no knowledge of it. We don't have a spy network that goes around checking people out. That's not the way the Church operates. Many, if not all, of those who run counter to the Church and its teachings or who commit sexual or other sins tell on themselves by their words and/or actions. Members or leaders who have knowledge of such transgressions or improprieties have an obligation to report it to the appropriate Church authority. If members are brought in for discipline, it is not necessarily because of some belief system they have. It's because they're openly teaching false doctrines or are privately or publicly breaking the commandments. It's the obligation of Church leaders to be alert and keep the Church morally clean and ethically straight. People who run around claiming to be Church members, who in fact are not in harmony with the Church and its teachings, alert members or leaders themselves by their own actions.

Philip: What is the Strengthening Church Members Committee?

Donald: It's a committee that seeks information that, in time, if the proper action is taken, does just that—it can strengthen Church members through proper discipline.

Philip: How so? Many excommunicants have claimed that it collected files on them in preparation for potential disciplinary courts.

Donald: They do it by caring about members of the Church. Discipline is designed to help members who have gone astray. The Church from its beginning has gathered anti-Mormon literature and derogatory or false information about the Church. If the source of this information comes from Church members of record, then action is taken. The Church must be aware of its critics and enemies. Again, Church leaders must keep the Church morally clean and ethically straight.

Philip: Should academics avoid publishing research if it could be understood as contradicting the Church's position on a given topic?

Donald: Members can publish whatever they want. There's no censorship. It depends on the context and the person's motive in doing what has been done. If a BYU professor, whose salary is paid with Church funds and who has signed an honor code of conduct to keep university rules, then publicly goes out and violates them, then that person is subject to discipline, but he or she is free to speak about any issue he or she wants to.

This makes sense. For example, if I hired you to be my employee for my widget company, then I wouldn't want you out there speaking out against the widgets in the name of freedom of academics. I don't want you to go out and misrepresent the company or perform actions that bring undesirable publicity and say my widgets are bad and people should buy other widgets. It's common sense that action should be taken. In the Church it is a serious matter. Jesus Christ set down certain rules, laws, regulations, doctrines, and practices, and if you join the Church, you ought to defend it. BYU has established standards that allow freedom to publish within university guidelines.

Philip: What about those topics not yet given much attention by Church leaders? Do members have free rein on those topics? Thomas Murphy was nearly excommunicated for doing genetic research that the Mormon Church had yet to conduct. How much freedom is one afforded on such controversial but relatively unaddressed topics? Mother in Heaven is another example of a controversial topic upon which people have published and been punished for doing so.

Donald: Well, in the case of Murphy, he says that because of DNA he has proven that the Book of Mormon is not true. How does he know? There were other groups of people here in America before Lehi arrived here. The Book of Mormon talks about other peoples who inhabited the American continent who were not discussed in what Murphy tried to prove in his research. How could DNA prove or disprove the truthfulness of a book brought here under the hand of God? The laws that govern mortality may not be sufficient to prove spiritual matters. To suppose that taking Lamanites today and saying their DNA doesn't match up and, therefore, the Book of Mormon is not true, seems somewhat inconsistent when one tries to match mortal processes with spiritual happenings.

I do not know anything regarding those who have been disciplined for publishing on the doctrine of a Mother in Heaven. Chances are they presented their ideas in a way that ran counter to true religion and to the Church and its teachings. Speculation on such matters can lead members astray and destroy faith in God the Father. Praying to a Mother in Heaven is not a true doctrine, no matter how it is defined or presented. It undermines faith in the true process of offering prayers, which is to pray to Heavenly Father in the name of Christ.

Members can believe anything they want. Church members may believe they have a Mother in Heaven, but to go out teaching that we ought to pray to her, or that we give details about her when both the prophets and the scriptures are silent—this violates the teachings of the Church. There's no Church-endorsed reference at all in the scriptures for praying to a Mother in Heaven. Reason suggests that we have a Mother in Heaven; even one of our hymns suggests such a teaching.[5] Those who got in trouble did so because they taught doctrines that are not in harmony with true religion and therefore run counter to the teachings of the Church. They can believe whatever they want. They can talk to their friends about it. But when they go about purporting that this doctrine has some semblance of truth, they will have to give account of their actions.

If Church members go to their friends and start talking about practicing plural marriage, they are not in harmony with the Church. Yes, there are some things where common sense says, "Don't discuss it in private or in public." Otherwise, hey, I've got the freedom to think anything I want, but I need to be careful that I'm not trying to represent the Church with my point of view or convince others that a certain doctrine or practice represents true religion or is what the Church teaches. As an individual, I can speculate all I want on any issue or topic as long as I keep to myself those matters that are not in harmony with truth and the Church and its teachings.

If I am a prominent or well thought of member of the Church, and I present a paper in the name of religious freedom that one might consider worshipping idols, I can expect Church discipline. That doctrine is contrary to true religion and the teachings of God. To bring up controversial topics in meetings such as sacrament meeting, Sunday School, priesthood meeting, Relief Society, etc., could raise questions and jeopardize one's standing in the Church. There are some members who have pure intent on undermining or destroying the faith of other Church members by suggesting or teaching doctrines that are not true. These members should be brought before a Church disciplinary council to give account of their actions.

However, everyone has the freedom to think, believe, and act as they wish. That's what agency is all about.

Philip: Yet Janice Allred was excommunicated in 1995 for her insistence on publishing a clearly speculative paper entitled "Toward a Theology of God the Mother."[4] Why was she disciplined for asserting her opinion?

Donald: I believe I have already established the fact that I can't comment on Church discipline, as that is confidential and would violate privacy issues. As a member of the Church, I don't know. I wasn't there and don't know the facts. Such a doctrine has not been revealed through a living prophet, and it is not appropriate to be a member of the Church and teach to others in any setting doctrines or practices that run counter to true religion and the Church and its teachings, such as practicing plural marriage or other theories that are not mainstream teachings of the living prophets. To speculate implies information that may not be in harmony with true religion and may undermine or destroy the faith of Church members and cause dissent and confusion in the Church. Ideas such as these are best kept to oneself. Heavenly Father or Jesus Christ have not revealed such doctrine.

I can tell you one thing, though. There was sufficient reason to hold a disciplinary council, or it never would have been called. The Church doesn't just go around disciplining its members without having sound evidence and looking at all facets of the situation. Church leaders know what they're doing and why something violates the rules, laws, and commandments of the Church. They're very careful before they ever do it. They are always on solid ground before they do it; they make it a matter of fervent prayer and fasting with a sincere desire to know the will of God on these matters.

The Church has no reason to remove members from the Church for what they say. Why would it? How does that help? The Church teaches the sacredness of the principle of agency. A war was fought in heaven over agency. This Church was organized by God the Father and His son, Jesus Christ, who therefore established the commandments and guidelines, and no one has a right to come along and say, "Why doesn't the Church consider this or do this or that?" It's not up to Church leaders to do as they please. Members can leave the Church and do and say anything they want. We expect Church leaders to always be in harmony with the teachings of the living prophets.

Philip: President Ezra Taft Benson told members to either follow Church leaders "and be blessed" or "reject them and suffer."[6] Does this principle still hold true today?

Donald: I think so. That's an eternal principle. All blessings a person receives are predicated upon obedience to the law that pertains to those blessings. If you break God's laws, you forfeit the blessings and suffer the consequences. The Old Testament talks about the rejection of the prophets. The New Testament talks about the rejection of Christ. This principle was set up long before the Church was restored in the latter days. That's the way it works. In our society today, "suffer" has a negative connotation. God gave His children commandments in order to bring them happiness. Church doctrine teaches "men are that they might have joy" (2 Ne. 2:25). For example, people who commit adultery while married cannot enjoy happiness in that they "suffer" from heartbreak and the negative emotions connected with the breach of trust. If someone steals and lies and breaks civil law, they are not going to be happy if they reap the consequences of being in jail or prison. The whole purpose of the gospel of Jesus Christ is to bring mankind peace and happiness through living the teachings and commandments, and to perfect them that they may return to live in the heavens with their family.

Philip: President Hinckley once commented, "People think in a very critical way before they come into this Church. When they come into this Church they're expected to conform. And they find happiness in that conformity."[7] So if one does not want to conform or perhaps relinquish his or her own judgment to that of Church leaders, then does not one belong in the LDS Church?

Donald: Why would you want to belong to something you can't conform to? The reason the Church is growing is because its members have a testimony of the truthfulness of its doctrines and ordinances. If you study true religion and find out that the Church teaches that we should observe the Word of Wisdom, be morally clean, and be honest in our dealings with others, and accept other doctrines or practices, and then you say, "I'm not going to do these things," then you've made a decision that you're not interested in receiving the blessings that come from membership in the Church.

If people or members are not honest in heart or do not have a sincere desire to conform, the Spirit of the Lord will withdraw from them, and they will have no foundation for a belief in religion. Yes, a person who has no intention of conforming should not join, for he or she will not find fellowship or happiness. Others who are members and who decide not to conform should request to have their membership withdrawn.

This does not undermine free thought. Thinking and acting are two different things. Members are free to think anything they want; however, they are encouraged to act in accordance with God's commandments as expressed through His prophets and leaders. I believe Church members are free to do whatever they want to do, but like anything else in life, their choices have consequences. Those who have freedom and power to make their own choices are not free to determine the consequences of their decisions.

Philip: The Church admonishes members to explore issues for themselves by prayerfully seeking out the answers to their questions. Their conclusions, it is assumed, will coincide with what the prophets say. What happens when prayer and Bible study lead a member to a conclusion not advocated by Church leadership? Are they allowed to believe that and stay in the Church?

Donald: Aren't they free to believe anything they want?

Philip: But what if they want to retain their membership?

Donald: You cannot have it both ways. You can believe whatever you want as long as you keep it to yourself. Church members are not compelled to believe in anything. If you have doubts, that's good. Just keep those doubts to yourself and keep trying to figure out through prayer and study and trying the principle to see if it is true. Discuss your concerns with family or friends or with Church leaders. Those who sincerely pray to Heavenly Father in the name of Christ are entitled to answers to their prayers. God made the promise in Matthew 7:7–11.[8] I think people who say they didn't get an answer to prayer may not have paid the price, but that's my opinion. I believe that God is consistent. If He organizes His Church and gives doctrines and ordinances as a part of true worship, He will confirm the truthfulness of those things to those who pray and ask in faith believing. If one were to pray for help with a personal problem, God's answer will be in harmony with His teachings and worship in His Church. The key is to understand the process of prayer. Answers to some may come in a way that they didn't expect, or they may not have been humble enough to accept God's will over theirs. When it comes to knowing if the doctrine is true, the Spirit will bear witness to those who ask in sincerity.

I think many thinking individuals may find some things about Church practices or doctrines of which they at times have doubts or don't understand, and may not have a testimony of their truthfulness. Members should read the scriptures and discuss their doubts with family members and others to get different points of view. The Church does not expect a blind obedience concerning what the leaders say. Church members have an obligation to listen to its leaders and then prayerfully determine if it is the leader's opinion or if what was said is prompted by the Spirit. Members are wise if they study, ponder, and pray to know the truth concerning all things and seek answers through the Spirit. The genius of the Church is that if members want to pay the price to study and pray, they can have a personal witness of the truthfulness of that which they pray. Testimonies don't come by lying around and philosophizing. You've got to try the thing out and see if it works, and ask God to witness to your spirit that it is true

Philip: You said a moment ago that members can believe whatever they want and not jeopardize their membership as long as they keep it to themselves, which directly relates to what has become the primary inquiry of this book. It appears that the LDS Church has appended a kind of Eleventh Commandment to the Old Testament Decalogue: "Thou shalt agree or be quiet." As long as divergent views are not printed or proclaimed in the media, then the Church doesn't bother with disciplinary action. However, when a member does publicly express his or her disagreement, then the Church's swift hand of justice moves into action. Is this an accurate observation?

Donald: Oh, I don't think so. The Church has not changed its approach in this matter. I think a majority of Church members talk with family and others and study the scriptures about their opinions on Church matters, and there is no reason for them to be disciplined, because they are not teaching false doctrines or practices that are contrary to true religion as taught by the Church. Some members have as their motives to destroy the faith of others. There were numerous times in the past when Church leaders spoke out on doctrinal and other issues as their own opinion and indicated that it was not official Church doctrine of teachings. So to say every time that's done they are disciplined is not a true statement. It depends on what they're talking about and what the circumstances are.

I am employed by the Church. I answer questions that come here. And if I went to the newspaper and published an article about why I think we ought to pray to Mother in Heaven, then I should expect disciplinary action. In the first place, it's a false doctrine. It's a doctrine that we don't have any knowledge about. We know next to nothing about our Mother in Heaven. So when I go out and say that we ought to be praying to her when I know that we ought to be praying to God the Father, I'm going contrary to the teachings and doctrines of the Church, and in my position I would deserve discipline.

Let's take another instance. Look at the Church's position on stem cell research. At this time, the Church does not take a position on many matters, including this one. When the Church president is inspired through revelation to take a stand, he will wait until there is accurate information and expert opinion, and then he will make it a matter of deliberation with other Church leaders and seek consensus, after which they will pray and seek guidance from the Spirit, and then the president will make public the Church's position.

Orrin Hatch, who is one of our U.S. Senators from Utah, gave a news conference that was printed in many news sources. Utah's elected government officials are free to speak their own mind on matters, and they may not be in harmony with the Church regarding specific issues. Hatch said in essence that he supported stem cell research, but he wasn't speaking for the Church. He was speaking for himself. In regards to these types of matters we have only one spokesman, and that's the living prophet, and he will only announce what the Lord would want him to give.

Philip: In sum, how free should a member of the LDS Church feel to explore theology and doctrine without incurring disciplinary action from the church?

Donald: Members have total freedom. They can do what they want, they can think anything they want, and they can believe anything they want, so long as they keep it to themselves.

The Church encourages honest scholarship and encourages the Saints to gain knowledge on matters pertaining to all disciplines of interest. Members have their agency to study and believe what they want; they can think anything they want, so long as they do not teach in public or private doctrines, philosophies, or practices that run counter to the Church or its teachings. On all matters, they are free to think as they will and not incur Church discipline.

Members can discuss with others their feelings on various matters and ask questions in appropriate Church meetings. However, they are accountable for what they say and do. Church members are obligated to sustain the General Authorities and other authorities of the Church. They are not to affiliate or be connected with those who run counter to the Church or its teachings. Latter-day Saints desiring to remain in good standing are obligated not to claim they represent the Church to the media or in private writings to teach anything that is contrary to the revealed doctrines and practices of true religion. Motive and intent play a vital role in this issue.

When a member is teaching, writing, or proclaiming doctrines or practices about the Church, key questions they should ask themselves include, What is the intent of doing this? Will it raise questions concerning my loyalty to the Church? Have I made it clear that this is my opinion and that it is not in harmony with the Church or its teachings? If so, then why am I not keeping this to myself? How will it benefit other Church members? Will it build faith in God and the Church, or will it be destructive and undermine the faith members have developed over years of study, worship and prayer?

Notes

1. At the time of this interview, Church membership numbered at more than 11 million, 3–4 percent of whom do not self-identify as Mormon. Tim B. Heaton, "Vital Statistics," in *Latter-day Saint Social Life*, edited by James T. Duke (Provo, Utah: Brigham Young University, 1998), 118. As of fall 2009, Church membership exceeds 13 million. The Church's full name is "The" Church of Jesus Christ of Latter-day Saints but is rendered in this interview as "the" for stylistic consistency.

2. Vern L. Bullough, "A Humanist View of Religious Universities," in *Religion, Feminism, and Freedom of Conscience: A Mormon/Humanist Dialogue*, edited by George D. Smith (Buffalo, N.Y.: Prometheus Books, 1994), 71.

3. In conjunction with some assertions made by disciplined Mormons in this volume, Allen D. Roberts claims, "It is now apparent that conservative members of the religion faculty, the Foundation for Ancient Research and Mormon Studies, the Church Educational System, and the Strengthening Church Members Committee secretly monitor colleagues and church members at large, collecting verbal and written information on what they consider to be questionable or unorthodox activity. Tapes of speeches and copies of offending articles and manuscripts are brought to the attention of high-ranking leaders and are forwarded to local leaders or university administrators responsible for exacting punishment. In some documented instances, spies have been sent into BYU classrooms." See "Academic Freedom at Brigham Young University: Free Inquiry in Religious Context" in *Religion, Feminism, and Freedom of Conscience: A Mormon/Humanist Dialogue*, edited by George D. Smith (Buffalo, N.Y.: Prometheus Books, 1994), 59.

4. Janice Allred, "Toward a Theology of God the Mother," *Dialogue: A Journal of Mormon Thought* 27, no. 2 (Summer 1994): 15–39.

5. Eliza R. Snow, "O My Father," Hymns of the Church of Jesus Christ of Latter-day Saints (Salt Lake City: Church of Jesus Christ of Latter-day Saints, 1985), #292.

6. Ezra Taft Benson, "Fourteen Fundamentals in Following the Prophets," BYU Devotional Address, February 26, 1980. An official version was published in *Devotional Speeches of the Year* (Provo, Utah: Brigham Young University Press, 1981), photocopy in Box 5, fd. 24, David John Buerger Papers, Special Collections, Marriott Library, University of Utah, quoted in D. Michael Quinn, "Ezra Taft Benson and Mormon Political Conflicts," *Dialogue: A Journal of Mormon Thought*

26, no. 2 (Summer 1993): 77. Benson delivered this address before he became president of the Church in 1985.

7. President Hinckley made this comment in an interview on *Compass* (ABC), which aired on November 9, 1997. For a complete transcript, see http://www.abc.net.au/compass/ intervs/hinckley.htm (accessed July 30, 2008).

8. "Ask, and it shall be given you; seek, and ye shall find; knock, and it shall be opened unto you: For every one that asketh receiveth; and he that seeketh findeth; and to him that knocketh it shall be opened. Or what man is there of you, whom if his son ask bread, will he give him a stone? Or if he ask a fish, will he give him a serpent? If ye then, being evil, know how to give good gifts unto your children, how much more shall your Father which is in heaven give good things to them that ask him?" (Matt. 7:7–11).

Index

Abbott, Scott, xi
Abel, Elijah, 175
academic freedom, x, xxvi note 1, 108–7, 217–18
Acts of John, 184
Alexander, Thomas G., xiv
"All Is Not Well in Zion," 47
Allen, James B., xiv
Allred, Ammon, 132
Allred, David, 132–33, 153
Allred, Enoch, 132
Allred, Janice Merrill, xii, xxxii note 46, 15, 131–55, 164–65, 219
Allred, Jared, 132
Allred, Joel, 132, 138, 144
Allred, John, 132, 153
Allred, Miriam, 132
Allred, Nephi, 132, 138, 145
Allred, Paul, 132
Allred, Rebecca, 132, 138
American Academy of Religion, 199
American Apocrypha, 193
Anderson, Christian, 86, 92, 100
Anderson, Lavina Fielding, xvi, xxxv, 4, 5, 16, 28, 85, 133, 135, 167, 192, 194, 201

Anderson, Paul, 86, 91, 96–97
Anderson, Vern, 140–41
Andrus, Hyrum, 22
apostasy, defined, xvii, 19 note 4, 142–44, 176, 195–96
Arrington, Leonard J., xiv, 87, 125, 127 note 6
Associated Press, 57, 116, 140, 195
authority/authoritarianism, xii, xix–xx, 7–9, 23–24, 46, 75–76, 92–95, 99, 145–47, 150, 152, 159, 164, 171–72, 178–79, 215–17, 220
Avery, Valeen Tippets, xi

B. H. Roberts Society, 2, 16
Baca, Angelo, 205
Bacon, Carl, 135, 136–37, 149–50
Ballard, M. Russell, 63
Barney, Kevin, 191, 207 note 11
Bartchy, Scott, 78, 82 note 31
baseball baptisms, 107–108
BBC, ix, 18, 142, 167
Beck, John and Martha, xi
Beecher, Maureen Ursenbach, xiv
Bennion, Lowell, xiv

Benson, Ezra Taft, x, xx, 8, 19 notes 6–7, 88, 220, 226 note 6
Benson, Steve, x
Bishop, Francis, xviii
Bitton, Davis, xiv
Blake, Dale, 166–68
Bloom, Harold, 67
Book of Mormon, xviii, 68–69, 71–75, 190–93, 95, 124, 186, 188, 193, 197, 200, 203, 207 note 9, 218
Bradley, Don, 238 note 20
Bradley, Martha Sonntag, xi
Brodie, Fawn M., xi, xiii, 187, 204
Brooks, Juanita, xi, xiii, 5, 19 note 3
Brothers Karamazov, The, 16–17
Brown, Pelatiah, xxvii note 14
Buchanan, Frederick S., xxviii note 14
Bullough, Vern L., 215
Busche, Enzio F., 63

"Call of Mormon Feminism, The," 39
careers. *See* women.
Case Reports of the Mormon Alliance, 54
Catholic Church, xxxi note 42, 123
Catholic University of America, xxxi note 42
censorship. *See* academic freedom.
Chronicle of Higher Education, 194
Chung, Connie, ix, 4
Church of Jesus Christ of Latter-day Saints. *See* authority, silence, *and* women.
  membership, ix, xxviii note 18, 210–12, 226 note 1
  origin and early history, xvii–xviii
  warns against symposium participation, xii–xiii, xxvi note 5
Church Handbook of Instructions, 193. See also *General Handbook of Instructions*.
Claremont Graduate University School of Religion, xxiv, 80 note 10
Clark, Stephen, 195
CNN, 4
collective unconscious, 80 note 6
Coltrin, Zebedee, 40, 50 note 26, 51 note 26
Community of Christ, 198, 200, 208 note 18
Compass (ABC), xxvii note 13
Cooley, Everett, xiii–xiv
Correlation Committee/Department, xiii–xv, xxvi note 8
Counterpoint (conference), 142–43, 155 note 5, 158, 181 note 1
Cowdery, Oliver, xviii–xix, 40, 65, 67
Curran, Charles, xxxi note 42

Daily Universe (BYU), 127
Decker, Ed, 184, 185, 200, 206 note 2
Delaney, Carol, 188, 206 note 7
Derr, Jill Mulvay, xiv
dialogical movement, xiv–xv, xxi, xxiv
Dialogue: A Journal of Mormon Thought, x–xi, xv, xxiv, 54, 56, 57, 100, 102, 106, 156, 167–68
Didier, Charles, xx
disfellowshipment, conditions of, 5, 109
DNA research, 189–93, 218. *See also* Book of Mormon.

DNA vs. the Book of Mormon, 208 note 17
Dostoyevsky, Feodor, 16
Dunn, Loren C., 3, 59

ecclesiastical/spiritual abuse, 22, 29, 88, 90–92, 133, 135
Eco Encore, 205
England, Eugene, xi, xx
Ensign, 22, 85–86
Episcopalian Church, 123
Equal Rights Amendment, 132, 152
Ether (Book of Mormon), 82 note 31
Evans, Vella, 55
excommunication, ix, 154, 170, 201–202, 213–14
Exponent II, xi

FAIR (Foundation for Apologetic Information and Research), 201, 205, 208 note 22
FARMS (Foundation for Ancient Research and Mormon Studies), 191, 201, 204, 208 note 22, 226 note 4
Farr, Cecilia Konchar, xi, 59, 138, 155 note 3
Faust, James E., xxvii note 9, 62, 181 note 4
feminism, and Mormonism, 9, 55–56, 58–59, 63–67, 81 note 11, 157–59, 165, 172–75, 193, 202
feminist studies, x, xii, 2
Ford, Thomas, xxviii note 16
Foster, Robert D., xix

"Fourteen Fundamentals in Following the Prophet," xx, xxix note 27
freedom of speech. *See* silence.

gay rights. *See* homosexuality.
Geer, Thelma, 186
Geiger, Juli, xxxv
General Handbook of Instructions, xii–xiii, xxvi note 5, xxx note 36, xxxii note 44, 19 note 4, 139, 141–42, 144, 150. See also *Church Handbook of Instructions.*
Gileadi, Avraham, xvii, xxi, 133
Givens, Terryl L., xvii, xxv
Gnosticism, 55, 61, 75, 76, 79, 123
God Makers, The, xx, 184, 206 note 2
God the Mother. *See* Mother in Heaven.
Godbe, William, 103 note 9
Godbeites, xi, 97
Grant, Heber J., 33
Gulf War, 187–88

Hafen, Bruce C., 63, 81 note 11
Hamblin, William J., 38
Hammond, F. Melvin, 159, 181 note 2
Hammond, Robert, 140–44, 149–51
Hanks (stake president), 57, 74
Hanks, D. Max, 53
Hanks, Ephraim, 57, 75
Hanks, Maxine, xvi, xxxv, 16, 53–84, 91, 133, 161, 195, 213
Harmon, Cheryl, 183
Harris, Martin, xviii–xix, 65, 67
Hatch, Orrin, 224

Hawker, Jeff, 28
Heavenly Mother. *See* Mother in Heaven.
Heinz, Kerry M., 23–28, 31, 45–46, 158–62, 166, 169–70, 176–77
Henetz, Patty, 194
Hickman, Martin, 208
Hinckley, Gordon B., xvii, xxvii note 13, 17, 33, 35, 40, 62, 75–76, 135–36, 139–41, 150, 221
history. *See* revisionist history.
homosexuality, 119–120, 126–127, 152, 193, 202
Houston, Gail Turley, xi
Howard W. Hunter Chair in Mormon Studies, xxiv, 80 note 10
Hunter, Howard W., 31
Hyde, Orson, xvii

identity, as Mormon, xxi–xxii, xxiv, xxxii note 46, 74
"If Women Have Had the Priesthood since 1843, Why Aren't They Using It?" 161
"Images of the Female Body, Human and Divine," 168, 160
Improvement Era, xix
Insider's View of Mormon Origins, An, xvi, 86
internet, xxiv–xxv

Jackson, Joseph H., xix
Jessee, Donald B., ix, xvii, xxi–xxiii, 209–27
John Whitmer Historical Association, 86
Johnson, Sonia, xi, 56, 132

Joseph Fielding Smith Institute for Latter-day Saint History, xiv
Journal of Mormon History, 86
Jung, Carl, 80 note 6

Kafka, Franz, 181 note 5
Kanavel, Edward, 1–2
Kanavel, Violet, 1–2
Kenney, Scott G., x
Kimball, Spencer W., 8, 19 note 6–7, 24, 75–76
King, Arthur Henry, 54, 73, 83 note 30
Kingdom of the Cults, 186
Knowlton, David Clark, xi, 59, 79, 138, 155 note 3
Kofford, Greg, xxxv
Kramer, Joel, 197, 208 note 17
Kronmeyer, Mattijs, xxxv
Küng, Hans, xxxi note 42

"Lamanites, Genesis, Genealogy, and Genetics," 191
Latimer, Matthew, 192–95, 199
Latter-day Saint Council on Mormon Studies, 80 note 10
Lee, Harold B., xiv
LeFevre, Don, xxx note 27
Leonard J. Arrington Chair in Mormon History and Culture, xxiv
Lewis, C. S., 43, 71, 84 note 26
Library of Congress, 80 note 10
Life on the Mississippi, 23
Lindholm, Lita, xxxv
Lindholm-Wood, Jessica, xxxv
Living Hope Ministries, 208 note 17
Los Angeles Times, ix, 116, 194, 195

Lucy's Book, 54
Lyon, T. Edgar, xiv

Madsen, Brigham D., xiii–xiv
Manifesto, xxviii note 19, 94
Martin, Walter, 186
Martin, Wilson, 23, 160, 166
Mary Magdalene, 76–77
Masonry, 65
Mauss, Armand, xxxii note 45
Maxwell, Neal A., 62
McConkie, Bruce R., xx, 89, 103 note 3
McKay, David O., xiv, xxvii note 10, 8, 19 note 6
McMurrin, Sterling, xiii–xiv, xxvii note 10, 203–204, 208 note 23
Merrill, John Arthur, 157
Merrill, Lenna Peterson, 157
Merrill, Virgil, 3–6
Metcalfe, Brent, xii, 192, 207 note 14
Metropolitan Community Church, 123
Miller, Marlin, 89–91, 100
"Missing Rib, The," 158, 177, 180
Mormonism, Mama & Me, 186
Modern Microfilm Company, 208 note 21
Morgan, Dale, xi, xiii
Mormon Alliance, xxiv, 22, 133–35
Mormon Enigma: Emma Hale Smith, xi
Mormon Hierarchy: Extensions of Power, The, 107
Mormon Hierarchy: Origins of Power, The, 107
Mormon History Association, xiv, 199
"Mormon Women Have Had the Priesthood since 1843," 115

Mormon Women's Forum, x, xvi, 2, 16, 132–134, 142–43, 155 note 5, 158, 165–66
Mother in Heaven, xii, 5, 16, 40, 75, 134–35, 142, 150, 169, 172–73, 177, 218–19, 224. *See also* feminist theology.
motherhood, 65–66, 175, 212–13
Mulder, William, xiv
Murphy, Greg, 184
Murphy, Jessyca, 185–86, 188
Murphy, Kerrie Sumner, 184–86, 188, 193, 202–203
Murphy, Roy, 183
Murphy, Thomas W., xii, 166, 183–208, 214, 218
"My Controversy with the Church," 142

National Post, 194
Nauvoo Expositor, xix
Neblett, Cameron, xxxv
Nelson, Russell M., xx–xxi, xxvii note 9, 27, 63, 181 note 4
New Approaches to the Book of Mormon, xii
New Mormon History, xiii
New York Times, 4, 14, 116
Newell, Linda King, xi, 161
Newsweek, 116

"O My Father," 40
Oaks, Dallin H., xii–xiii, xx, xxvi note 9, 36, 50 note 14, 63, 181 note 4
"On Being a Mormon Historian," 109, 124
Oxford, Earl of, 82 note 28

Packer, Boyd K., xii–xiii, 4, 6, 16, 19 note 2, 23–24, 30–31, 45–47, 59, 62, 122–125, 159, 161
Palmer, Grant H., xvi, 54, 103 note 10, 198
Paramore, James M., 111
Petersen, Mark E., 107, 128 note 2
"Plea to the Leadership of the Church, A," 37–38
Poelman, Ronald E., 63
polygamy, 41–42, 110
Priddis, Ron, 195
priesthood, and women's ordination, x, 12, 41, 171, 173–75, 102–203, 212–13
probation, conditions of, 141
public discourse, xx, xxii, xxv, 149. *See also* silence.

Quakers, 122
Quinn, Adam, 106, 121–122
Quinn, D. Michael, xiv, xvi, xxxii note 46, 16, 57–58, 62, 67, 105–129, 133, 161
Quinn, Janice Darley, 106, 119
Quinn, Lisa, 106
Quinn, Mary, 106
Quinn, Moshe, 106

race, and Mormonism, 191–93, 205
Relief Society, 9, 55, 64–65
Relief Society Magazine, 85
revisionist history, x, xiii–xv, 63–65, 108–110, 121
Rigdon, Sidney, xix, 51 note 26, 67
Riggs, Burr, xviii
Road to Serfdom, The, 33

Roberts, Allen Dale, xxiv, 216, 226 note 4
Roberts, Brigham H., 197, 204, 207 note 16

Saints Alive, 206 note 2
Salamander Society, 194
Salt Lake Tribune, 116, 140
Same-Sex Dynamics among Nineteenth-Century Americans: A Mormon Example, 107
Sanctity of Dissent, The, 33, 38
Scott, Richard G., 62
Seventh East Press, 54
Shipps, Jan, x, xxxii note 46, xxxv, 67
Signature Books, x, 86
silence, and divergent views, xii, xv–xvii, xx–xxiii, xxxi note 40, 12, 88, 161, 169, 177–78, 222–23, 225
Sillito, John, xxi
Smith, Alvin, 67
Smith, Emma Hale, 65, 67
Smith, George D., xxviii note 16
Smith, Hyrum, xix, 67
Smith, Joseph, xvii–xix, xxi, xxvii note 14, xxix note 21, 34–35, 37, 40–41, 44, 50 notes 17 and 26, 64–65, 67–72, 75–77, 95, 98, 102, 117, 126, 152, 172, 174–75, 178–79, 184, 188, 198, 200–201, 213
Smith, Joseph, Sr., 67
Smith, Joseph, III, 208 note 18
Smith, Joseph F., 46
Smith, Lucy Mack, 65, 67
Smith, Sylvester, xviii
Snow, Eliza R., 40, 50 note 24, 60, 65, 87

Southern Methodist University, xxxi note 42
Southerton, Simon, 191, 207 note 11
Spaulding, Solomon, 72, 82 note 28
spiritual abuse. See ecclesiastical/ spiritual abuse.
Stack, Peggy Fletcher, 140, 155 note 4
Staker, Susan, xxi
Stark, Rodney, xxviii note 18
stem cell research, 224
Steven Christensen Award, 86
Strangers in Paradox, 39, 171, 174, 178
Strengthening Church Members Committee, 6, xxvi note 9, 136, 167, 181 note 4, 217, 226 note 4
Sunstone (magazine/symposium), x–xi, xv, 2, 16, 22–23, 26–27, 30, 47, 88, 132, 134, 137, 139–40, 148, 158, 161, 188–89, 199–200
Swearing Elders, xiv

Tanner, Jerald and Sandra, 200, 208 note 21
Tanner, N. Eldon, xx, xxix note 26
Tanner, O. C., xiii–xiv
Taylor, John, xxi
Temple of the God Makers, 206 note 2
Todd, Jay M., 85–86
Tolkien, J. R. R., 71, 82 note 26
Toscano, Margaret Ann Merrill, xii, xxxii note 46, 5, 16, 22, 28, 31, 132–133, 135, 157
Toscano, Paul James, xvi, xxiv, xxxii note 46, 16, 86, 21–51, 133, 135, 157–58, 160–64, 167–68, 171, 176
Toscano, Rose, 21

Toscano, Sam, 21
Toscano, Sarah, 162–63
"Toward a Mormon Theology of God the Mother," 135, 138, 146, 219–20
trammel, xxviii note 14
Twain, Mark, 23
Tyler, Jan, 56

Ulrich, Laurel Thatcher, xi, 181 note 1
Unitarian Church, 123
unrighteous dominion. See ecclesiastical/ spiritual abuse.
Utah Lighthouse Ministry, 208 note 21
Utah State University, xxiv

Vanocur, Chris, 2, 3
vigils, 4, 28, 49 note 6, 141, 166–67, 170
Voice (club), 159
Von Hayek, Friedrich Augustus, 33, 49
Voros, Fred, 28, 31, 135, 167; and wife, 167

Wall Street Journal, ix, 195
Washington Post, 116
Wells, Emmeline B., 87
Wesley, John, 198
Whitesides, Alan, 2, 4
Whitesides, Lynn Kanavel, xvi, xxiv, xxxii note 46, 1–20, 91, 133–34, 214

Widtsoe, John A., 98
Wight, Lyman, xviii
Wilson, Frank, xxxv

women, place in Mormonism, 12–15, 19 note 7, 30, 87–88, 117, 212–13. *See also* feminism, priesthood *and* motherhood.

Women and Authority: Re-emerging Mormon Feminism, 54–61, 63, 115

Wood, Dustin, xxxv

Woodruff, Wilford, 10, 94

"Worlds of Joseph Smith, The," 80 note 10

Wright, David, xii

Yale University Divinity School, 80 note 10

Young, Brigham, xviii, xxiv, 57, 103 note 9, 172, 174, 208 notes 18 and 21

Also available from
GREG KOFFORD BOOKS

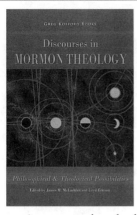

Discourses in Mormon Theology: Philosophical and Theological Possibilities

Edited by
James M. McLachlan and Loyd Ericson

Hardcover, ISBN: 978-1-58958-103-6

A mere two hundred years old, Mormonism is still in its infancy compared to other theological disciplines (Judaism, Catholicism, Buddhism, etc.). This volume will introduce its reader to the rich blend of theological viewpoints that exist within Mormonism. The essays break new ground in Mormon studies by exploring the vast expanse of philosophical territory left largely untouched by traditional approaches to Mormon theology. It presents philosophical and theological essays by many of the finest minds associated with Mormonism in an organized and easy-to-understand manner and provides the reader with a window into the fascinating diversity amongst Mormon philosophers. Open-minded students of pure religion will appreciate this volume's thoughtful inquiries.

These essays were delivered at the first conference of the Society for Mormon Philosophy and Theology. Authors include Grant Underwood, Blake T. Ostler, Dennis Potter, Margaret Merrill Toscano, James E. Faulconer, and Robert L. Millet

Praise for *Discourses in Mormon Theology*:

"In short, *Discourses in Mormon Theology* is an excellent compilation of essays that are sure to feed both the mind and soul. It reminds all of us that beyond the white shirts and ties there exists a universe of theological and moral sensitivity that cries out for study and acclamation."
-Jeff Needle, Association for Mormon Letters

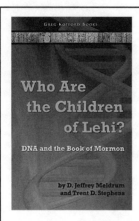

Who Are the Children of Lehi? DNA and the Book of Mormon

D. Jeffrey Meldrum and Trent D. Stephens

Hardcover, ISBN: 978-1-58958-048-0
Paperback, ISBN: 978-1-58958-129-6

How does the Book of Mormon, keystone of the LDS faith, stand up to data about DNA sequencing that puts the ancestors of modern Native Americans in northeast Asia instead of Palestine?

In *Who Are the Children of Lehi?* Meldrum and Stephens examine the merits and the fallacies of DNA-based interpretations that challenge the Book of Mormon's historicity. They provide clear guides to the science, summarize the studies, illuminate technical points with easy-to-grasp examples, and spell out the data's implications.

The results? There is no straight-line conclusion between DNA evidence and "Lamanites." The Book of Mormon's validity lies beyond the purview of scientific empiricism—as it always has. And finally, inspiringly, they affirm Lehi's kinship as one of covenant, not genes.

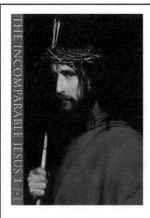

The Incomparable Jesus

Grant H. Palmer

Paperback, ISBN: 978-1-58958-092-3

Distilled from his personal experiences in teaching Jesus to the hard-to-reach, this professional educator has produced a tender testament to the incomparable Jesus. It describes a Savior who walked with him through the halls of the county jail where he served as chaplain, succoring those in need.

In this slim volume, Palmer sensitively shares his understanding of what it means to know Jesus by doing his works. He lists the qualities of divine character attested to by the Apostles Peter and Paul, and also those that Jesus revealed about himself in his masterful Sermon on the Mount, particularly in the beatitudes.

With reverence Palmer shares personal spiritual experiences that were life-changing assurances of Jesus's love for him—a love poured out unstintingly in equally life-changing blessings on prisoners whose crimes had not stopped short of sexual abuse and murder. Reading this book offers a deeper understanding of the Savior's mercy, a stronger sense of his love, and a deeper commitment to follow him.

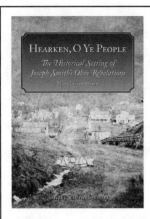

Hearken, O Ye People: The Historical Setting of Joseph Smith's Ohio Revelations

Mark Lyman Staker

Hardcover, ISBN: 978-1-58958-113-5

Awarded 2010 Best Book Award - John Whitmer Historical Association

More of Mormonism's canonized revelations originated in or near Kirtland than any other place. Yet many of the events connected with those revelations and their 1830s historical context have faded over time. Mark Staker reconstructs the cultural experiences by which Kirtland's Latter-day Saints made sense of the revelations Joseph Smith pronounced. This volume rebuilds that exciting decade using clues from numerous archives, privately held records, museum collections, and even the soil where early members planted corn and homes. From this vast array of sources he shapes a detailed narrative of weather, religious backgrounds, dialect differences, race relations, theological discussions, food preparation, frontier violence, astronomical phenomena, and myriad daily customs of nineteenth-century life. The result is a "from the ground up" experience that today's Latter-day Saints can all but walk into and touch.

Praise for *Hearken O Ye People***:**

"I am not aware of a more deeply researched and richly contextualized study of any period of Mormon church history than Mark Staker's study of Mormons in Ohio. We learn about everything from the details of Alexander Campbell's views on priesthood authority to the road conditions and weather on the four Lamanite missionaries' journey from New York to Ohio. All the Ohio revelations and even the First Vision are made to pulse with new meaning. This book sets a new standard of in-depth research in Latter-day Saint history."
        -Richard Bushman, author of *Joseph Smith: Rough Stone Rolling*

"To be well-informed, any student of Latter-day Saint history and doctrine must now be acquainted with the remarkable research of Mark Staker on the important history of the church in the Kirtland, Ohio, area."
        -Neal A. Maxwell Institute, Brigham Young University

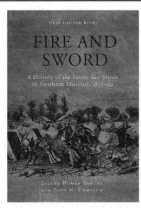

Fire and Sword: A History of the Latter-day Saints in Northern Missouri, 1836-39

Leland Homer Gentry and Todd M. Compton

Hardcover, ISBN: 978-1-58958-103-6

Many Mormon dreams flourished in Missouri. So did many Mormon nightmares.

The Missouri period—especially from the summer of 1838 when Joseph took over vigorous, personal direction of this new Zion until the spring of 1839 when he escaped after five months of imprisonment—represents a moment of intense crisis in Mormon history. Representing the greatest extremes of devotion and violence, commitment and intolerance, physical suffering and terror—mobbings, battles, massacres, and political "knockdowns"—it shadowed the Mormon psyche for a century.

Leland Gentry was the first to step beyond this disturbing period as a one-sided symbol of religious persecution and move toward understanding it with careful documentation and evenhanded analysis. In Fire and Sword, Todd Compton collaborates with Gentry to update this foundational work with four decades of new scholarship, more insightful critical theory, and the wealth of resources that have become electronically available in the last few years.

Compton gives full credit to Leland Gentry's extraordinary achievement, particularly in documenting the existence of Danites and in attempting to tell the Missourians' side of the story; but he also goes far beyond it, gracefully drawing into the dialogue signal interpretations written since Gentry and introducing the raw urgency of personal writings, eyewitness journalists, and bemused politicians seesawing between human compassion and partisan harshness. In the lush Missouri landscape of the Mormon imagination where Adam and Eve had walked out of the garden and where Adam would return to preside over his posterity, the towering religious creativity of Joseph Smith and clash of religious stereotypes created a swift and traumatic frontier drama that changed the Church.

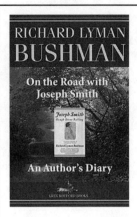

On the Road with Joseph Smith: An Author's Diary

Richard L. Bushman

Paperback, ISBN 978-1-58958-102-9

After living with Joseph Smith for seven years and delivering the final proofs of his landmark study, *Joseph Smith: Rough Stone Rolling* to Knopf in July 2005, biographer Richard Lyman Bushman went "on the road" for a year, crisscrossing the country from coast to coast, delivering addresses on Joseph Smith and attending book-signings for the new biography.

Bushman confesses to hope and humility as he awaits reviews. He frets at the polarization that dismissed the book as either too hard on Joseph Smith or too easy. He yields to a very human compulsion to check sales figures on Amazon. com, but partway through the process stepped back with the recognition, "The book seems to be cutting its own path now, just as [I] hoped."

For readers coming to grips with the ongoing puzzle of the Prophet and the troublesome dimensions of their own faith, Richard Bushman, openly but not insistently presents himself as a believer. "I believe enough to take Joseph Smith seriously," he says. He draws comfort both from what he calls his "mantra" ("Today I will be a follower of Jesus Christ") and also from ongoing engagement with the intellectual challenges of explaining Joseph Smith.

Praise for *On the Road With Joseph Smith*:

"The diary is possibly unparalleled—an author of a recent book candidly dissecting his experiences with both Mormon and non-Mormon audiences ... certainly deserves wider distribution—in part because it shows a talented historian laying open his vulnerabilities, and also because it shows how much any historian lays on the line when he writes about Joseph Smith."
  -Dennis Lythgoe, *Deseret News*

"By turns humorous and poignant, this behind-the-scenes look at Richard Bushman's public and private ruminations about Joseph Smith reveals a great deal—not only about the inner life of one of our greatest scholars, but about Mormonism at the dawn of the 21st century."
  -Jana Riess, co-author of *Mormonism for Dummies*

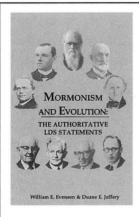

Mormonism and Evolution: The Authoritative LDS Statements

Edited by William E. Evenson and Duane E. Jeffrey

Paperback, ISBN: 978-1-58958-093-0

The Church of Jesus Christ of Latter-day Saints (the Mormon Church) has generally been viewed by the public as anti-evolutionary in its doctrine and teachings. But official statements on the subject by the Church's highest governing quorum and/or president have been considerably more open and diverse than is popularly believed.

This book compiles in full all known authoritative statements (either authored or formally approved for publication) by the Church's highest leaders on the topics of evolution and the origin of human beings. The editors provide historical context for these statements that allows the reader to see what stimulated the issuing of each particular document and how they stand in relation to one another.

"Let the Earth Bring Forth" Evolution and Scripture

Howard C. Stutz

Paperback, ISBN: 978-1-58958-126-5

A century ago in 1809, Charles Darwin was born. Fifty years later, he published a scientific treatise describing the process of speciation that launched what appeared to be a challenge to the traditional religious interpretation of how life was created on earth. The controversy has erupted anew in the last decade as Creationists and Young Earth adherents challenge school curricula and try to displace "the theory of evolution."

This book is filled with fascinating examples of speciation by the well-known process of mutation but also by the less well-known processes of sexual recombination and polyploidy. In addition to the fossil record, Howard Stutz examines the evidence from the embryo stages of human beings and other creatures to show how selection and differentiation moved development in certain favored directions while leaving behind evidence of earlier, discarded developments. Anatomy, biochemistry, and genetics are all examined in their turn.

With rigorously scientific clarity but in language accessible to a popular audience, the book proceeds to its conclusion, reached after a lifetime of study: the divine map of creation is one supported by both scientific evidence and the scriptures. This is a book to be read, not only for its fascinating scientific insights, but also for a new appreciation of well-known scriptures.

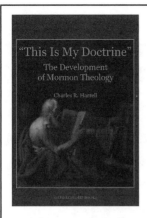

"This is My Doctrine": The Development of Mormon Theology

Charles R. Harrell

Hardcover, ISBN: 978-1-58958-103-6

The principal doctrines defining Mormonism today often bear little resemblance to those it started out with in the early 1830s. This book shows that these doctrines did not originate in a vacuum but were rather prompted and informed by the religious culture from which Mormonism arose. Early Mormons, like their early Christian and even earlier Israelite predecessors, brought with them their own varied culturally conditioned theological presuppositions (a process of convergence) and only later acquired a more distinctive theological outlook (a process of differentiation).

In this first-of-its-kind comprehensive treatment of the development of Mormon theology, Charles Harrell traces the history of Latter-day Saint doctrines from the times of the Old Testament to the present. He describes how Mormonism has carried on the tradition of the biblical authors, early Christians, and later Protestants in reinterpreting scripture to accommodate new theological ideas while attempting to uphold the integrity and authority of the scriptures. In the process, he probes three questions: How did Mormon doctrines develop? What are the scriptural underpinnings of these doctrines? And what do critical scholars make of these same scriptures? In this enlightening study, Harrell systematically peels back the doctrinal accretions of time to provide a fresh new look at Mormon theology.

"*This Is My Doctrine*" will provide those already versed in Mormonism's theological tradition with a new and richer perspective of Mormon theology. Those unacquainted with Mormonism will gain an appreciation for how Mormon theology fits into the larger Jewish and Christian theological traditions.

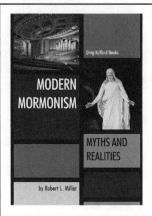

Modern Mormonism: Myths and Realities

Robert L. Millet

Paperback, ISBN: 978-1-58958-127-2

What answer may a Latter-day Saint make to accusations from those of other faiths that "Mormons aren't Christians," or "You think God is a man," and "You worship a different Jesus"? Not only are these charges disconcerting, but the hostility with which they are frequently hurled is equally likely to catch Latter-day Saints off guard.

Now Robert L. Millet, veteran of hundreds of such verbal battles, cogently, helpfully, and scripturally provides important clarifications for Latter-day Saints about eleven of the most frequent myths used to discredit the Church. Along the way, he models how to conduct such a Bible based discussion respectfully, weaving in enlightenment from LDS scriptures and quotations from religious figures in other faiths, ranging from the early church fathers to the archbishop of Canterbury.

Millet enlivens this book with personal experiences as a boy growing up in an area where Mormons were a minuscule and not particularly welcome minority, in one-on-one conversations with men of faith who believed differently, and with his own BYU students who also had lessons to learn about interfaith dialogue. He pleads for greater cooperation in dealing with the genuine moral and social evils afflicting the world, and concludes with his own ardent and reverent testimony of the Savior.

Modern Polygamy and Mormon Fundamentalism: The Generations after the Manifesto

Brian C. Hales

Hardcover, ISBN: 978-1-58958-035-0

Winner of the John Whitmer Historical Association's Smith-Pettit Best Book Award

This fascinating study seeks to trace the historical tapestry that is early Mormon polygamy, details the official discontinuation of the practice by the Church, and, for the first time, describes the many zeal-driven organizations that arose in the wake of that decision. Among the polygamous groups discussed are the LeBaronites, whose "blood atonement" killings sent fear throughout Mormon communities in the late seventies and the eighties; the FLDS Church, which made news recently over its construction of a compound and temple in Texas (Warren Jeffs, the leader of that church, is now standing trial on two felony counts after his being profiled on America's Most Wanted resulted in his capture); and the Allred and Kingston groups, two major factions with substantial membership statistics both in and out of the United States. All these fascinating histories, along with those of the smaller independent groups, are examined and explained in a way that all can appreciate.

Praise for *Modern Polygamy and Mormon Fundamentalism*:

"This book is the most thorough and comprehensive study written on the sugbject to date, providing readers with a clear, candid, and broad sweeping overview of the history, teachings, and practices of modern fundamentalist groups."
—Alexander L. Baugh, Associate Professor of Church History and Doctrine, Brigham Young University

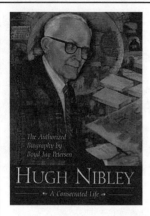

Hugh Nibley:
A Consecrated Life

Boyd Jay Petersen

Hardcover, ISBN: 978-1-58958-019-0

Winner of the Mormon History Association's Best Biography Award

As one of the LDS Church's most widely recognized scholars, Hugh Nibley is both an icon and an enigma. Through complete access to Nibley's correspondence, journals, notes, and papers, Petersen has painted a portrait that reveals the man behind the legend.

Starting with a foreword written by Zina Nibley Petersen and finishing with appendices that include some of the best of Nibley's personal correspondence, the biography reveals aspects of the tapestry of the life of one who has truly consecrated his life to the service of the Lord.

Praise for *A Consecrated Life*:

"Hugh Nibley is generally touted as one of Mormonism's greatest minds and perhaps its most prolific scholarly apologist. Just as hefty as some of Nibley's largest tomes, this authorized biography is delightfully accessible and full of the scholar's delicious wordplay and wit, not to mention some astonishing war stories and insights into Nibley's phenomenal acquisition of languages. Introduced by a personable foreword from the author's wife (who is Nibley's daughter), the book is written with enthusiasm, respect and insight.... On the whole, Petersen is a careful scholar who provides helpful historical context.... This project is far from hagiography. It fills an important gap in LDS history and will appeal to a wide Mormon audience."
—Publishers Weekly

"Well written and thoroughly researched, Petersen's biography is a must-have for anyone struggling to reconcile faith and reason."
—Greg Taggart, Association for Mormon Letters

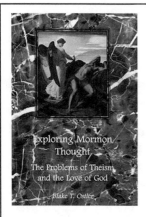

Exploring Mormon Thought Series

Blake T. Ostler

IN VOLUME ONE, *The Attributes of God*, Blake T. Ostler explores Christian and Mormon notions about God. ISBN: 978-1-58958-003-9

IN VOLUME TWO, *The Problems of Theism and the Love of God*, Blake Ostler explores issues related to soteriology, or the theory of salvation. ISBN: 978-1-58958-095-4

IN VOLUME THREE, *Of God and Gods*, Ostler analyzes and responds to the arguments of contemporary international theologians, reconstructs and interprets Joseph Smith's important King Follett Discourse and Sermon in the Grove, and argues persuasively for the Mormon doctrine of "robust deification." ISBN: 978-1-58958-107-4

Praise for the *Exploring Mormon Thought* series:

"These books are the most important works on Mormon theology ever written. There is nothing currently available that is even close to the rigor and sophistication of these volumes. B. H. Roberts and John A. Widtsoe may have had interesting insights in the early part of the twentieth century, but they had neither the temperament nor the training to give a rigorous defense of their views in dialogue with a wider stream of Christian theology. Sterling McMurrin and Truman Madsen had the capacity to engage Mormon theology at this level, but neither one did."
—Neal A. Maxwell Institute, Brigham Young University

Perspectives on Mormon Theology Series

Brian D. Birch and Loyd Ericson, series editors

(forthcoming)

This series will feature multiple volumes published on particular theological topics of interest in Latter-day Saint thought. Volumes will be co-edited by leading scholars and graduate students whose interests and knowledge will ensure that the essays in each volume represent quality scholarship and acknowledge the diversity of thought found and expressed in Mormon theological studies. Topics for the first few volumes include: revelation, apostasy, atonement, scripture, and grace.

The *Perspectives on Mormon Theology* series will bring together the best of new and previously published essays on various theological subjects. Each volume will be both a valued resource for academics in Mormon Studies and an illuminating introduction to the broad and sophisticated approaches to Mormon theology.